A MARVEL COMICS EVEN

CIVIL WAR

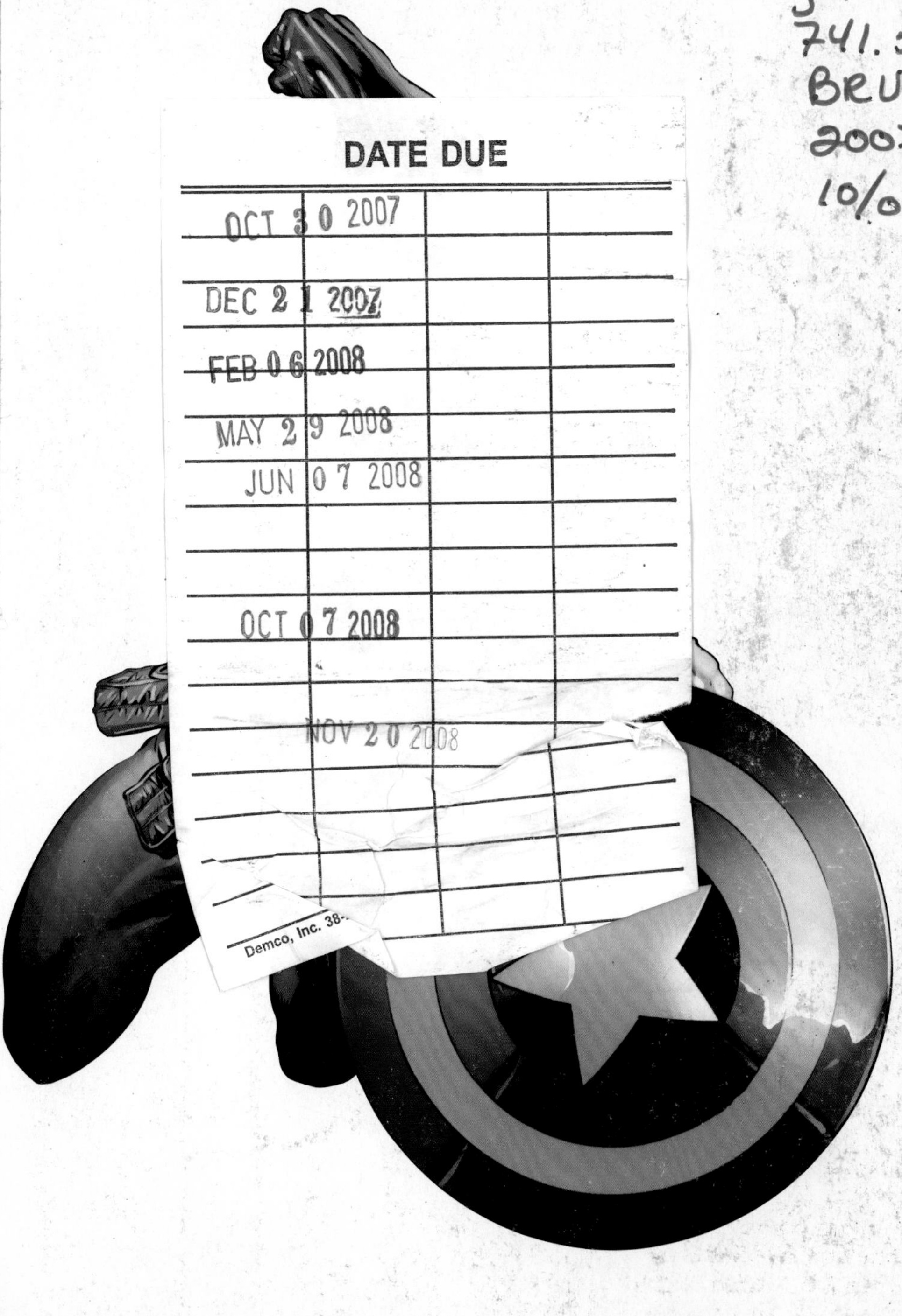

APTAIN AMERICA

A

MARVEL COMICS

PRESENTATION

CIVIL

CA

WRITER
ED BRUBAKER

THE DRUMS OF WAR

ART
MIKE PERKINS

COLOR ART
FRANK D'ARMATA

WINTER SOLDIER:
WINTER KILLS

ART
LEE WEEKS &
STEFANO GAUDIANO
WITH RICK HOBERG

COLORIST
MATT MILLA

LETTERER
VIRTUAL CALLIGRAPHY'S
JOE CARAMAGNA

COVER ART
STEVE EPTING

ASSISTANT EDITORS
MOLLY LAZER &
AUBREY SITTERSON

EDITOR
TOM BREVOORT

CAPTAIN AMERICA
CREATED BY
JOE SIMON & JACK KIRBY

COLLECTION EDITOR
JENNIFER GRÜNWALD

ASSISTANT EDITORS
MICHAEL SHORT &
CORY LEVINE

ASSOCIATE EDITOR
MARK D. BEAZLEY

SENIOR EDITOR,
SPECIAL PROJECTS
JEFF YOUNGQUIST

SENIOR VICE PRESIDENT
OF SALES
DAVID GABRIEL

BOOK DESIGNER
DAYLE CHESLER

VICE PRESIDENT OF CREATIVE
TOM MARVELLI

EDITOR IN CHIEF
JOE QUESADA

PUBLISHER
DAN BUCKLEY

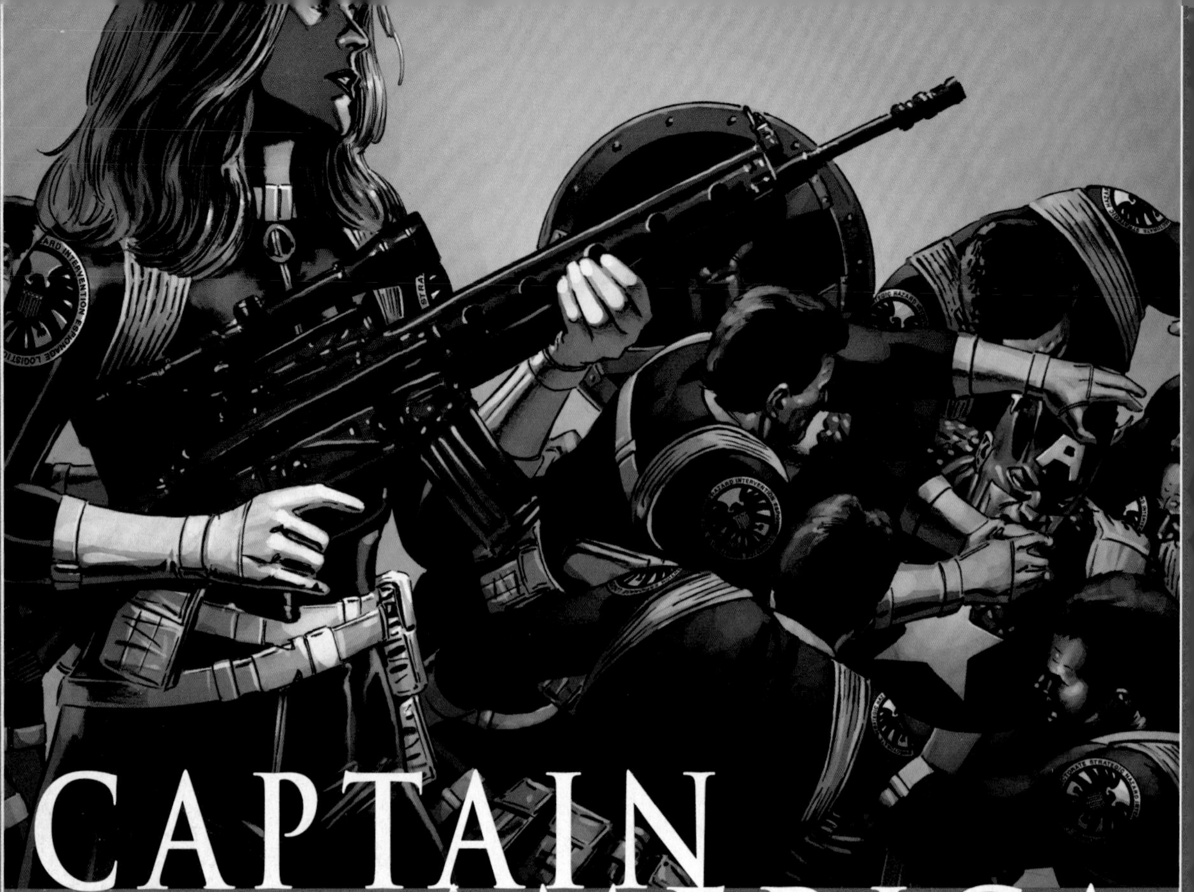

CAPTAIN AMERICA

A MARVEL COMICS EVENT

CIVIL WAR

CAPTAIN AMERICA #22

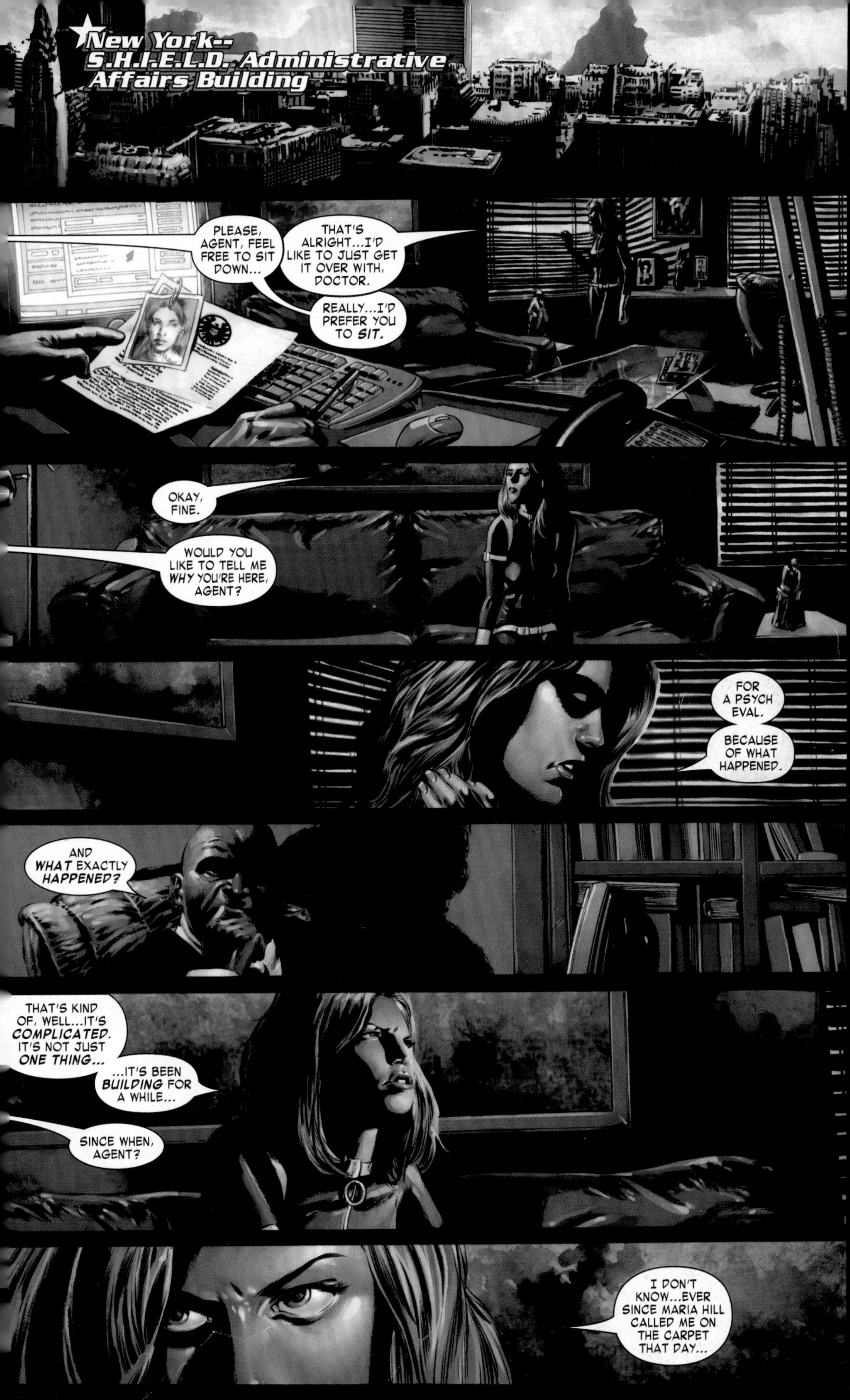
New York--
S.H.I.E.L.D. Administrative Affairs Building
PLEASE, AGENT, FEEL FREE TO SIT DOWN...
THAT'S ALRIGHT...I'D LIKE TO JUST GET IT OVER WITH, DOCTOR.
REALLY...I'D PREFER YOU TO SIT.
OKAY, FINE.
WOULD YOU LIKE TO TELL ME WHY YOU'RE HERE, AGENT?
FOR A PSYCH EVAL.
BECAUSE OF WHAT HAPPENED.
AND WHAT EXACTLY HAPPENED?
THAT'S KIND OF, WELL...IT'S COMPLICATED. IT'S NOT JUST ONE THING...
...IT'S BEEN BUILDING FOR A WHILE...
SINCE WHEN, AGENT?
I DON'T KNOW...EVER SINCE MARIA HILL CALLED ME ON THE CARPET THAT DAY...

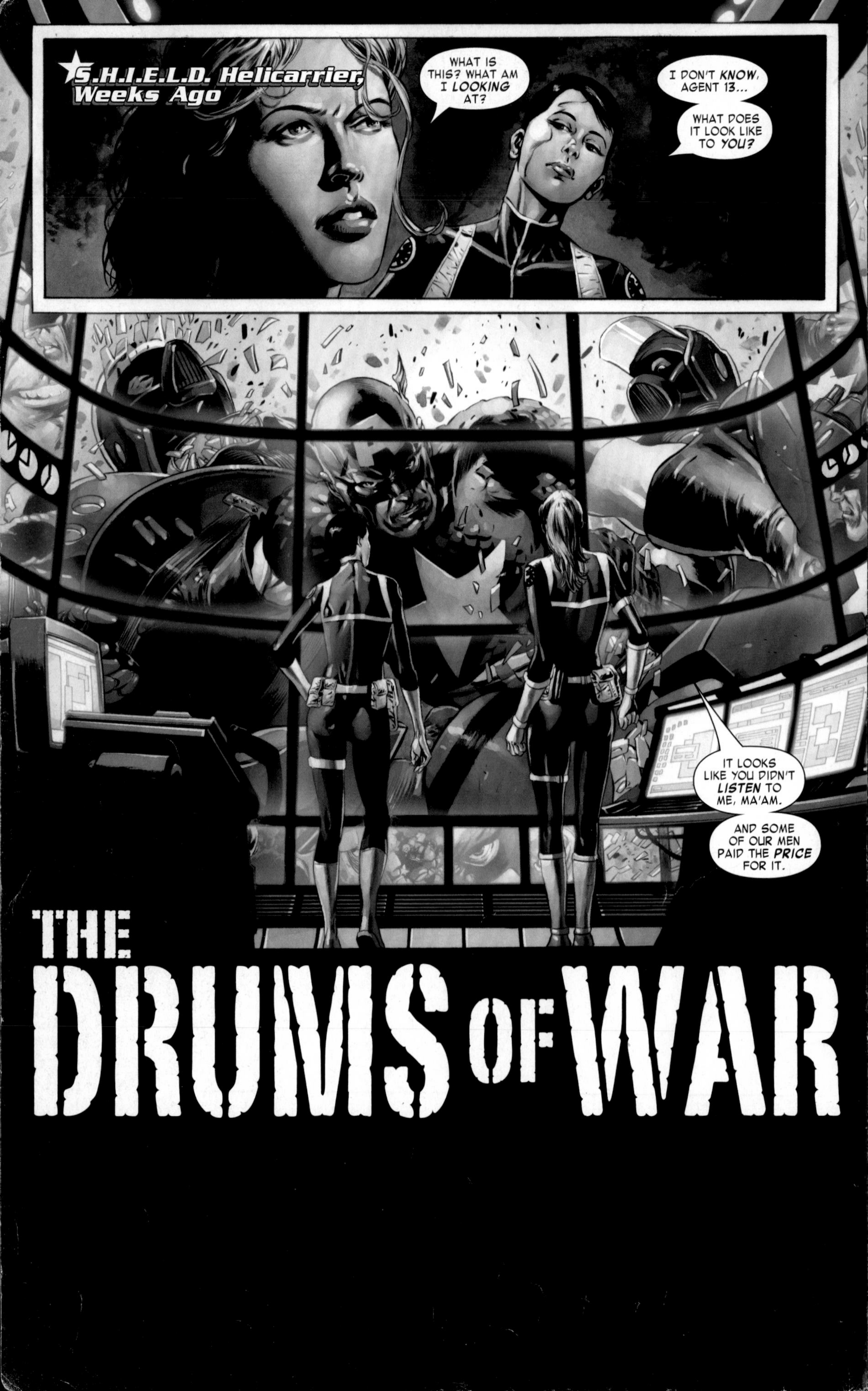
S.H.I.E.L.D. Helicarrier, Weeks Ago
WHAT IS THIS? WHAT AM I LOOKING AT?
I DON'T KNOW, AGENT 13...
WHAT DOES IT LOOK LIKE TO YOU?
IT LOOKS LIKE YOU DIDN'T LISTEN TO ME, MA'AM.
AND SOME OF OUR MEN PAID THE PRICE FOR IT.
THE DRUMS OF WAR

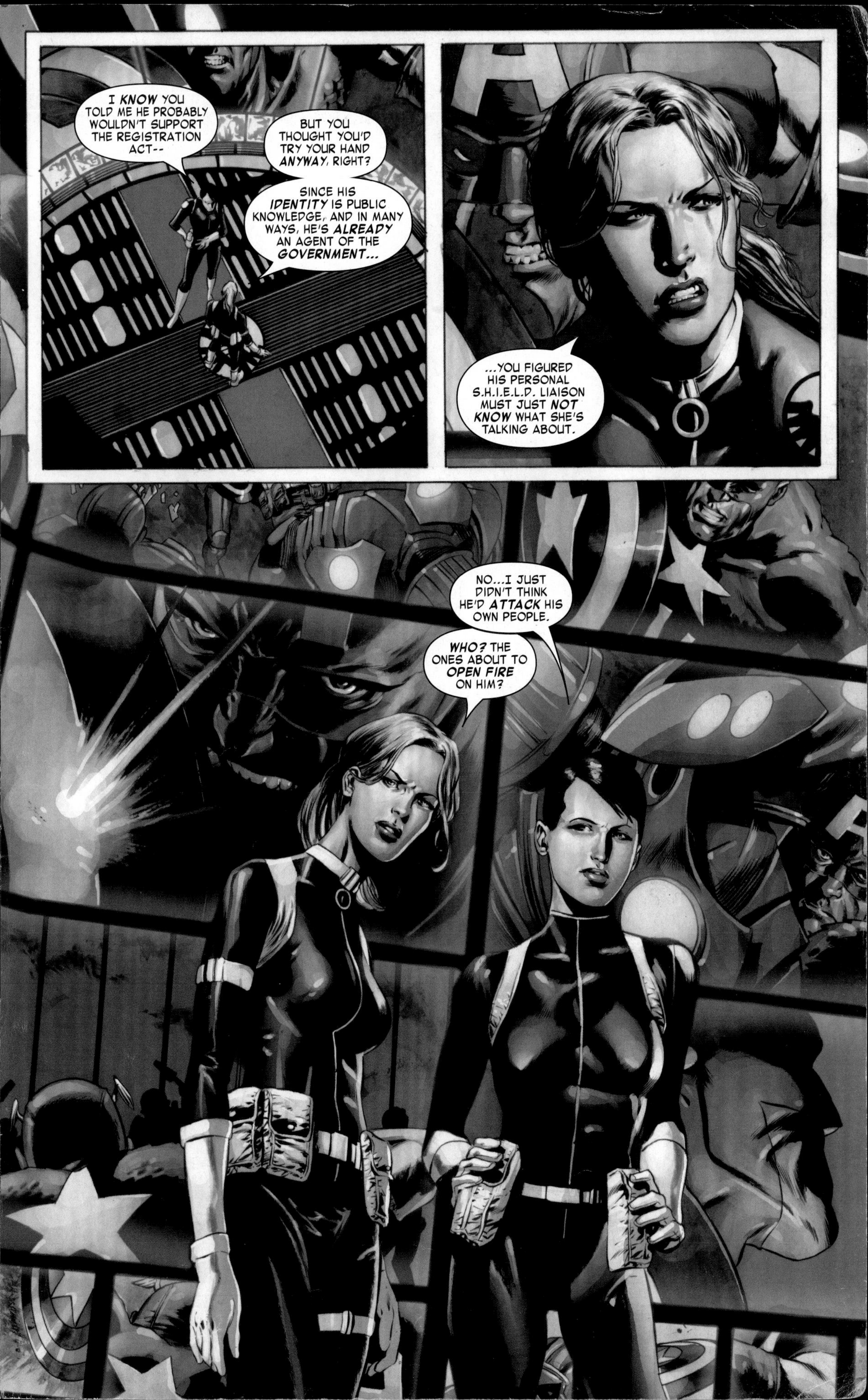
I KNOW YOU TOLD ME HE PROBABLY WOULDN'T SUPPORT THE REGISTRATION ACT--
BUT YOU THOUGHT YOU'D TRY YOUR HAND ANYWAY, RIGHT?
SINCE HIS IDENTITY IS PUBLIC KNOWLEDGE, AND IN MANY WAYS, HE'S ALREADY AN AGENT OF THE GOVERNMENT...
...YOU FIGURED HIS PERSONAL S.H.I.E.L.D. LIAISON MUST JUST NOT KNOW WHAT SHE'S TALKING ABOUT.
NO...I JUST DIDN'T THINK HE'D ATTACK HIS OWN PEOPLE.
WHO? THE ONES ABOUT TO OPEN FIRE ON HIM?

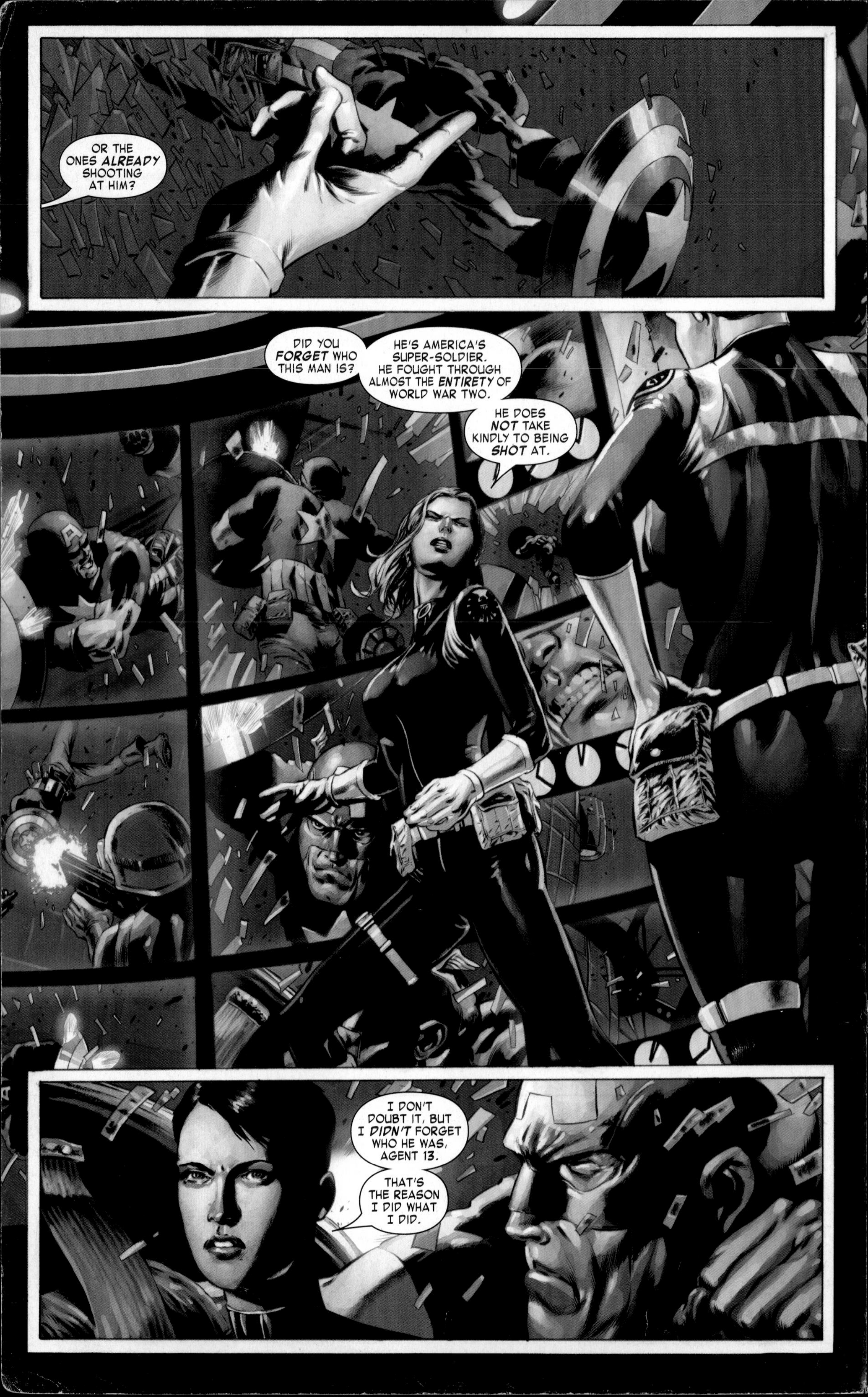
OR THE ONES ALREADY SHOOTING AT HIM?
DID YOU FORGET WHO THIS MAN IS?
HE'S AMERICA'S SUPER-SOLDIER. HE FOUGHT THROUGH ALMOST THE ENTIRETY OF WORLD WAR TWO.
HE DOES NOT TAKE KINDLY TO BEING SHOT AT.
I DON'T DOUBT IT, BUT I DIDN'T FORGET WHO HE WAS, AGENT 13.
THAT'S THE REASON I DID WHAT I DID.

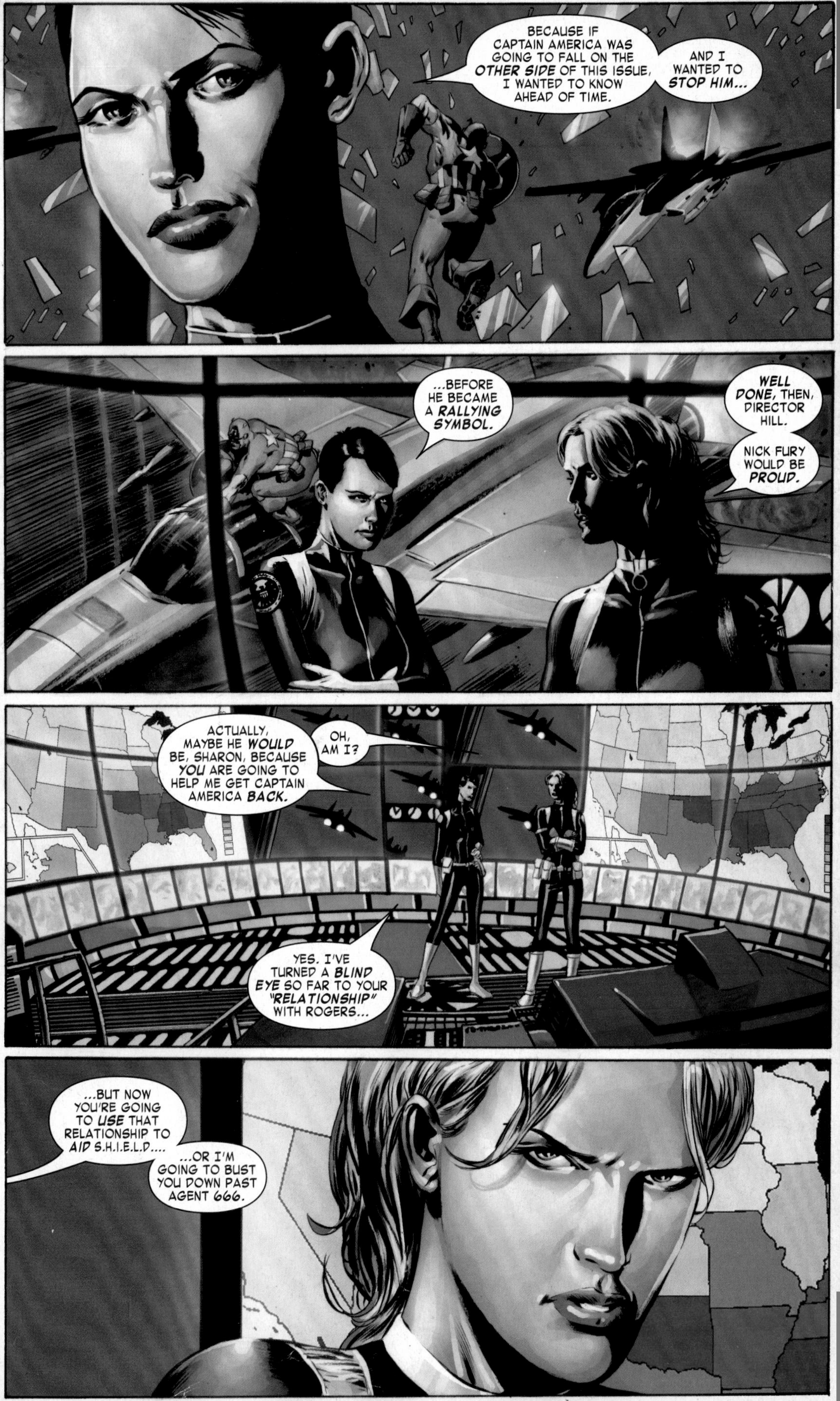
BECAUSE IF CAPTAIN AMERICA WAS GOING TO FALL ON THE OTHER SIDE OF THIS ISSUE, I WANTED TO KNOW AHEAD OF TIME.
AND I WANTED TO STOP HIM...
...BEFORE HE BECAME A RALLYING SYMBOL.
WELL DONE, THEN, DIRECTOR HILL.
NICK FURY WOULD BE PROUD.
ACTUALLY, MAYBE HE WOULD BE, SHARON, BECAUSE YOU ARE GOING TO HELP ME GET CAPTAIN AMERICA BACK.
OH, AM I?
YES. I'VE TURNED A BLIND EYE SO FAR TO YOUR "RELATIONSHIP" WITH ROGERS...
...BUT NOW YOU'RE GOING TO USE THAT RELATIONSHIP TO AID S.H.I.E.L.D....
...OR I'M GOING TO BUST YOU DOWN PAST AGENT 666.

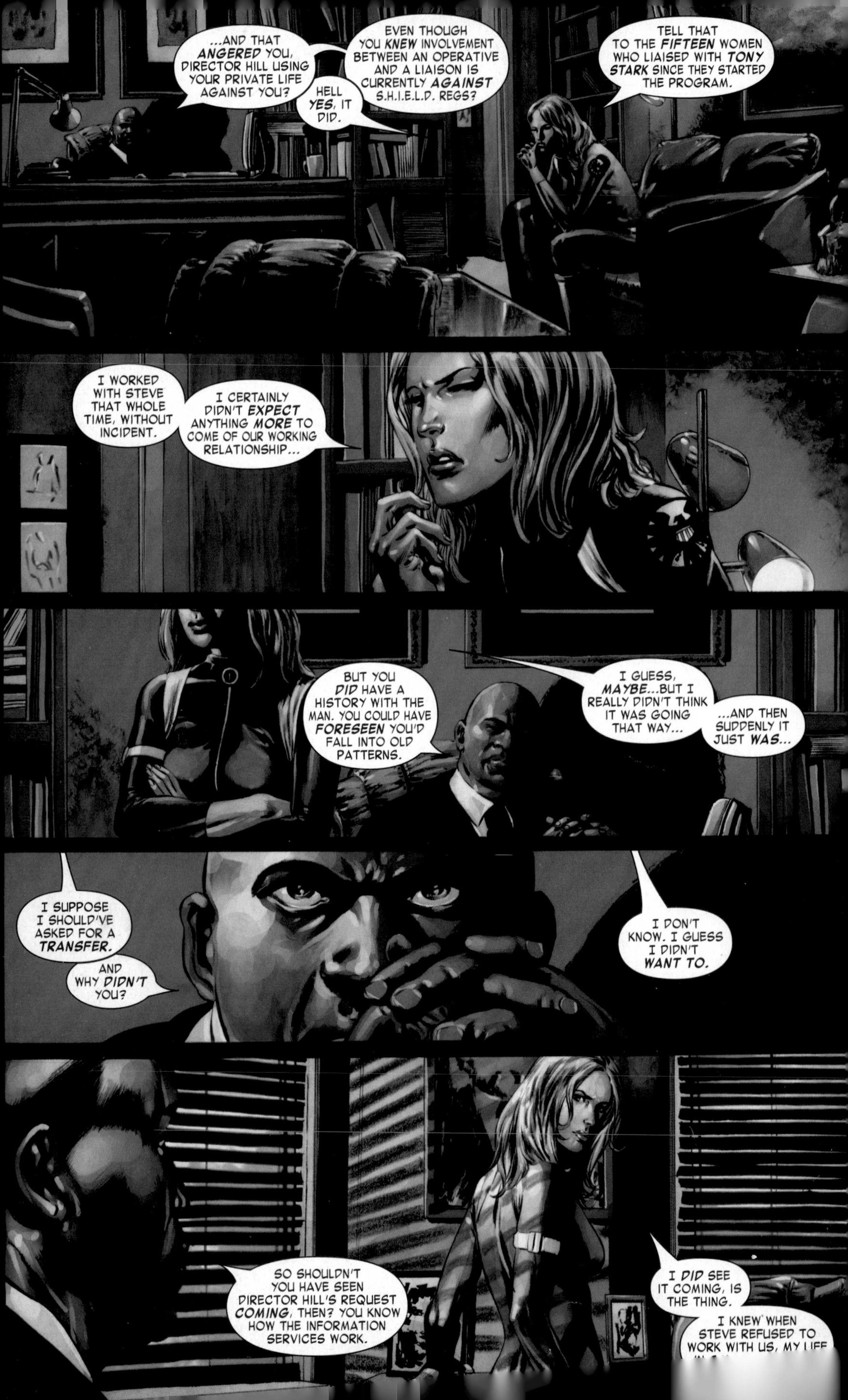

...AND THAT ANGERED YOU, DIRECTOR HILL USING YOUR PRIVATE LIFE AGAINST YOU?
HELL YES, IT DID.
EVEN THOUGH YOU KNEW INVOLVEMENT BETWEEN AN OPERATIVE AND A LIAISON IS CURRENTLY AGAINST S.H.I.E.L.D. REGS?
TELL THAT TO THE FIFTEEN WOMEN WHO LIAISED WITH TONY STARK SINCE THEY STARTED THE PROGRAM.
I WORKED WITH STEVE THAT WHOLE TIME, WITHOUT INCIDENT.
I CERTAINLY DIDN'T EXPECT ANYTHING MORE TO COME OF OUR WORKING RELATIONSHIP...
BUT YOU DID HAVE A HISTORY WITH THE MAN. YOU COULD HAVE FORESEEN YOU'D FALL INTO OLD PATTERNS.
I GUESS, MAYBE...BUT I REALLY DIDN'T THINK IT WAS GOING THAT WAY...
...AND THEN SUDDENLY IT JUST WAS...
I SUPPOSE I SHOULD'VE ASKED FOR A TRANSFER.
AND WHY DIDN'T YOU?
I DON'T KNOW. I GUESS I DIDN'T WANT TO.
SO SHOULDN'T YOU HAVE SEEN DIRECTOR HILL'S REQUEST COMING, THEN? YOU KNOW HOW THE INFORMATION SERVICES WORK.
I DID SEE IT COMING, IS THE THING.
I KNEW WHEN STEVE REFUSED TO WORK WITH US, MY LIFE

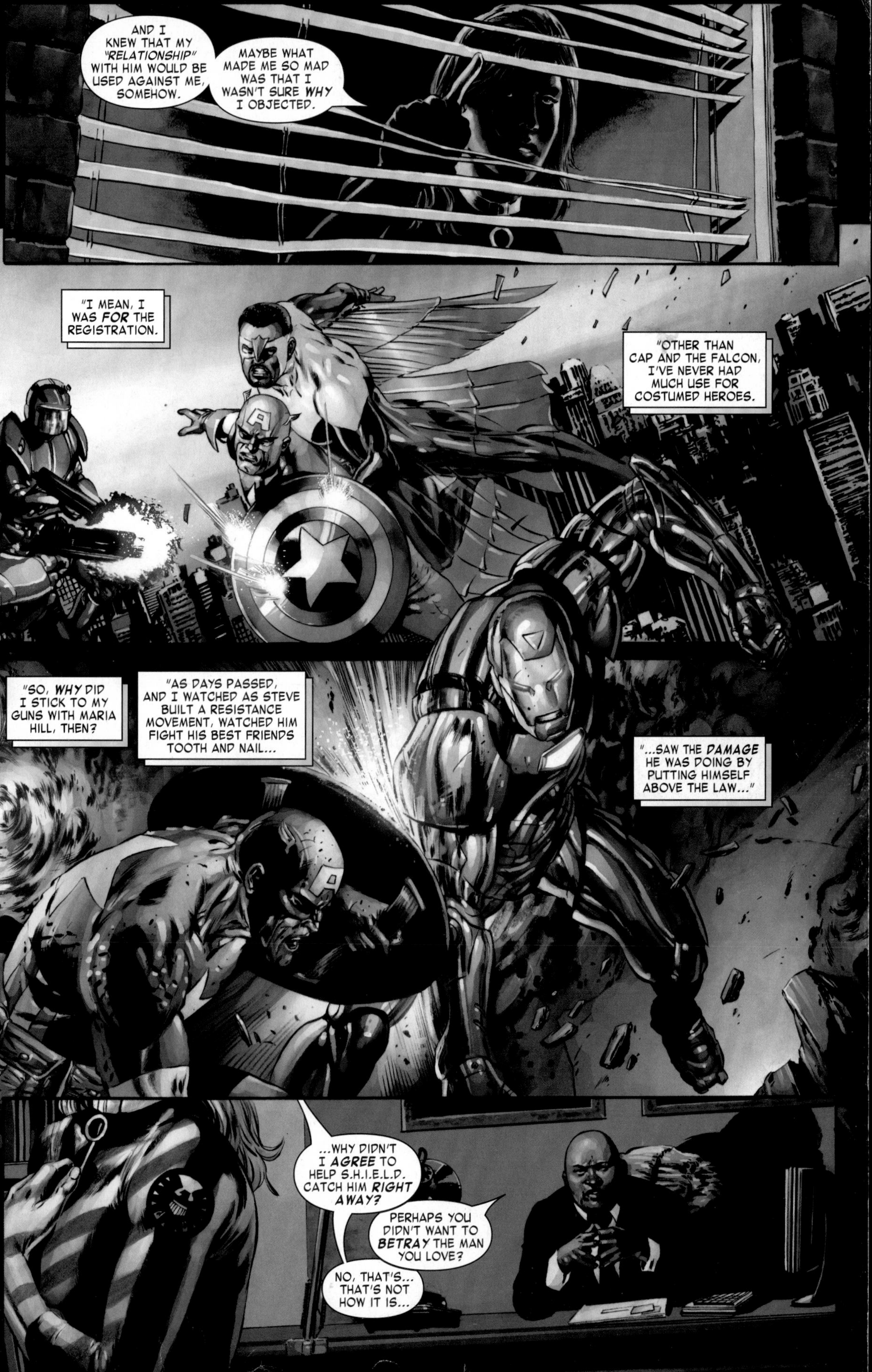
AND I KNEW THAT MY "RELATIONSHIP" WITH HIM WOULD BE USED AGAINST ME, SOMEHOW.
MAYBE WHAT MADE ME SO MAD WAS THAT I WASN'T SURE WHY I OBJECTED.
"I MEAN, I WAS FOR THE REGISTRATION.
"OTHER THAN CAP AND THE FALCON, I'VE NEVER HAD MUCH USE FOR COSTUMED HEROES.
"SO, WHY DID I STICK TO MY GUNS WITH MARIA HILL, THEN?
"AS DAYS PASSED, AND I WATCHED AS STEVE BUILT A RESISTANCE MOVEMENT, WATCHED HIM FIGHT HIS BEST FRIENDS TOOTH AND NAIL...
"...SAW THE DAMAGE HE WAS DOING BY PUTTING HIMSELF ABOVE THE LAW..."
...WHY DIDN'T I AGREE TO HELP S.H.I.E.L.D. CATCH HIM RIGHT AWAY?
PERHAPS YOU DIDN'T WANT TO BETRAY THE MAN YOU LOVE?
NO, THAT'S... THAT'S NOT HOW IT IS...

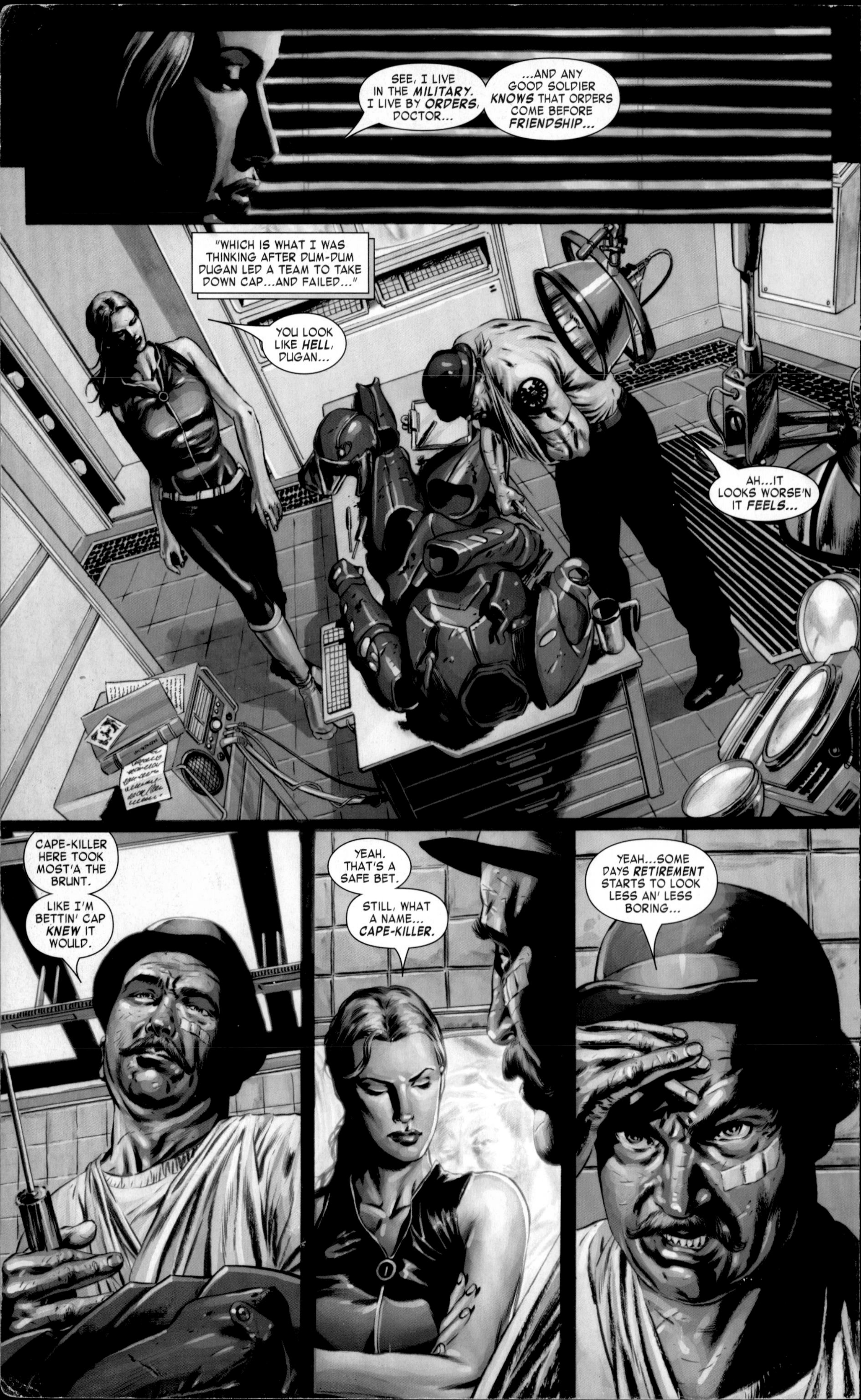
SEE, I LIVE IN THE MILITARY. I LIVE BY ORDERS, DOCTOR...
...AND ANY GOOD SOLDIER KNOWS THAT ORDERS COME BEFORE FRIENDSHIP...
"WHICH IS WHAT I WAS THINKING AFTER DUM-DUM DUGAN LED A TEAM TO TAKE DOWN CAP...AND FAILED..."
YOU LOOK LIKE HELL, DUGAN...
AH...IT LOOKS WORSE'N IT FEELS...
CAPE-KILLER HERE TOOK MOST'A THE BRUNT.
LIKE I'M BETTIN' CAP KNEW IT WOULD.
YEAH. THAT'S A SAFE BET.
STILL, WHAT A NAME... CAPE-KILLER.
YEAH...SOME DAYS RETIREMENT STARTS TO LOOK LESS AN' LESS BORING...

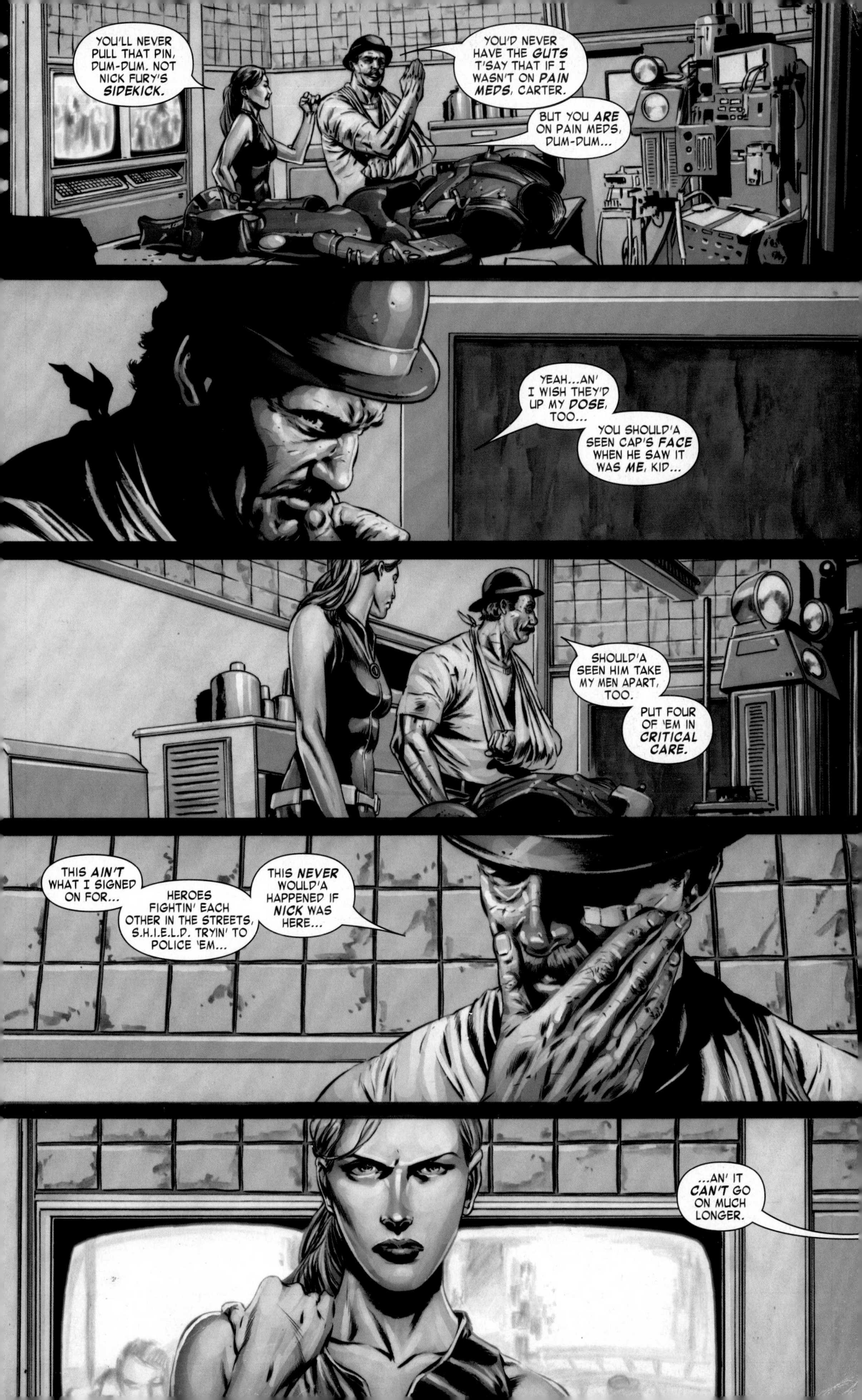
YOU'LL NEVER PULL THAT PIN, DUM-DUM. NOT NICK FURY'S SIDEKICK.
YOU'D NEVER HAVE THE GUTS T'SAY THAT IF I WASN'T ON PAIN MEDS, CARTER.
BUT YOU ARE ON PAIN MEDS, DUM-DUM...
YEAH...AN' I WISH THEY'D UP MY DOSE, TOO...
YOU SHOULD'A SEEN CAP'S FACE WHEN HE SAW IT WAS ME, KID...
SHOULD'A SEEN HIM TAKE MY MEN APART, TOO.
PUT FOUR OF 'EM IN CRITICAL CARE.
THIS AIN'T WHAT I SIGNED ON FOR...
HEROES FIGHTIN' EACH OTHER IN THE STREETS, S.H.I.E.L.D. TRYIN' TO POLICE 'EM...
THIS NEVER WOULD'A HAPPENED IF NICK WAS HERE...
...AN' IT CAN'T GO ON MUCH LONGER.

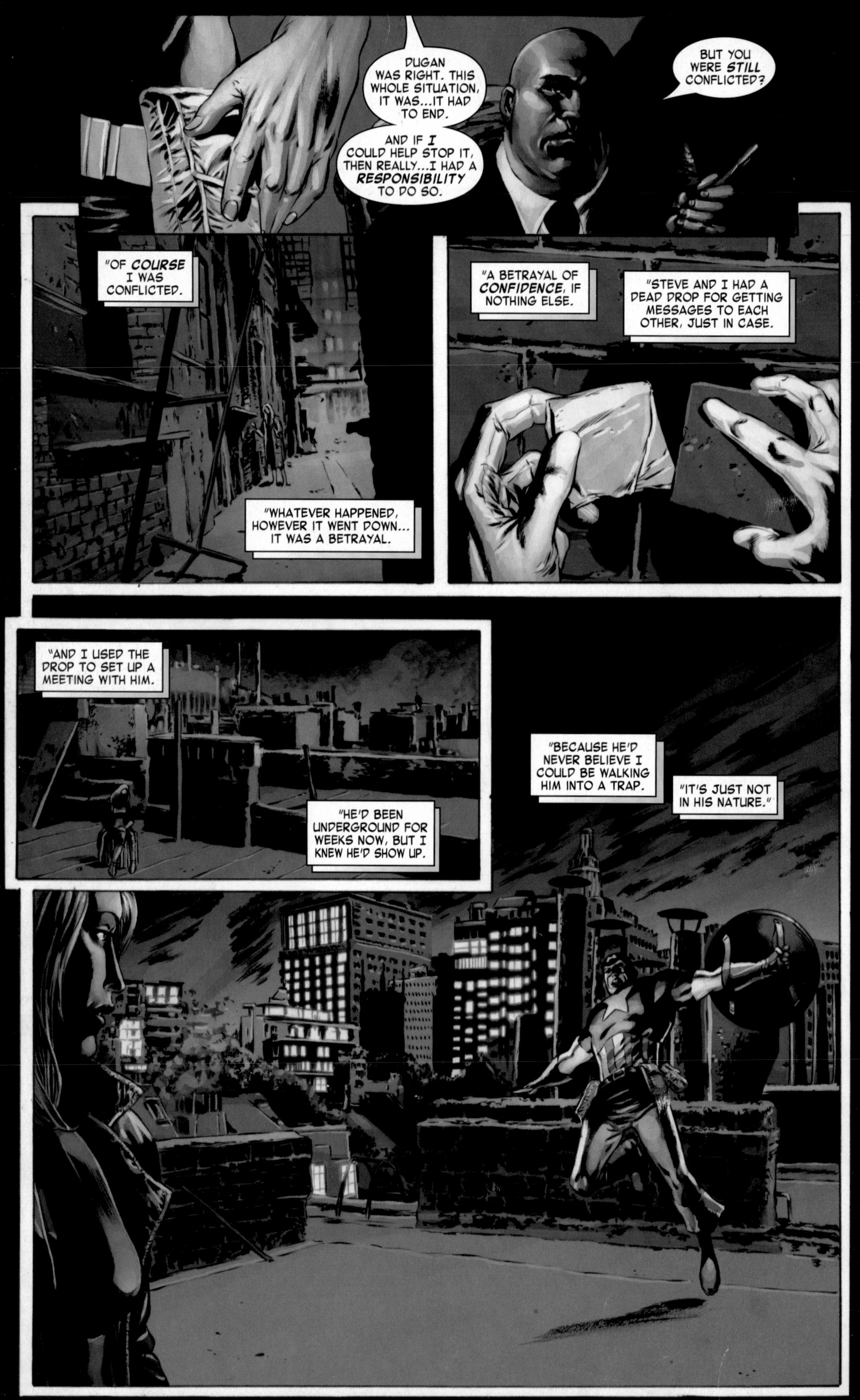
DUGAN WAS RIGHT. THIS WHOLE SITUATION, IT WAS...IT HAD TO END.
AND IF I COULD HELP STOP IT, THEN REALLY...I HAD A RESPONSIBILITY TO DO SO.
BUT YOU WERE STILL CONFLICTED?
"OF COURSE I WAS CONFLICTED.
"WHATEVER HAPPENED, HOWEVER IT WENT DOWN... IT WAS A BETRAYAL.
"A BETRAYAL OF CONFIDENCE, IF NOTHING ELSE.
"STEVE AND I HAD A DEAD DROP FOR GETTING MESSAGES TO EACH OTHER, JUST IN CASE.
"AND I USED THE DROP TO SET UP A MEETING WITH HIM.
"HE'D BEEN UNDERGROUND FOR WEEKS NOW, BUT I KNEW HE'D SHOW UP.
"BECAUSE HE'D NEVER BELIEVE I COULD BE WALKING HIM INTO A TRAP.
"IT'S JUST NOT IN HIS NATURE."

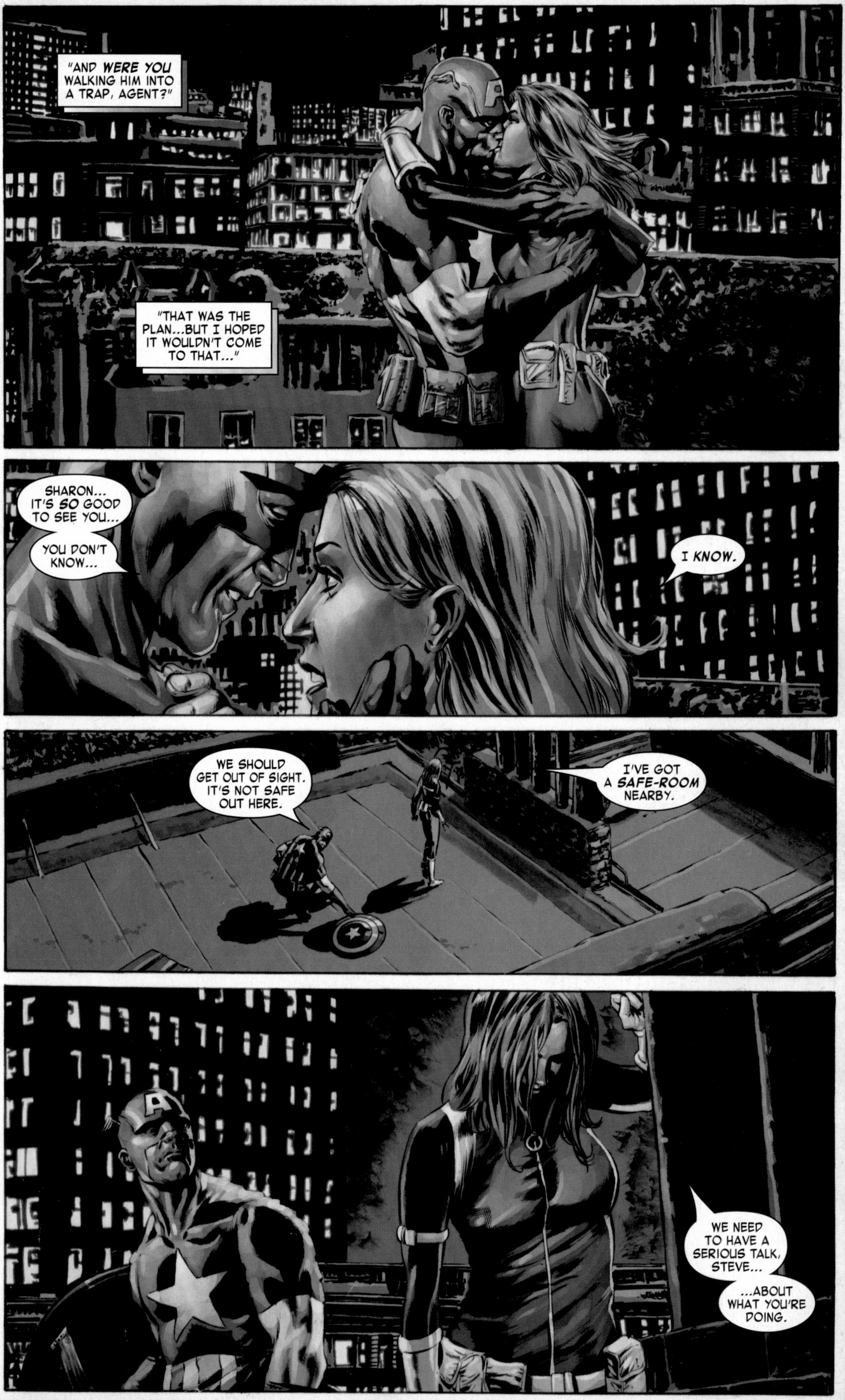
"AND WERE YOU WALKING HIM INTO A TRAP, AGENT?"
"THAT WAS THE PLAN...BUT I HOPED IT WOULDN'T COME TO THAT..."
SHARON... IT'S SO GOOD TO SEE YOU...
YOU DON'T KNOW...
I KNOW.
WE SHOULD GET OUT OF SIGHT. IT'S NOT SAFE OUT HERE.
I'VE GOT A SAFE-ROOM NEARBY.
WE NEED TO HAVE A SERIOUS TALK, STEVE...
...ABOUT WHAT YOU'RE DOING.

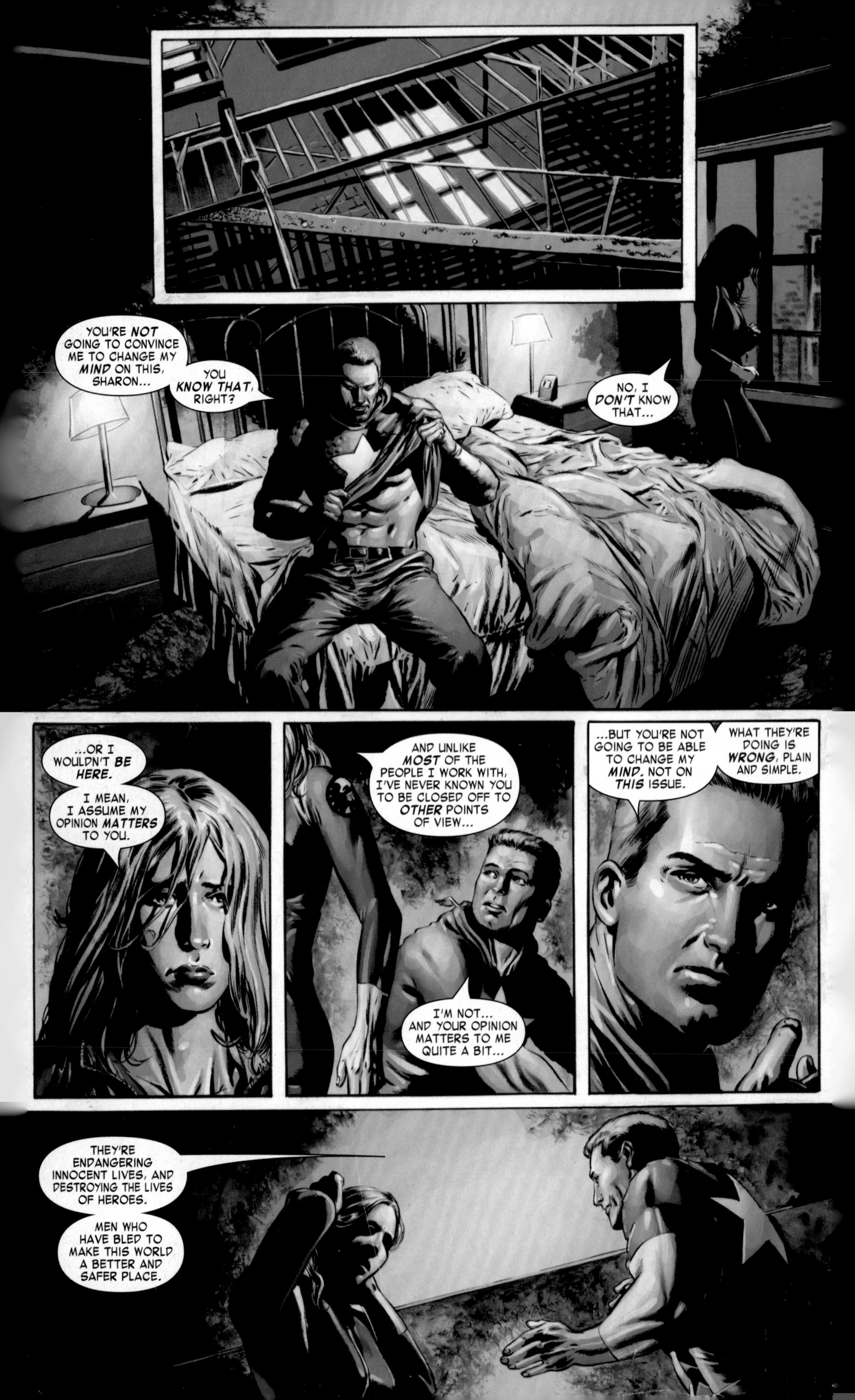
YOU'RE NOT GOING TO CONVINCE ME TO CHANGE MY MIND ON THIS, SHARON...
YOU KNOW THAT, RIGHT?
NO, I DON'T KNOW THAT...
...OR I WOULDN'T BE HERE.
I MEAN, I ASSUME MY OPINION MATTERS TO YOU.
AND UNLIKE MOST OF THE PEOPLE I WORK WITH, I'VE NEVER KNOWN YOU TO BE CLOSED OFF TO OTHER POINTS OF VIEW...
I'M NOT... AND YOUR OPINION MATTERS TO ME QUITE A BIT...
...BUT YOU'RE NOT GOING TO BE ABLE TO CHANGE MY MIND. NOT ON THIS ISSUE.
WHAT THEY'RE DOING IS WRONG, PLAIN AND SIMPLE.
THEY'RE ENDANGERING INNOCENT LIVES, AND DESTROYING THE LIVES OF HEROES.
MEN WHO HAVE BLED TO MAKE THIS WORLD A BETTER AND SAFER PLACE.

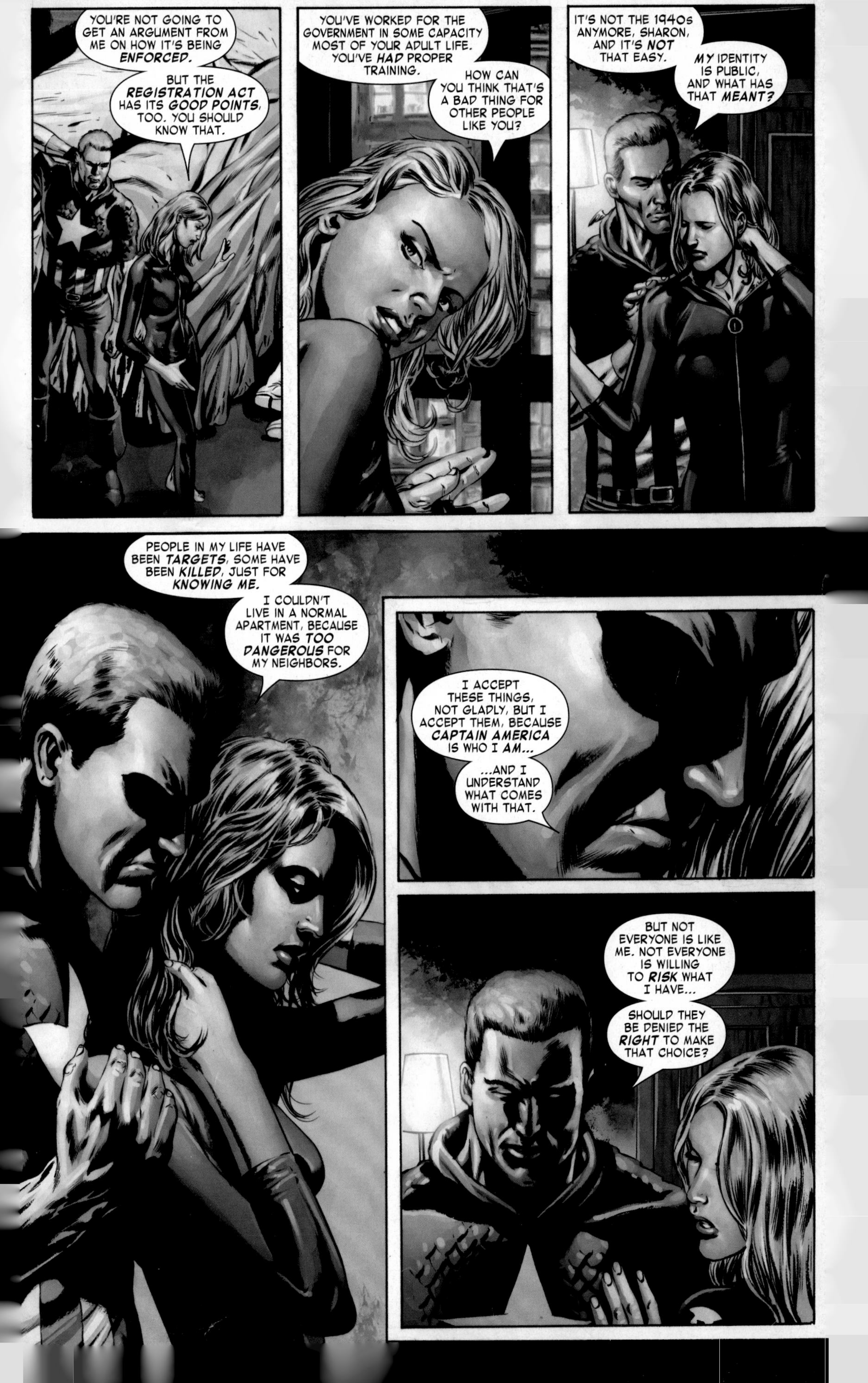
YOU'RE NOT GOING TO GET AN ARGUMENT FROM ME ON HOW IT'S BEING ENFORCED.
BUT THE REGISTRATION ACT HAS ITS GOOD POINTS, TOO. YOU SHOULD KNOW THAT.
YOU'VE WORKED FOR THE GOVERNMENT IN SOME CAPACITY MOST OF YOUR ADULT LIFE. YOU'VE HAD PROPER TRAINING.
HOW CAN YOU THINK THAT'S A BAD THING FOR OTHER PEOPLE LIKE YOU?
IT'S NOT THE 1940s ANYMORE, SHARON, AND IT'S NOT THAT EASY.
MY IDENTITY IS PUBLIC, AND WHAT HAS THAT MEANT?
PEOPLE IN MY LIFE HAVE BEEN TARGETS, SOME HAVE BEEN KILLED, JUST FOR KNOWING ME.
I COULDN'T LIVE IN A NORMAL APARTMENT, BECAUSE IT WAS TOO DANGEROUS FOR MY NEIGHBORS.
I ACCEPT THESE THINGS, NOT GLADLY, BUT I ACCEPT THEM, BECAUSE CAPTAIN AMERICA IS WHO I AM...
...AND I UNDERSTAND WHAT COMES WITH THAT.
BUT NOT EVERYONE IS LIKE ME. NOT EVERYONE IS WILLING TO RISK WHAT I HAVE...
SHOULD THEY BE DENIED THE RIGHT TO MAKE THAT CHOICE?

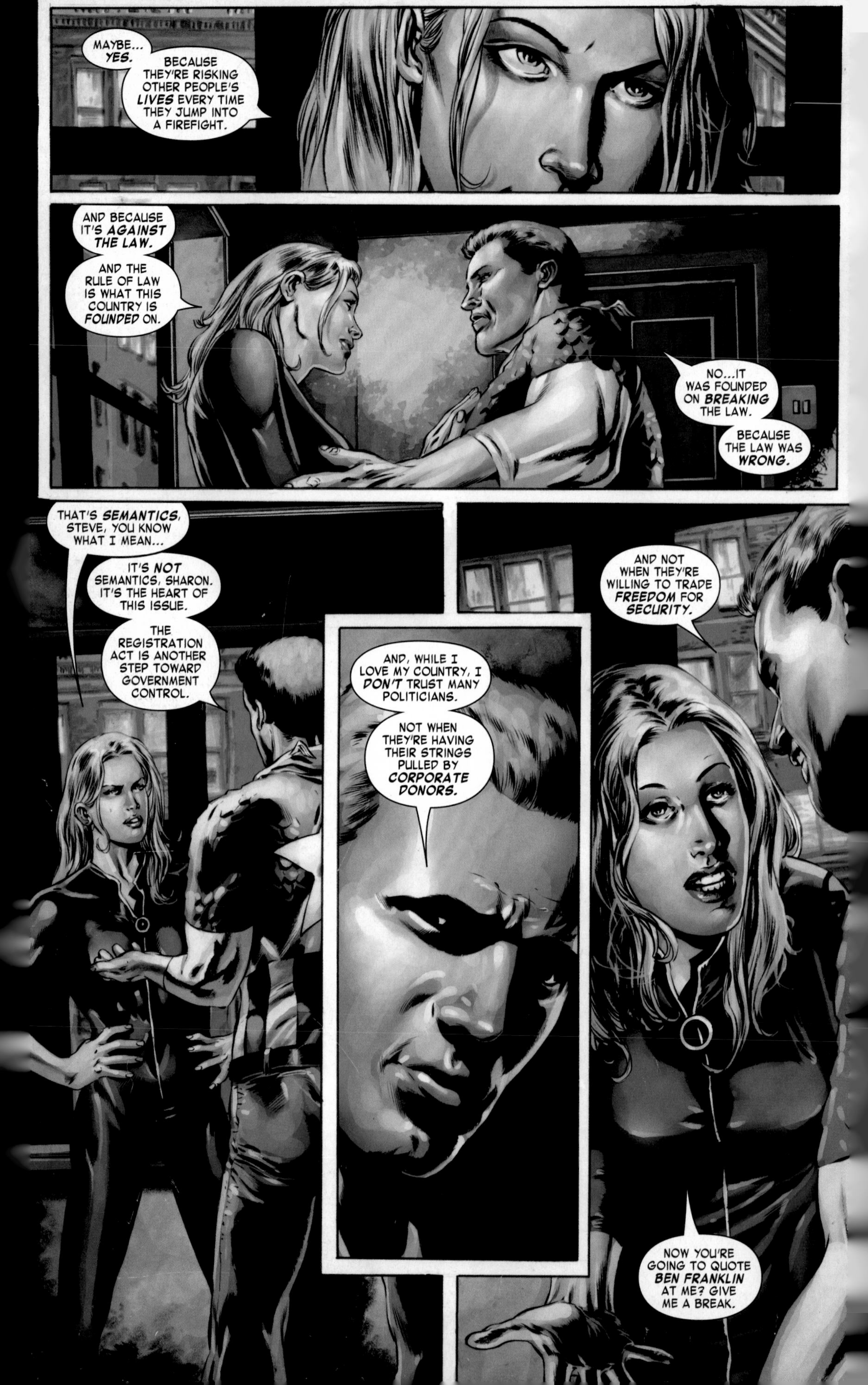
MAYBE... YES.
BECAUSE THEY'RE RISKING OTHER PEOPLE'S LIVES EVERY TIME THEY JUMP INTO A FIREFIGHT.
AND BECAUSE IT'S AGAINST THE LAW.
AND THE RULE OF LAW IS WHAT THIS COUNTRY IS FOUNDED ON.
NO...IT WAS FOUNDED ON BREAKING THE LAW.
BECAUSE THE LAW WAS WRONG.
THAT'S SEMANTICS, STEVE, YOU KNOW WHAT I MEAN...
IT'S NOT SEMANTICS, SHARON. IT'S THE HEART OF THIS ISSUE.
THE REGISTRATION ACT IS ANOTHER STEP TOWARD GOVERNMENT CONTROL.
AND, WHILE I LOVE MY COUNTRY, I DON'T TRUST MANY POLITICIANS.
NOT WHEN THEY'RE HAVING THEIR STRINGS PULLED BY CORPORATE DONORS.
AND NOT WHEN THEY'RE WILLING TO TRADE FREEDOM FOR SECURITY.
NOW YOU'RE GOING TO QUOTE BEN FRANKLIN AT ME? GIVE ME A BREAK.

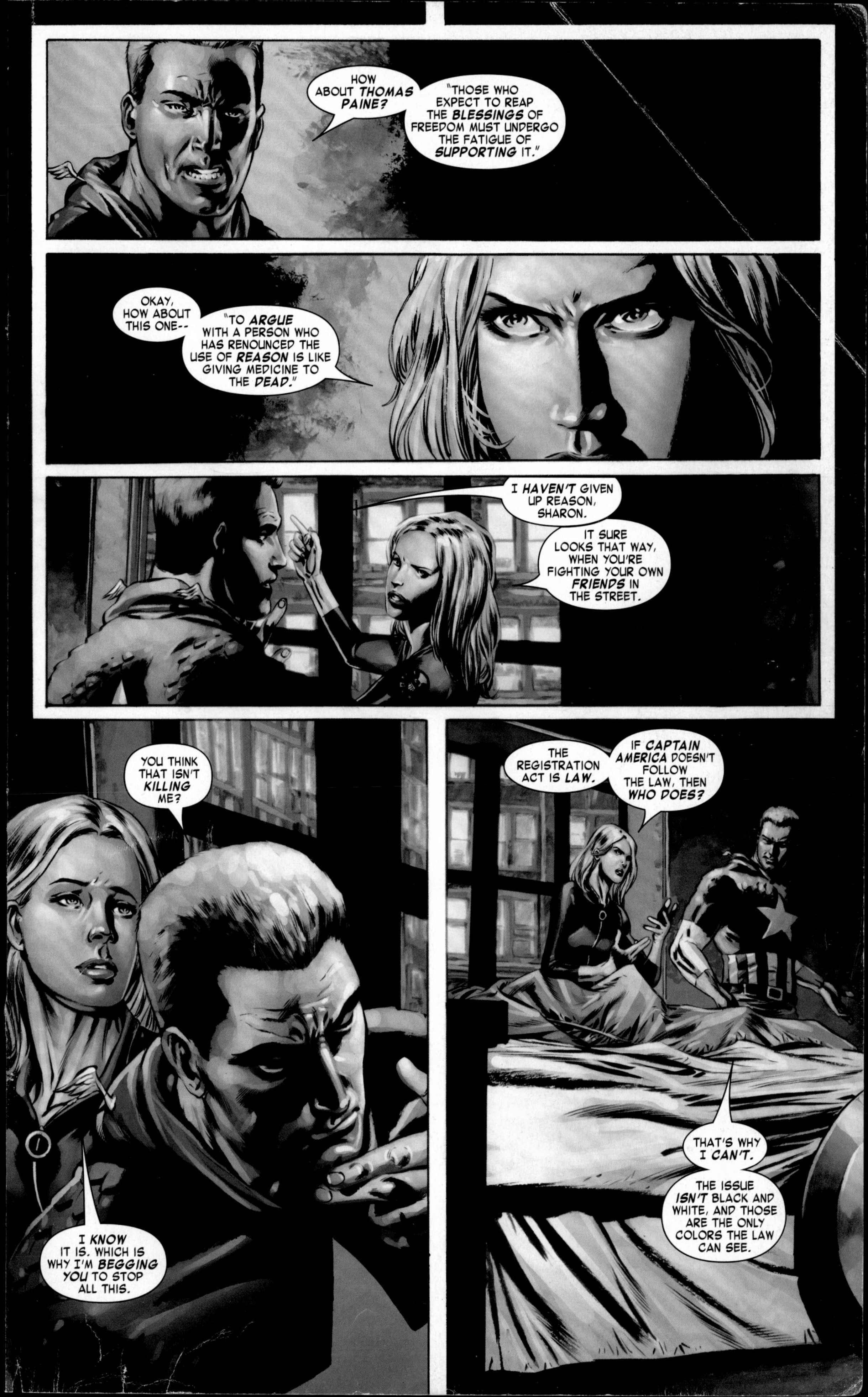
HOW ABOUT THOMAS PAINE?
"THOSE WHO EXPECT TO REAP THE BLESSINGS OF FREEDOM MUST UNDERGO THE FATIGUE OF SUPPORTING IT."
OKAY, HOW ABOUT THIS ONE--
"TO ARGUE WITH A PERSON WHO HAS RENOUNCED THE USE OF REASON IS LIKE GIVING MEDICINE TO THE DEAD."
I HAVEN'T GIVEN UP REASON, SHARON.
IT SURE LOOKS THAT WAY, WHEN YOU'RE FIGHTING YOUR OWN FRIENDS IN THE STREET.
YOU THINK THAT ISN'T KILLING ME?
I KNOW IT IS. WHICH IS WHY I'M BEGGING YOU TO STOP ALL THIS.
THE REGISTRATION ACT IS LAW.
IF CAPTAIN AMERICA DOESN'T FOLLOW THE LAW, THEN WHO DOES?
THAT'S WHY I CAN'T.
THE ISSUE ISN'T BLACK AND WHITE, AND THOSE ARE THE ONLY COLORS THE LAW CAN SEE.

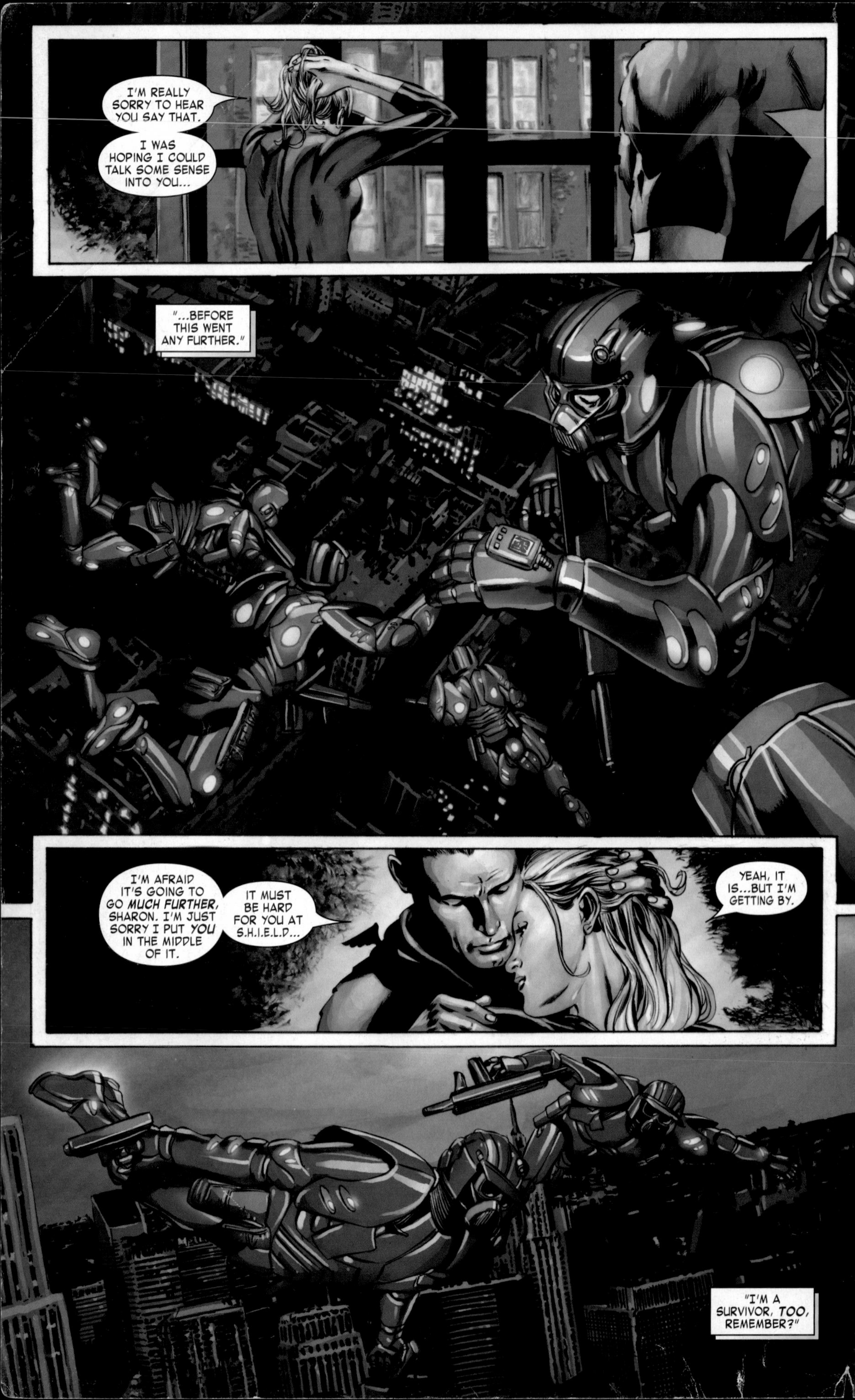
I'M REALLY SORRY TO HEAR YOU SAY THAT.
I WAS HOPING I COULD TALK SOME SENSE INTO YOU...
"...BEFORE THIS WENT ANY FURTHER."
I'M AFRAID IT'S GOING TO GO *MUCH FURTHER*, SHARON. I'M JUST SORRY I PUT *YOU* IN THE MIDDLE OF IT.
IT MUST BE HARD FOR YOU AT S.H.I.E.L.D...
YEAH, IT IS...BUT I'M GETTING BY.
"I'M A SURVIVOR, *TOO*, REMEMBER?"

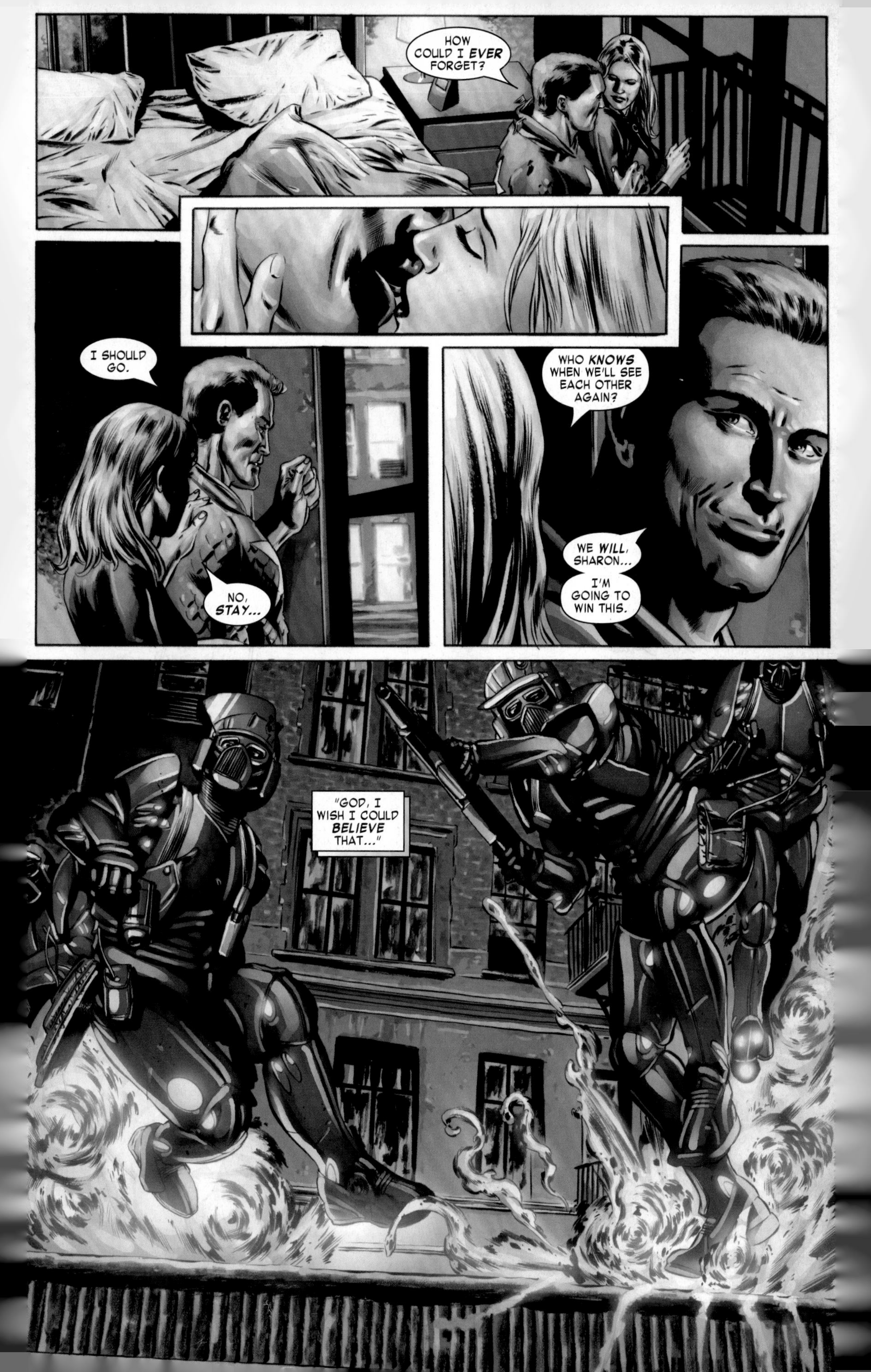
HOW COULD I EVER FORGET?
I SHOULD GO.
NO, STAY...
WHO KNOWS WHEN WE'LL SEE EACH OTHER AGAIN?
WE WILL, SHARON...
I'M GOING TO WIN THIS.
"GOD, I WISH I COULD BELIEVE THAT..."

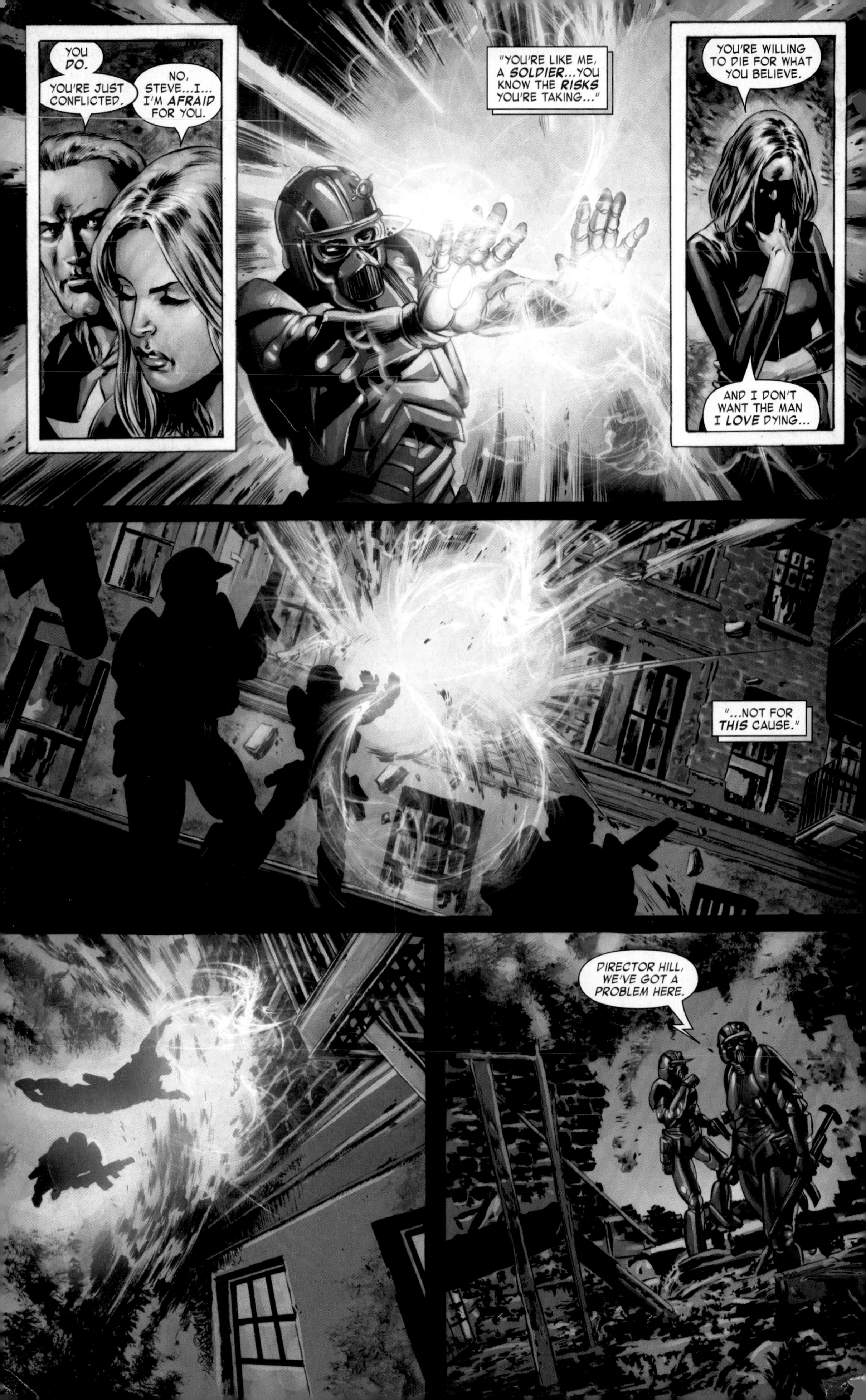
YOU DO.
YOU'RE JUST CONFLICTED.
NO, STEVE...I... I'M AFRAID FOR YOU.
"YOU'RE LIKE ME, A SOLDIER...YOU KNOW THE RISKS YOU'RE TAKING..."
YOU'RE WILLING TO DIE FOR WHAT YOU BELIEVE.
AND I DON'T WANT THE MAN I LOVE DYING...
"...NOT FOR THIS CAUSE."
DIRECTOR HILL, WE'VE GOT A PROBLEM HERE.

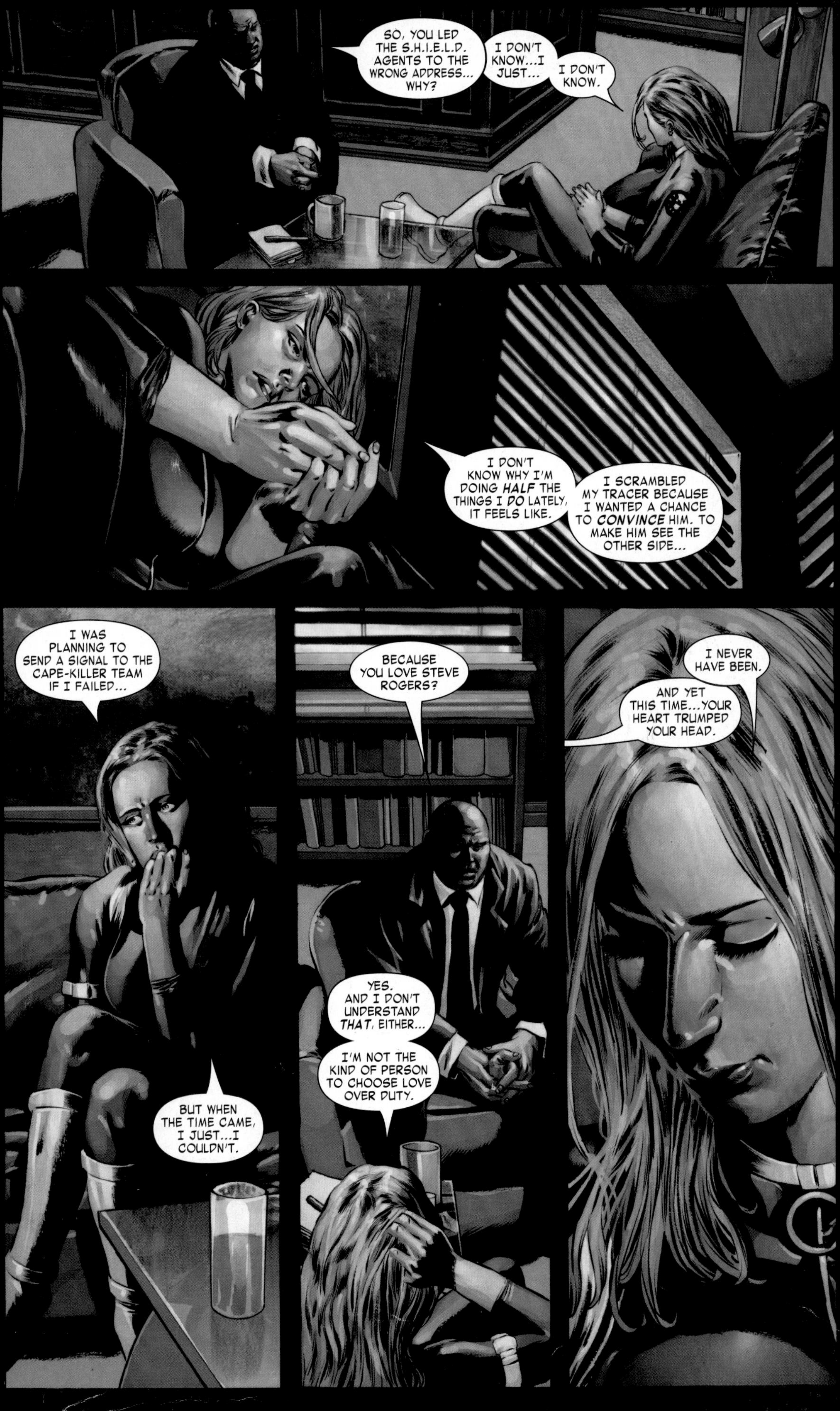
SO, YOU LED THE S.H.I.E.L.D. AGENTS TO THE WRONG ADDRESS... WHY?
I DON'T KNOW...I JUST...
I DON'T KNOW.
I DON'T KNOW WHY I'M DOING HALF THE THINGS I DO LATELY, IT FEELS LIKE.
I SCRAMBLED MY TRACER BECAUSE I WANTED A CHANCE TO CONVINCE HIM. TO MAKE HIM SEE THE OTHER SIDE...
I WAS PLANNING TO SEND A SIGNAL TO THE CAPE-KILLER TEAM IF I FAILED...
BUT WHEN THE TIME CAME, I JUST...I COULDN'T.
BECAUSE YOU LOVE STEVE ROGERS?
YES. AND I DON'T UNDERSTAND THAT, EITHER...
I'M NOT THE KIND OF PERSON TO CHOOSE LOVE OVER DUTY.
I NEVER HAVE BEEN.
AND YET THIS TIME...YOUR HEART TRUMPED YOUR HEAD.

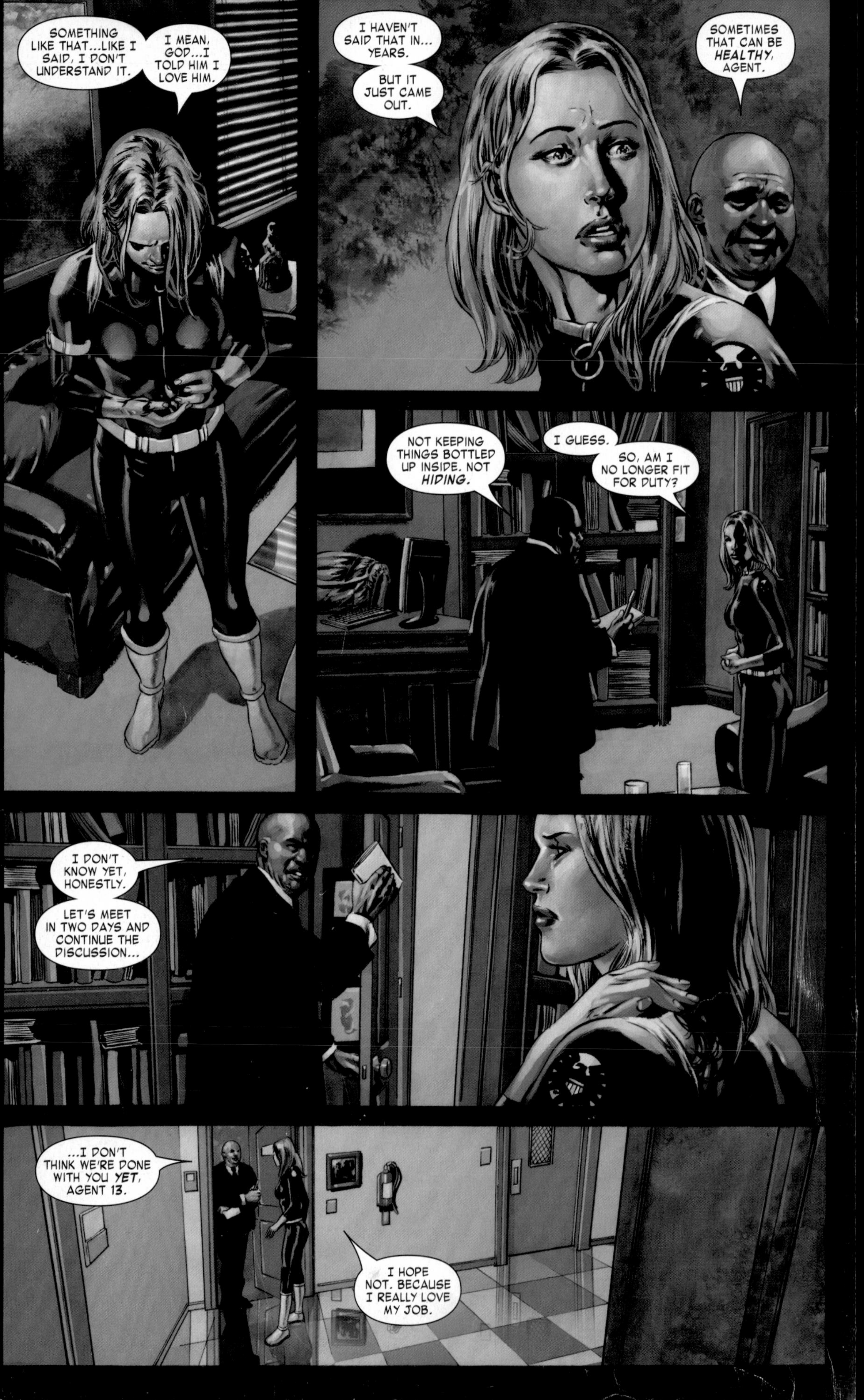
SOMETHING LIKE THAT...LIKE I SAID, I DON'T UNDERSTAND IT.
I MEAN, GOD...I TOLD HIM I LOVE HIM.
I HAVEN'T SAID THAT IN... YEARS.
BUT IT JUST CAME OUT.
SOMETIMES THAT CAN BE *HEALTHY*, AGENT.
NOT KEEPING THINGS BOTTLED UP INSIDE. NOT *HIDING*.
I GUESS.
SO, AM I NO LONGER FIT FOR DUTY?
I DON'T KNOW YET, HONESTLY.
LET'S MEET IN TWO DAYS AND CONTINUE THE DISCUSSION...
...I DON'T THINK WE'RE DONE WITH YOU *YET*, AGENT 13.
I HOPE NOT. BECAUSE I REALLY LOVE MY JOB.

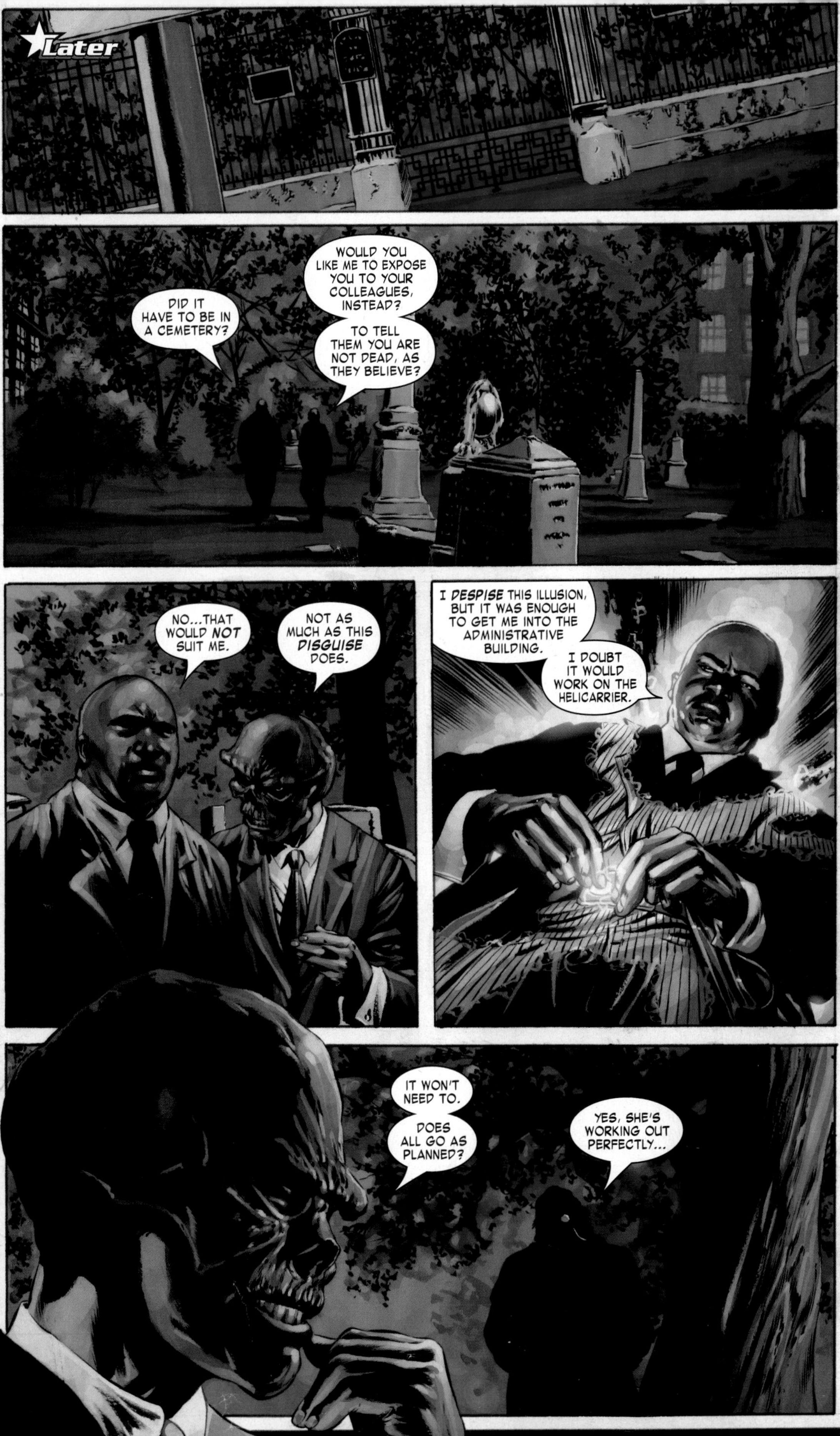
Later
DID IT HAVE TO BE IN A CEMETERY?
WOULD YOU LIKE ME TO EXPOSE YOU TO YOUR COLLEAGUES, INSTEAD?
TO TELL THEM YOU ARE NOT DEAD, AS THEY BELIEVE?
NO...THAT WOULD NOT SUIT ME.
NOT AS MUCH AS THIS DISGUISE DOES.
I DESPISE THIS ILLUSION, BUT IT WAS ENOUGH TO GET ME INTO THE ADMINISTRATIVE BUILDING.
I DOUBT IT WOULD WORK ON THE HELICARRIER.
IT WON'T NEED TO.
DOES ALL GO AS PLANNED?
YES, SHE'S WORKING OUT PERFECTLY...

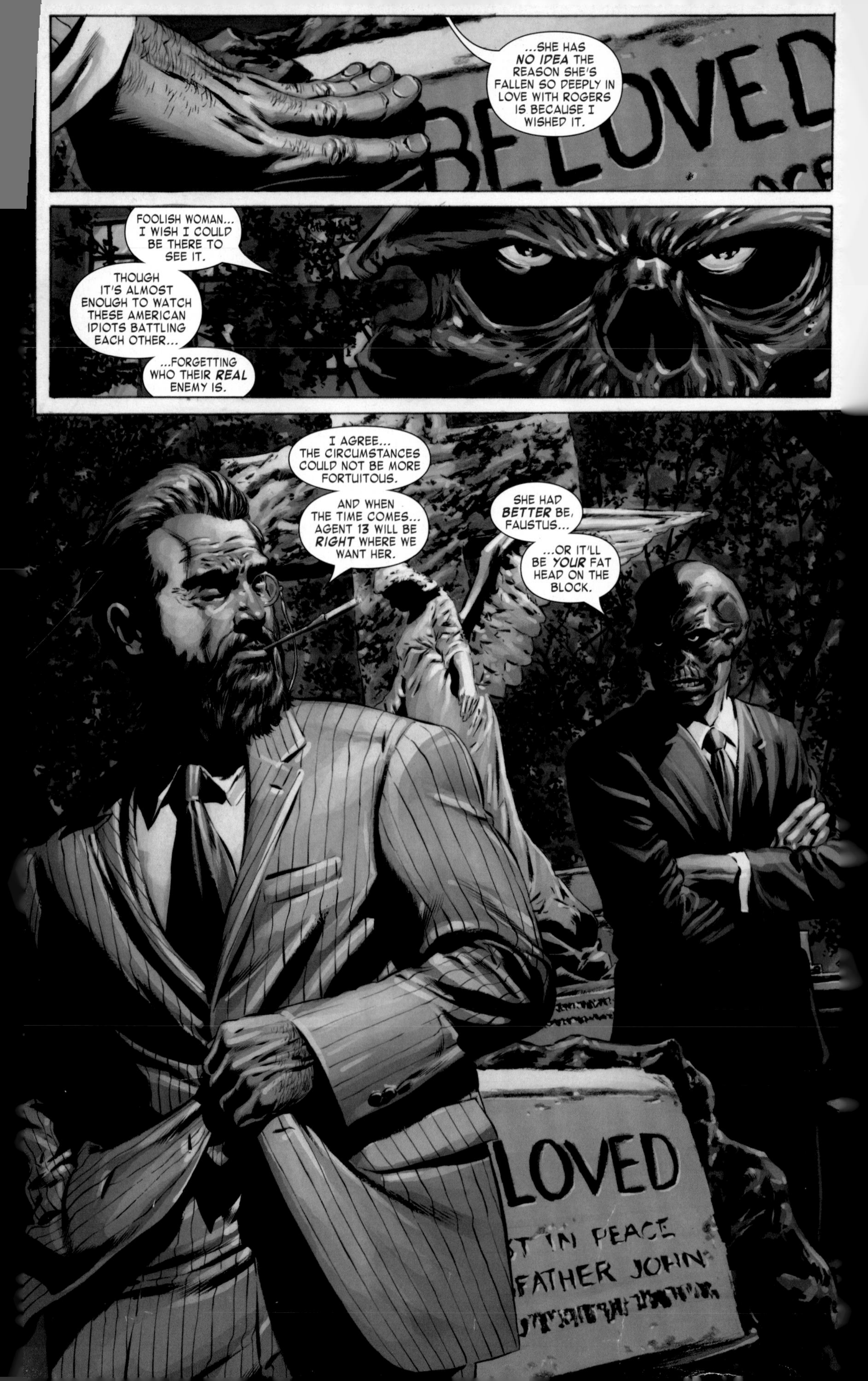
...SHE HAS NO IDEA THE REASON SHE'S FALLEN SO DEEPLY IN LOVE WITH ROGERS IS BECAUSE I WISHED IT.
BELOVED
FOOLISH WOMAN... I WISH I COULD BE THERE TO SEE IT.
THOUGH IT'S ALMOST ENOUGH TO WATCH THESE AMERICAN IDIOTS BATTLING EACH OTHER...
...FORGETTING WHO THEIR REAL ENEMY IS.
I AGREE... THE CIRCUMSTANCES COULD NOT BE MORE FORTUITOUS.
AND WHEN THE TIME COMES... AGENT 13 WILL BE RIGHT WHERE WE WANT HER.
SHE HAD BETTER BE, FAUSTUS...
...OR IT'LL BE YOUR FAT HEAD ON THE BLOCK.
LOVED
ST IN PEACE
FATHER JOHN

CAPTAIN
AMERICA
A MARVEL COMICS EVENT

CIVIL
WAR

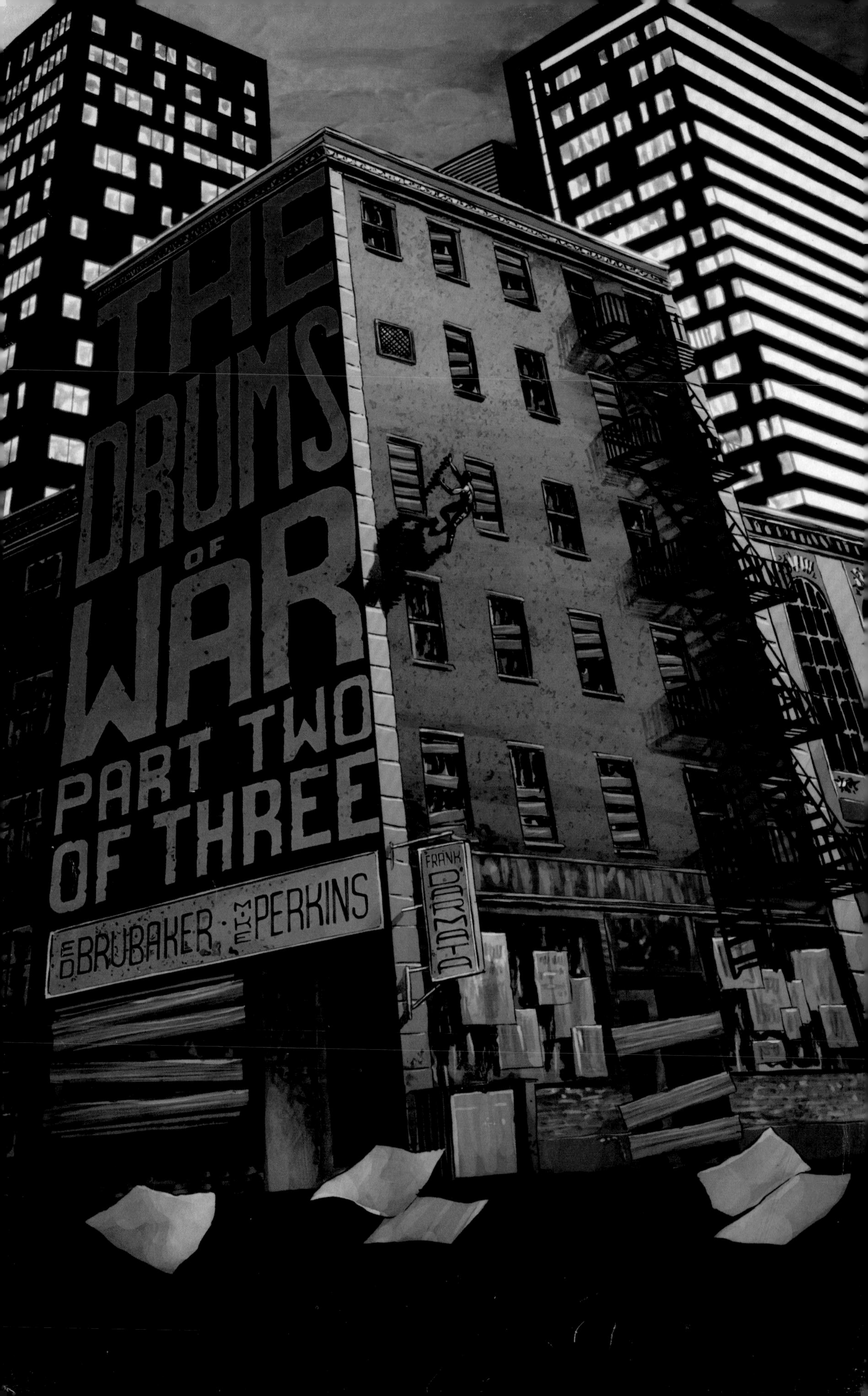
THE DRUMS OF WAR
PART TWO OF THREE
ED BRUBAKER · MIKE PERKINS
FRANK D'ARMATA

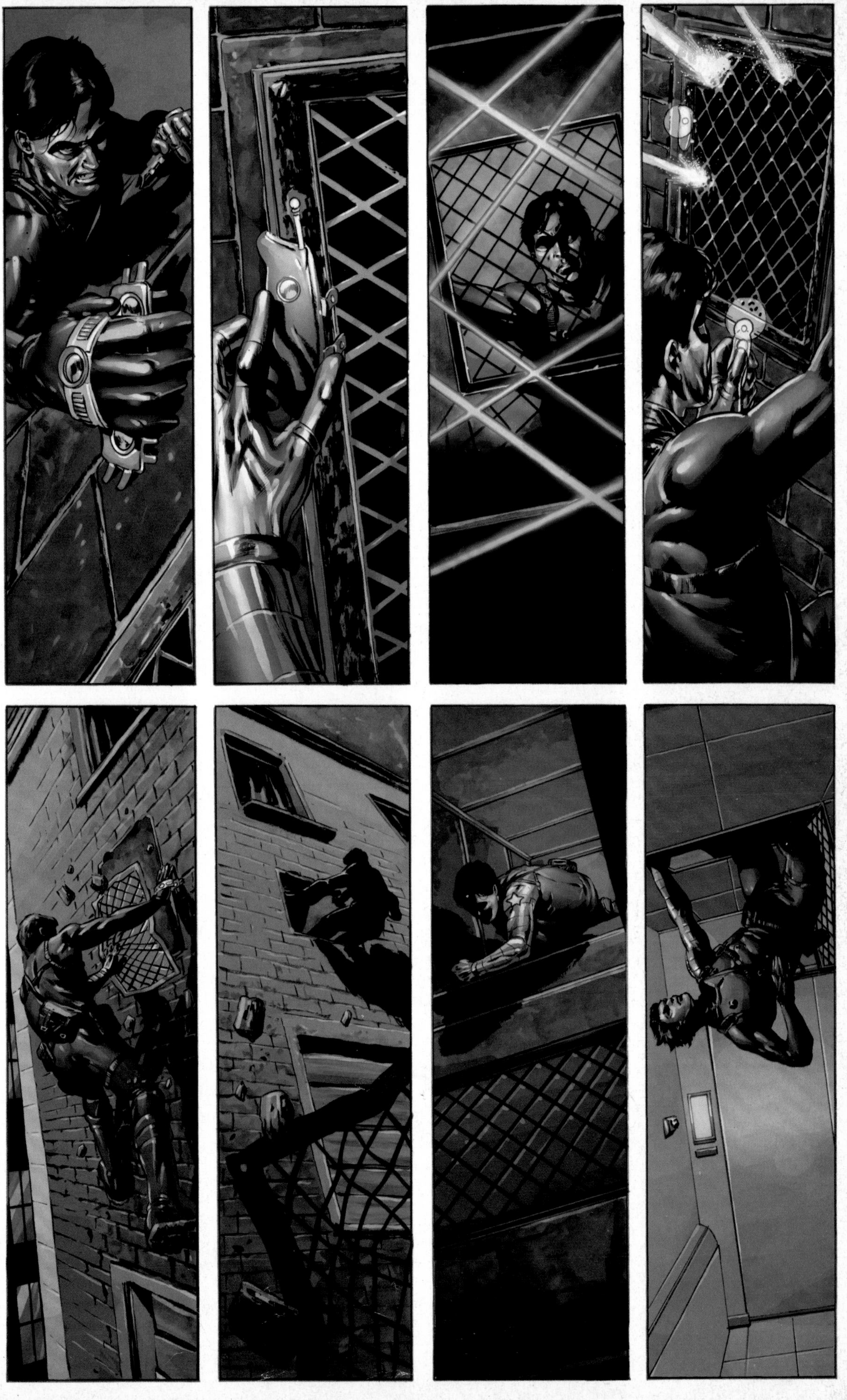

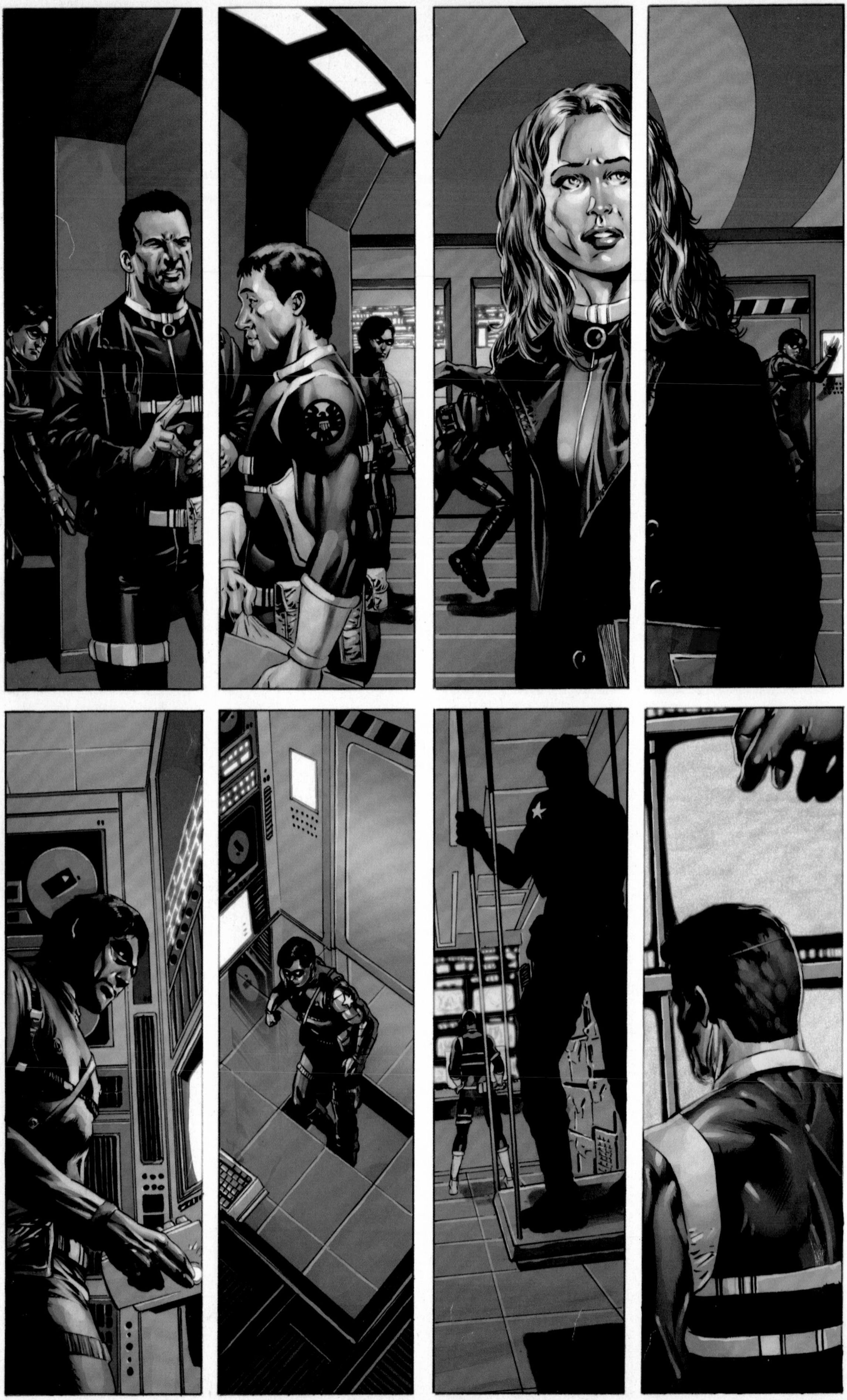

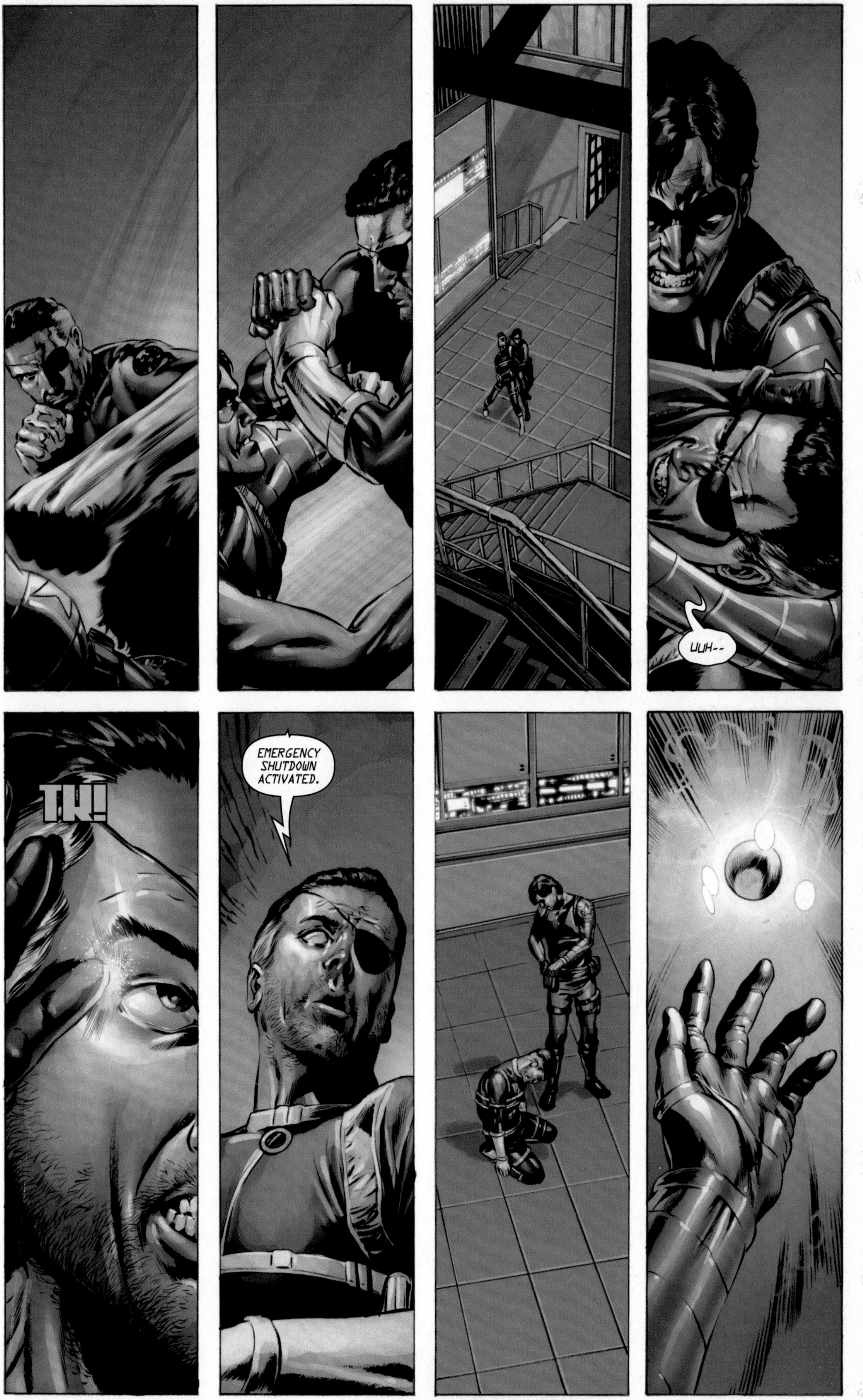
UUH--
TK!
EMERGENCY SHUTDOWN ACTIVATED.

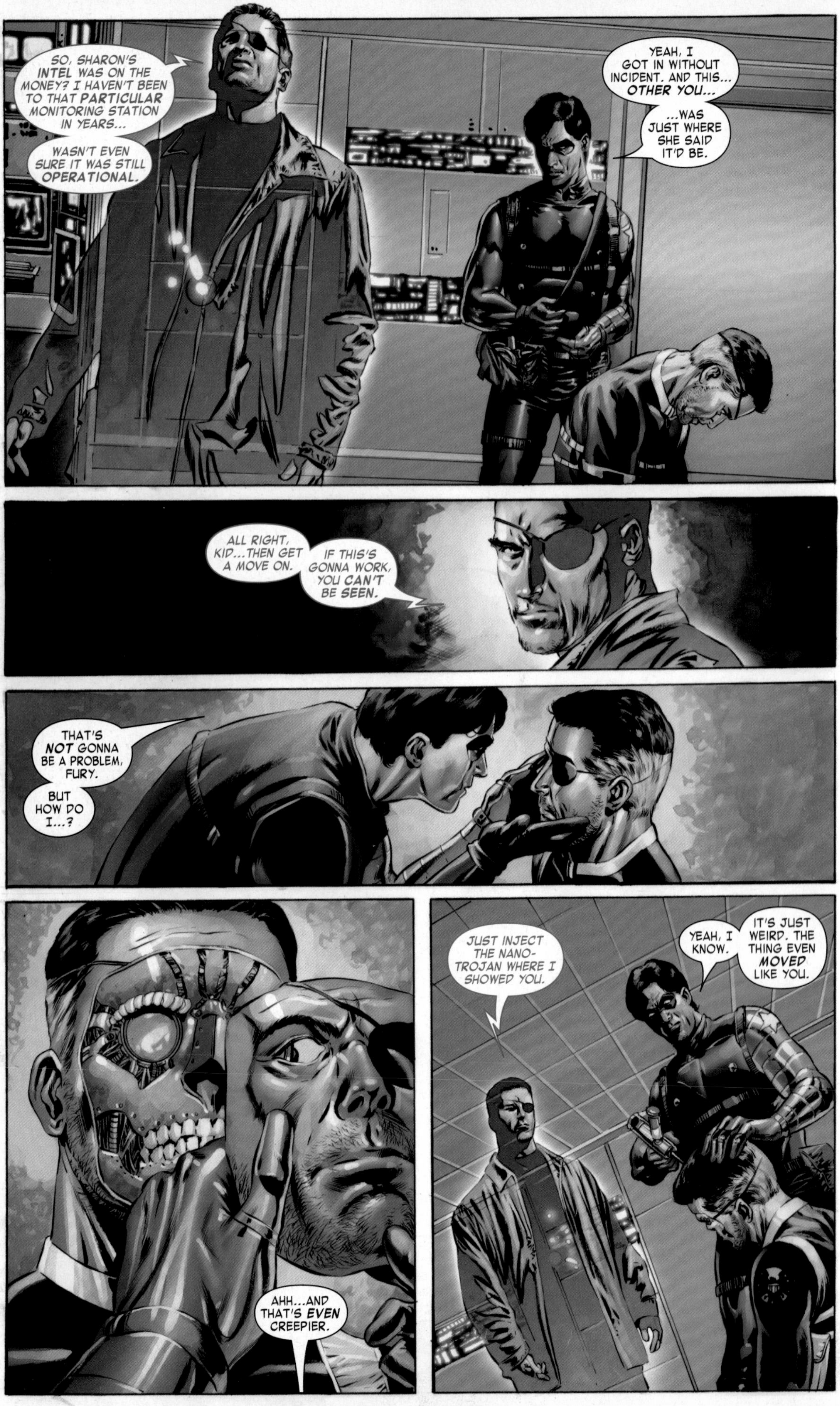
SO, SHARON'S INTEL WAS ON THE MONEY? I HAVEN'T BEEN TO THAT PARTICULAR MONITORING STATION IN YEARS...
WASN'T EVEN SURE IT WAS STILL OPERATIONAL.
YEAH, I GOT IN WITHOUT INCIDENT. AND THIS... OTHER YOU...
...WAS JUST WHERE SHE SAID IT'D BE.
ALL RIGHT, KID...THEN GET A MOVE ON.
IF THIS'S GONNA WORK, YOU CAN'T BE SEEN.
THAT'S NOT GONNA BE A PROBLEM, FURY.
BUT HOW DO I...?
AHH...AND THAT'S EVEN CREEPIER.
JUST INJECT THE NANO-TROJAN WHERE I SHOWED YOU.
YEAH, I KNOW.
IT'S JUST WEIRD. THE THING EVEN MOVED LIKE YOU.

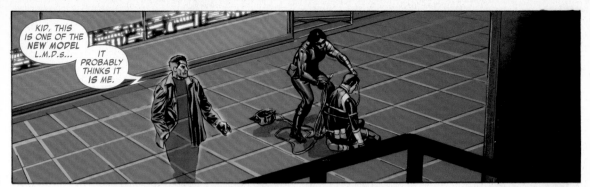

KID, THIS IS ONE OF THE NEW MODEL L.M.D.s... IT PROBABLY THINKS IT IS ME.

AND FROM WHAT MY SOURCES SAY, S.H.I.E.L.D. DOESN'T MIND THAT ONE BIT.

THEY'RE USIN' THIS THING TO COVER THEIR BUTTS.

OKAY... NOW WHERE DO I...?

RIGHT THERE. JUST HOOK THEM TO THAT INPUT...

THEY WANNA PLAY LIKE THEY STILL GOT NICK FURY ON THEIR PAYROLL...

WELL...GOOD FOR THEM... AND US.

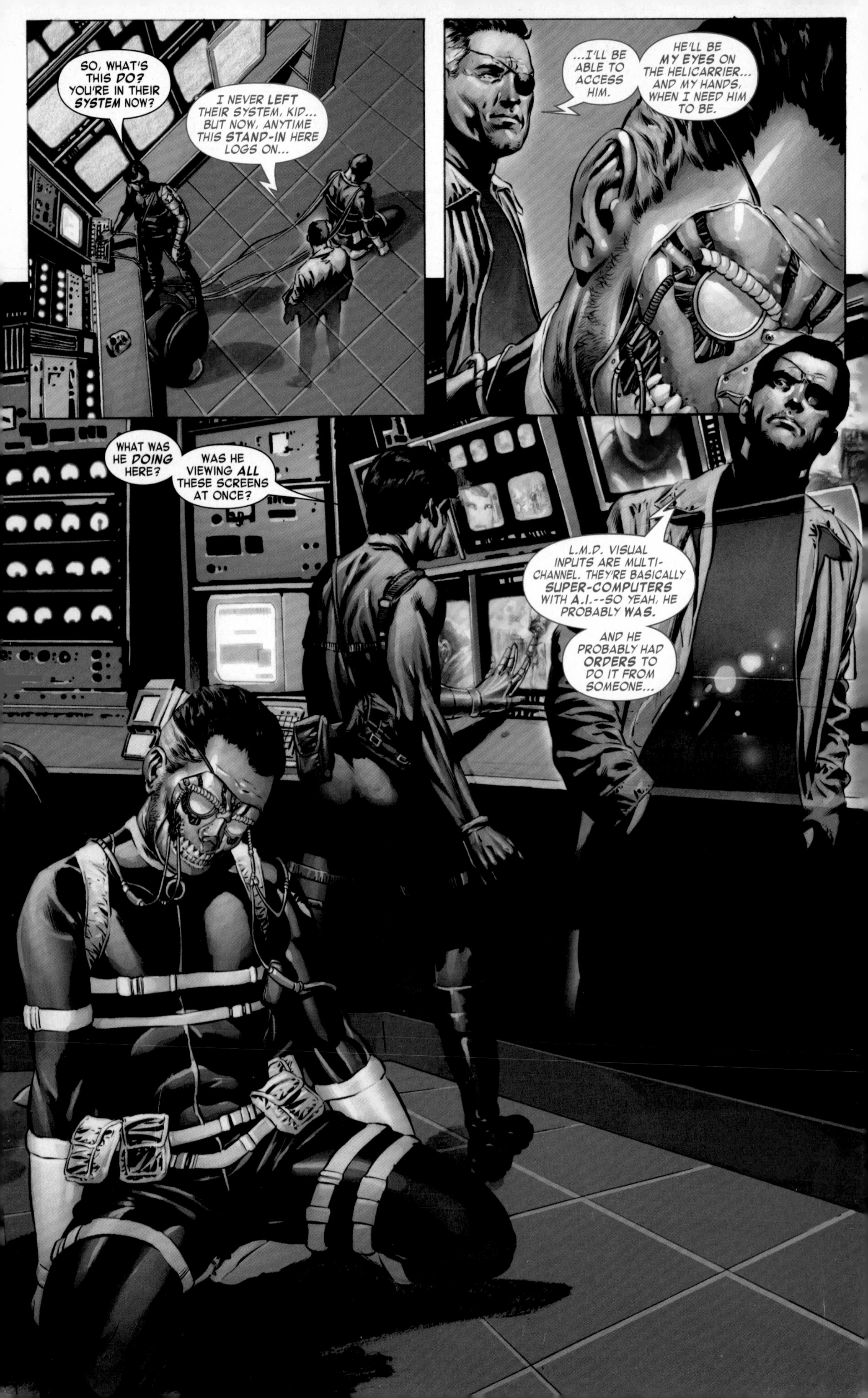
SO, WHAT'S THIS DO? YOU'RE IN THEIR SYSTEM NOW?
I NEVER LEFT THEIR SYSTEM, KID... BUT NOW, ANYTIME THIS STAND-IN HERE LOGS ON...
...I'LL BE ABLE TO ACCESS HIM.
HE'LL BE MY EYES ON THE HELICARRIER... AND MY HANDS, WHEN I NEED HIM TO BE.
WHAT WAS HE DOING HERE?
WAS HE VIEWING ALL THESE SCREENS AT ONCE?
L.M.D. VISUAL INPUTS ARE MULTI-CHANNEL. THEY'RE BASICALLY SUPER-COMPUTERS WITH A.I.--SO YEAH, HE PROBABLY WAS.
AND HE PROBABLY HAD ORDERS TO DO IT FROM SOMEONE...

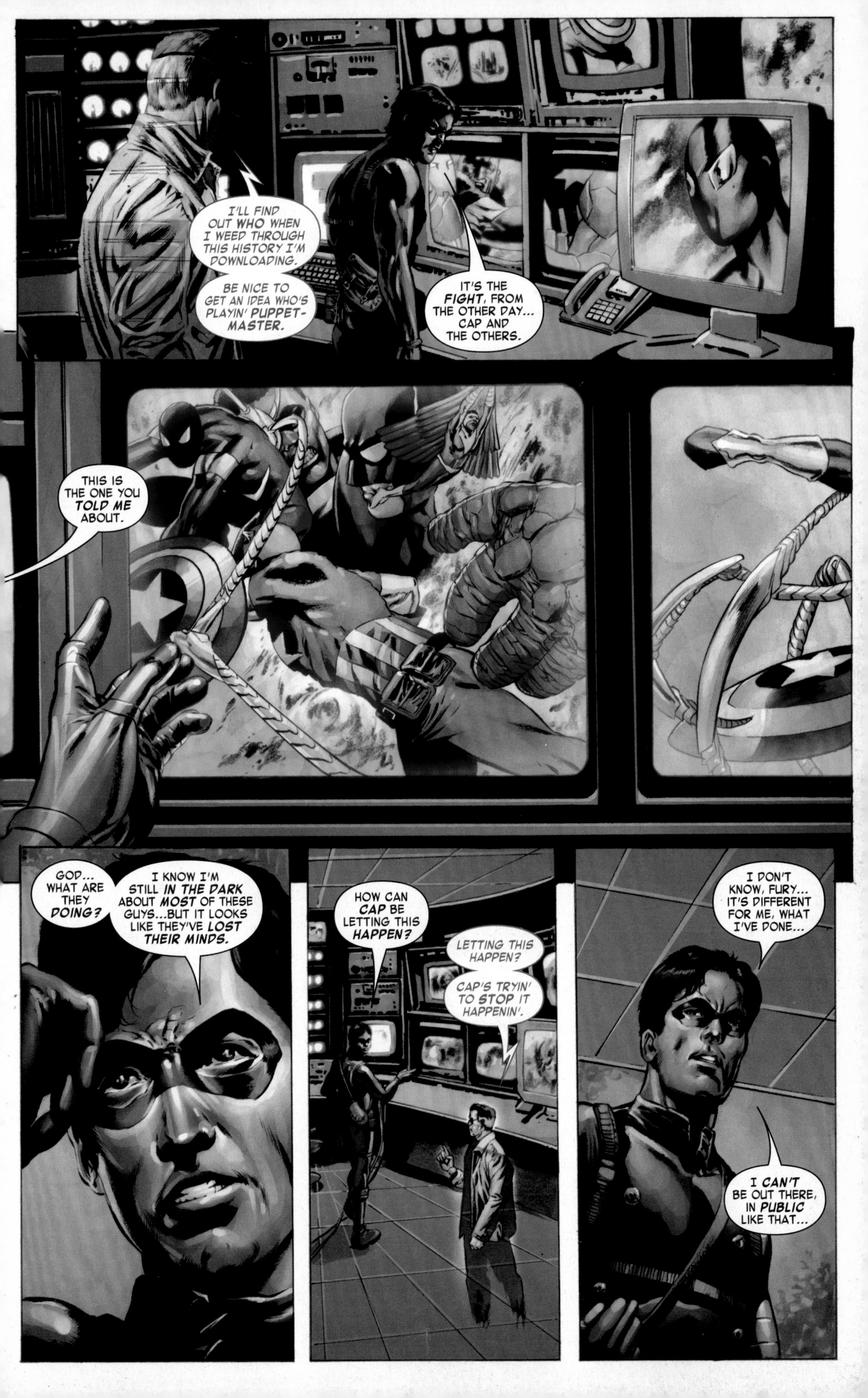
I'LL FIND OUT WHO WHEN I WEED THROUGH THIS HISTORY I'M DOWNLOADING.
BE NICE TO GET AN IDEA WHO'S PLAYIN' PUPPET-MASTER.
IT'S THE FIGHT, FROM THE OTHER DAY... CAP AND THE OTHERS.
THIS IS THE ONE YOU TOLD ME ABOUT.
GOD... WHAT ARE THEY DOING?
I KNOW I'M STILL IN THE DARK ABOUT MOST OF THESE GUYS...BUT IT LOOKS LIKE THEY'VE LOST THEIR MINDS.
HOW CAN CAP BE LETTING THIS HAPPEN?
LETTING THIS HAPPEN?
CAP'S TRYIN' TO STOP IT HAPPENIN'.
I DON'T KNOW, FURY... IT'S DIFFERENT FOR ME, WHAT I'VE DONE...
I CAN'T BE OUT THERE, IN PUBLIC LIKE THAT...

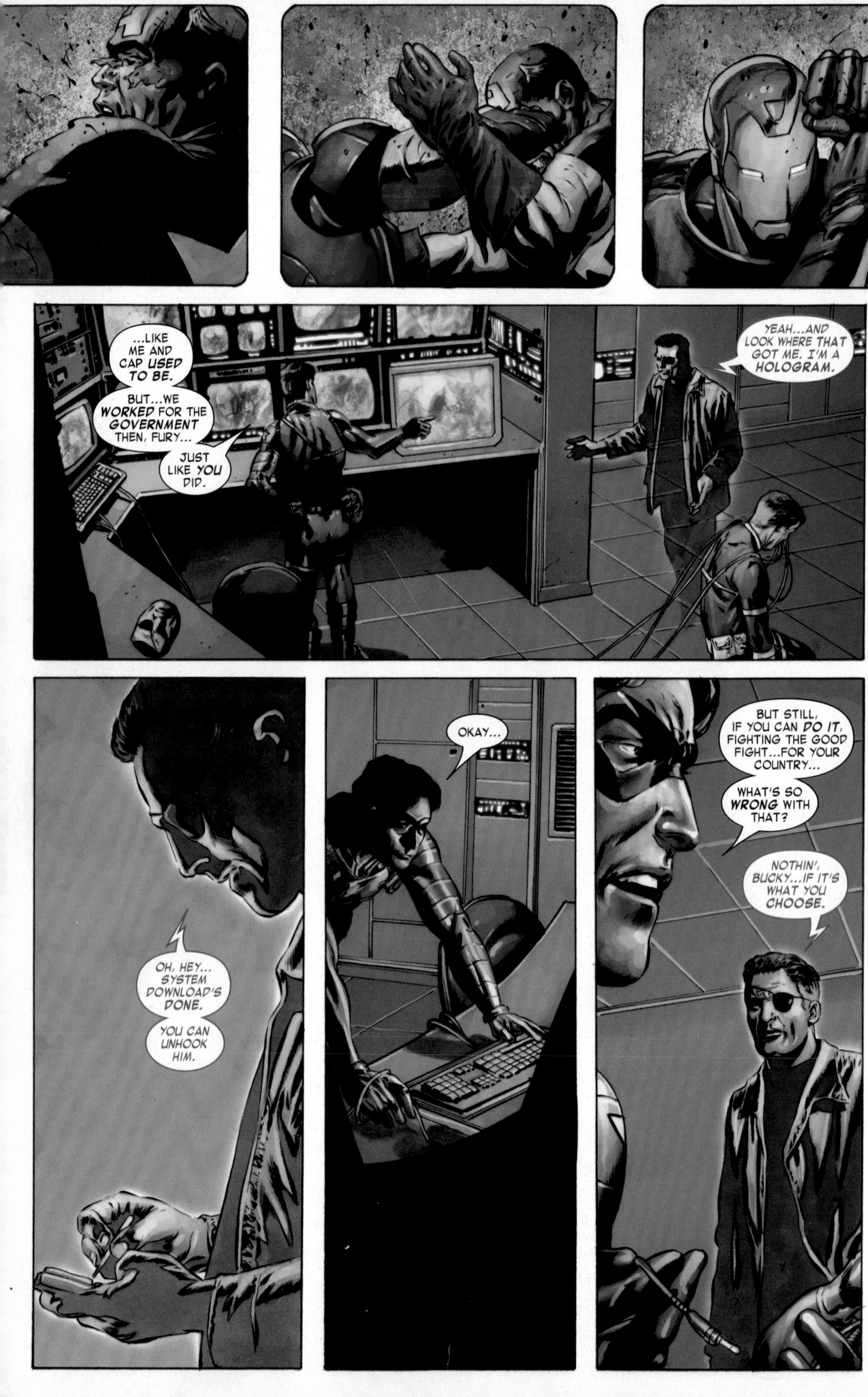
...LIKE ME AND CAP USED TO BE.
BUT...WE WORKED FOR THE GOVERNMENT THEN, FURY...
JUST LIKE YOU DID.
YEAH...AND LOOK WHERE THAT GOT ME. I'M A HOLOGRAM.
OH, HEY... SYSTEM DOWNLOAD'S DONE.
YOU CAN UNHOOK HIM.
OKAY...
BUT STILL, IF YOU CAN DO IT, FIGHTING THE GOOD FIGHT...FOR YOUR COUNTRY...
WHAT'S SO WRONG WITH THAT?
NOTHIN', BUCKY...IF IT'S WHAT YOU CHOOSE.

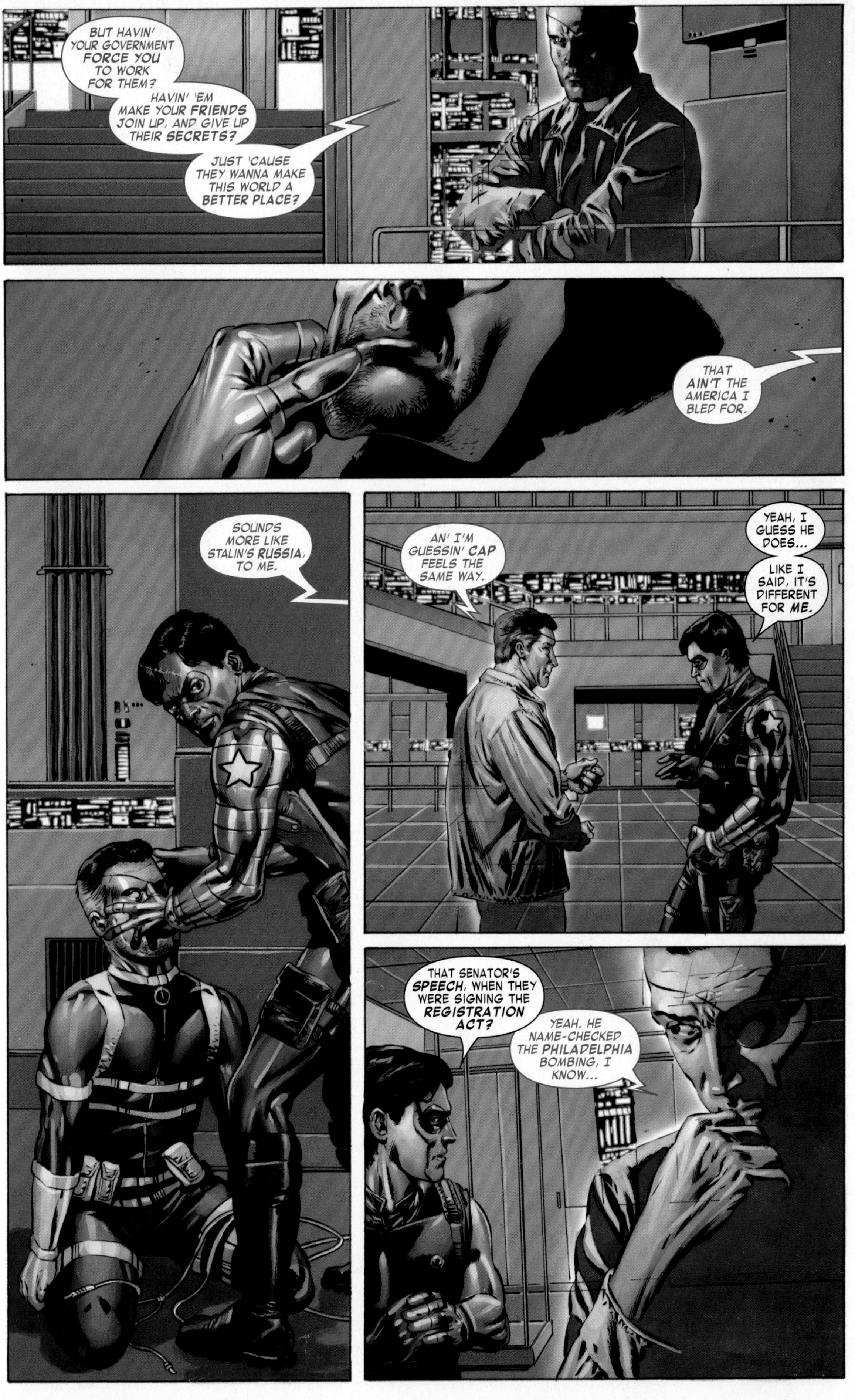
BUT HAVIN' YOUR GOVERNMENT FORCE YOU TO WORK FOR THEM?
HAVIN' 'EM MAKE YOUR FRIENDS JOIN UP, AND GIVE UP THEIR SECRETS?
JUST 'CAUSE THEY WANNA MAKE THIS WORLD A BETTER PLACE?
THAT AIN'T THE AMERICA I BLED FOR.
SOUNDS MORE LIKE STALIN'S RUSSIA, TO ME.
AN' I'M GUESSIN' CAP FEELS THE SAME WAY.
YEAH, I GUESS HE DOES...
LIKE I SAID, IT'S DIFFERENT FOR ME.
THAT SENATOR'S SPEECH, WHEN THEY WERE SIGNING THE REGISTRATION ACT?
YEAH. HE NAME-CHECKED THE PHILADELPHIA BOMBING, I KNOW...

THAT MEANS, ON SOME LEVEL, I'M PART OF THE REASON FOR THIS...

...THIS *MESS* THAT CAP'S CAUGHT UP IN.

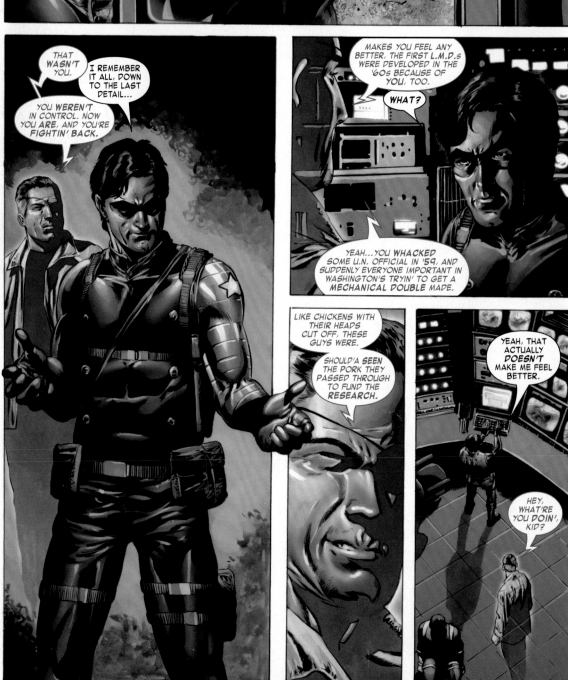

THAT WASN'T YOU.

I REMEMBER IT ALL, DOWN TO THE LAST DETAIL...

YOU WEREN'T IN CONTROL. NOW YOU ARE, AND YOU'RE FIGHTIN' BACK.

MAKES YOU FEEL ANY BETTER, THE FIRST L.M.D.s WERE DEVELOPED IN THE '60s BECAUSE OF YOU, TOO.

WHAT?

YEAH... YOU WHACKED SOME U.N. OFFICIAL IN '59, AND SUDDENLY EVERYONE IMPORTANT IN WASHINGTON'S TRYIN' TO GET A MECHANICAL DOUBLE MADE.

LIKE CHICKENS WITH THEIR HEADS CUT OFF, THESE GUYS WERE.

SHOULD'A SEEN THE PORK THEY PASSED THROUGH TO FUND THE RESEARCH.

YEAH, THAT ACTUALLY *DOESN'T* MAKE ME FEEL BETTER.

HEY, WHAT'RE YOU DOIN', KID?

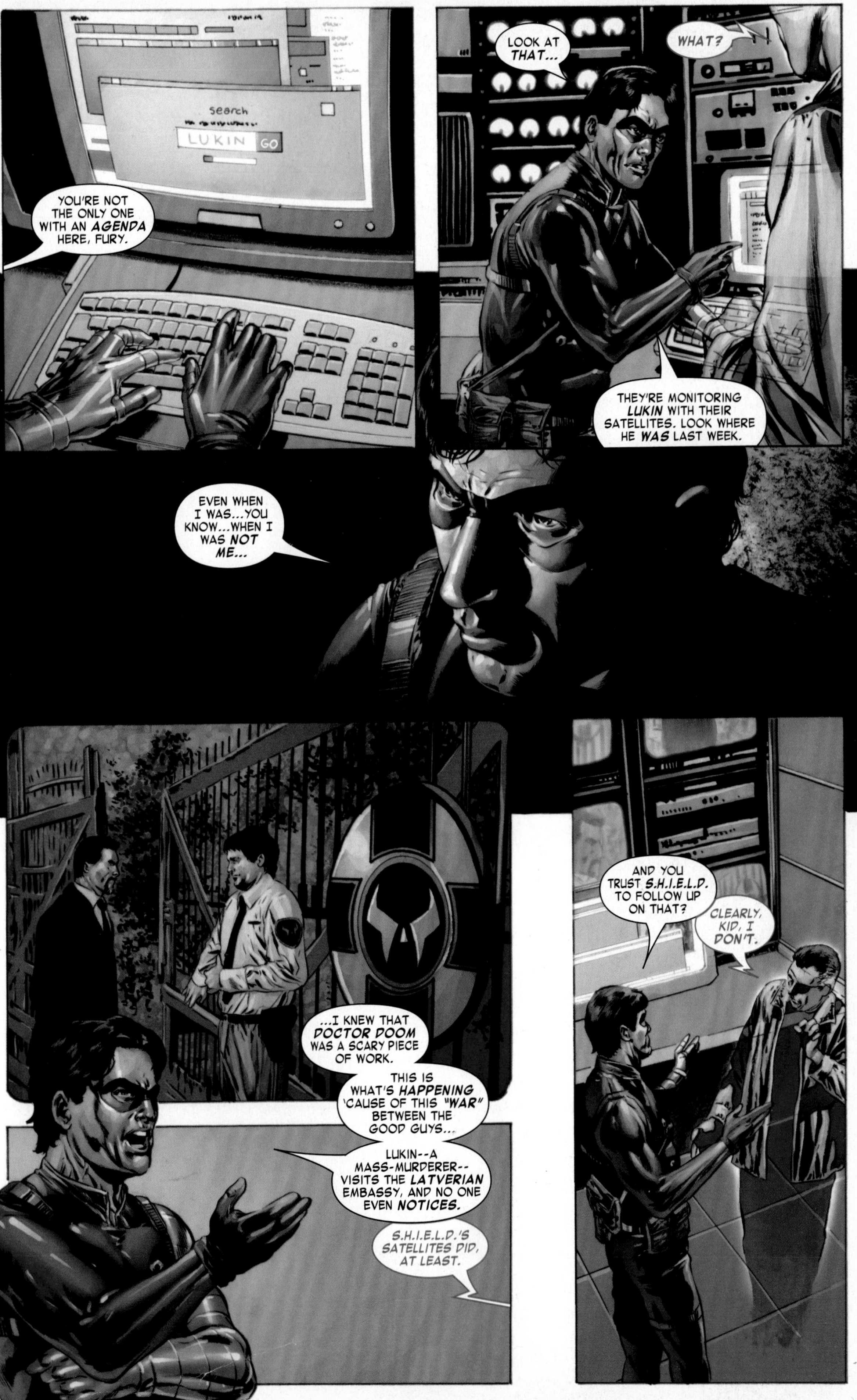
search
LUKIN GO
YOU'RE NOT THE ONLY ONE WITH AN AGENDA HERE, FURY.
LOOK AT THAT...
WHAT?
THEY'RE MONITORING LUKIN WITH THEIR SATELLITES. LOOK WHERE HE WAS LAST WEEK.
EVEN WHEN I WAS...YOU KNOW...WHEN I WAS NOT ME...
...I KNEW THAT DOCTOR DOOM WAS A SCARY PIECE OF WORK.
THIS IS WHAT'S HAPPENING 'CAUSE OF THIS "WAR" BETWEEN THE GOOD GUYS...
LUKIN--A MASS-MURDERER--VISITS THE LATVERIAN EMBASSY, AND NO ONE EVEN NOTICES.
S.H.I.E.L.D.'S SATELLITES DID, AT LEAST.
AND YOU TRUST S.H.I.E.L.D. TO FOLLOW UP ON THAT?
CLEARLY, KID, I DON'T.

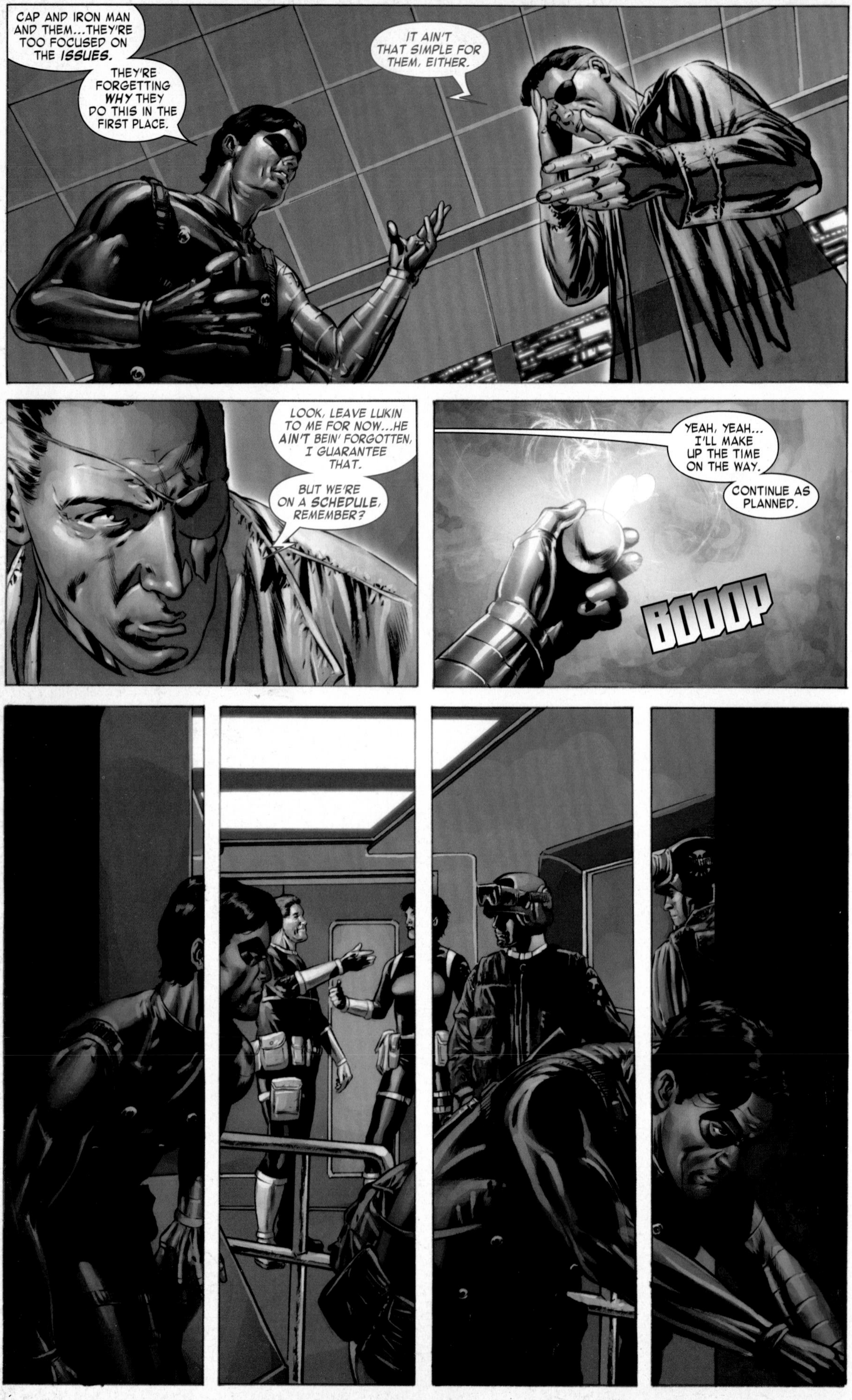
CAP AND IRON MAN AND THEM...THEY'RE TOO FOCUSED ON THE *ISSUES.*
THEY'RE FORGETTING *WHY* THEY DO THIS IN THE FIRST PLACE.
IT AIN'T THAT SIMPLE FOR THEM, EITHER.
LOOK, LEAVE LUKIN TO ME FOR NOW...HE AIN'T BEIN' FORGOTTEN, I GUARANTEE THAT.
BUT WE'RE ON A *SCHEDULE,* REMEMBER?
YEAH, YEAH... I'LL MAKE UP THE TIME ON THE WAY.
CONTINUE AS PLANNED.
BOOOP

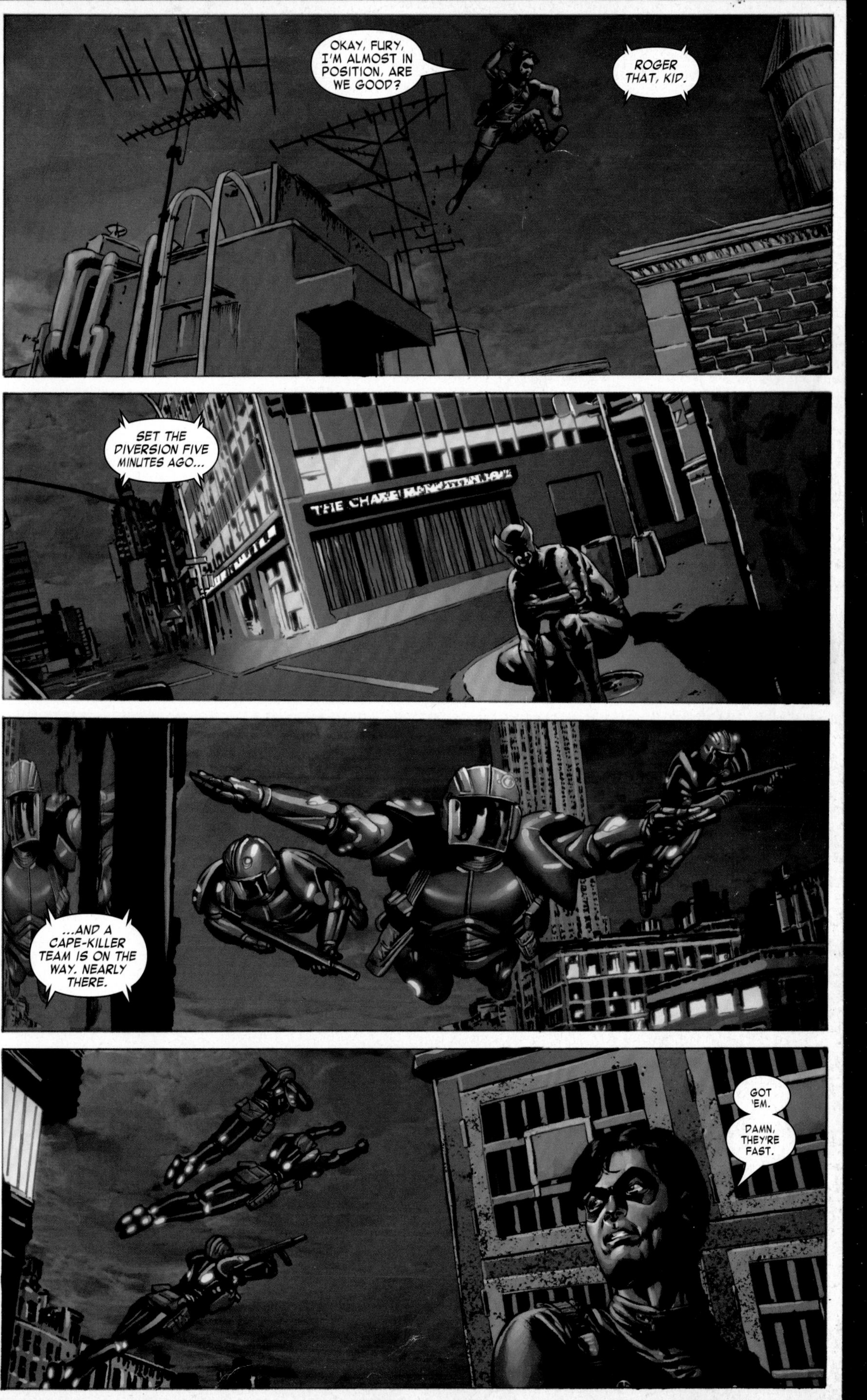

OKAY, FURY, I'M ALMOST IN POSITION, ARE WE GOOD?
ROGER THAT, KID.
SET THE DIVERSION FIVE MINUTES AGO...
...AND A CAPE-KILLER TEAM IS ON THE WAY. NEARLY THERE.
GOT 'EM.
DAMN, THEY'RE FAST.

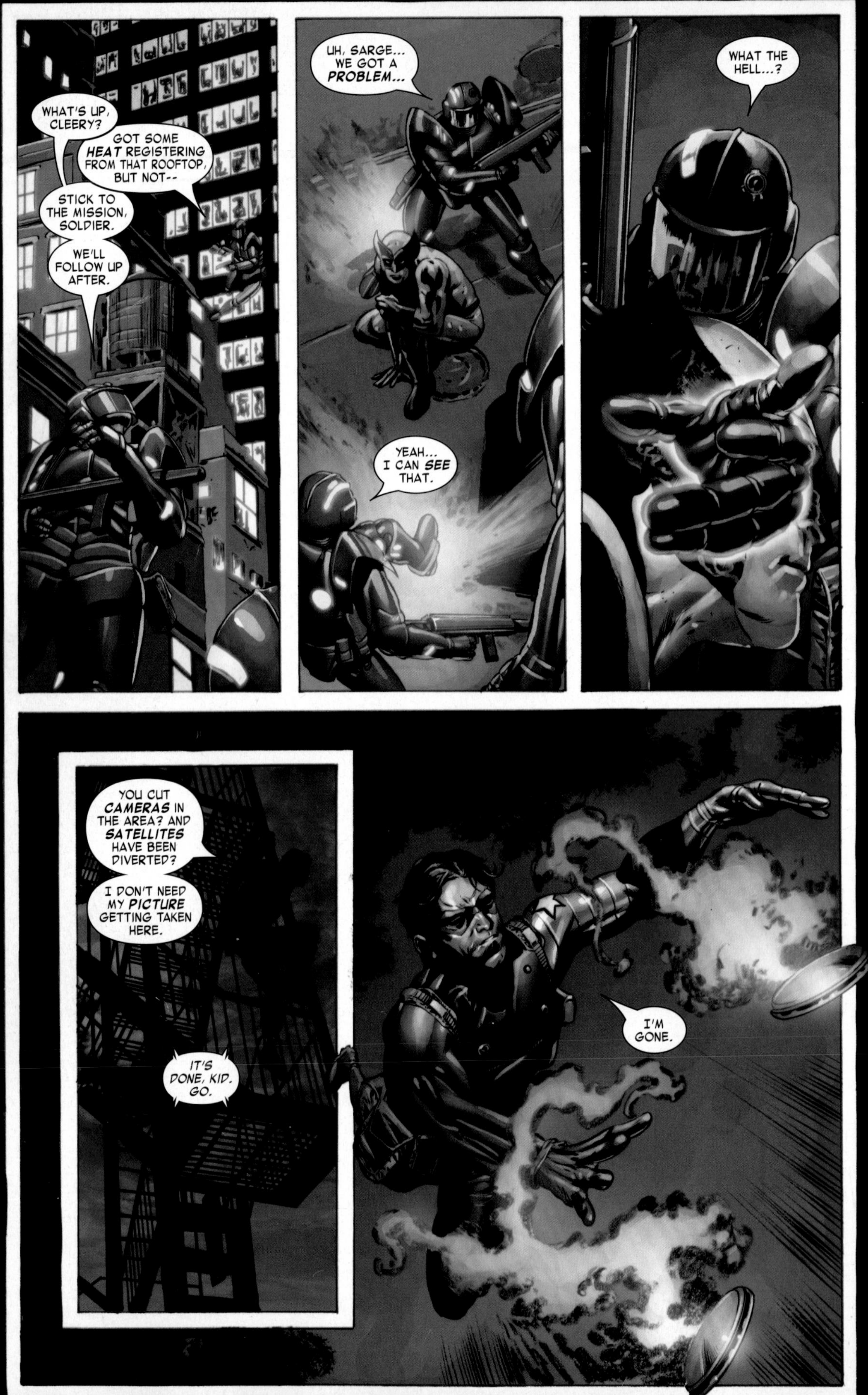
WHAT'S UP, CLEERY?
GOT SOME HEAT REGISTERING FROM THAT ROOFTOP, BUT NOT--
STICK TO THE MISSION, SOLDIER.
WE'LL FOLLOW UP AFTER.
UH, SARGE... WE GOT A PROBLEM...
YEAH... I CAN SEE THAT.
WHAT THE HELL...?
YOU CUT CAMERAS IN THE AREA? AND SATELLITES HAVE BEEN DIVERTED?
I DON'T NEED MY PICTURE GETTING TAKEN HERE.
IT'S DONE, KID. GO.
I'M GONE.

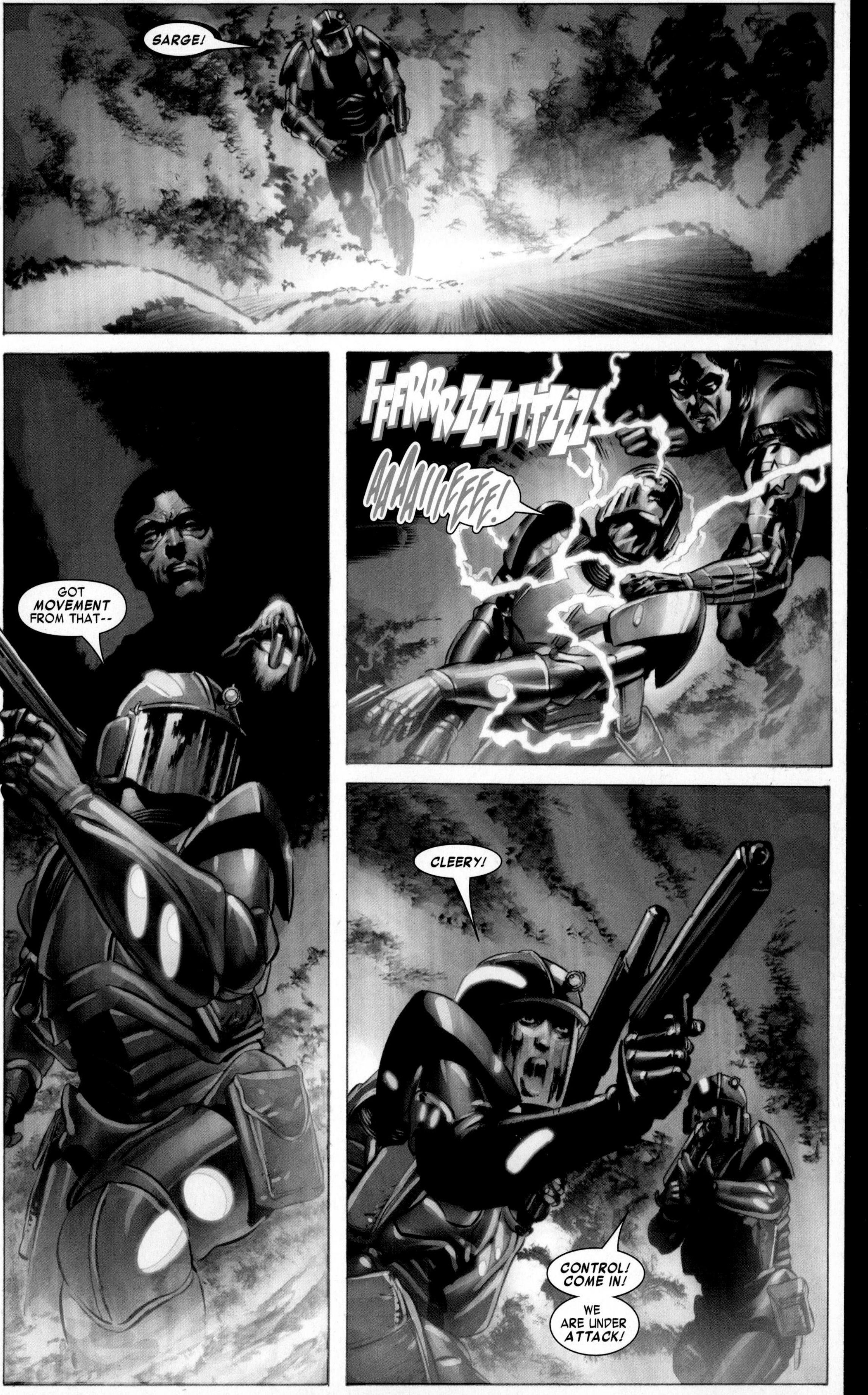
SARGE!
GOT MOVEMENT FROM THAT--
FFFRRRZZZTTTZZZ
AAAAIIIEEEE!
CLEERY!
CONTROL! COME IN!
WE ARE UNDER ATTACK!

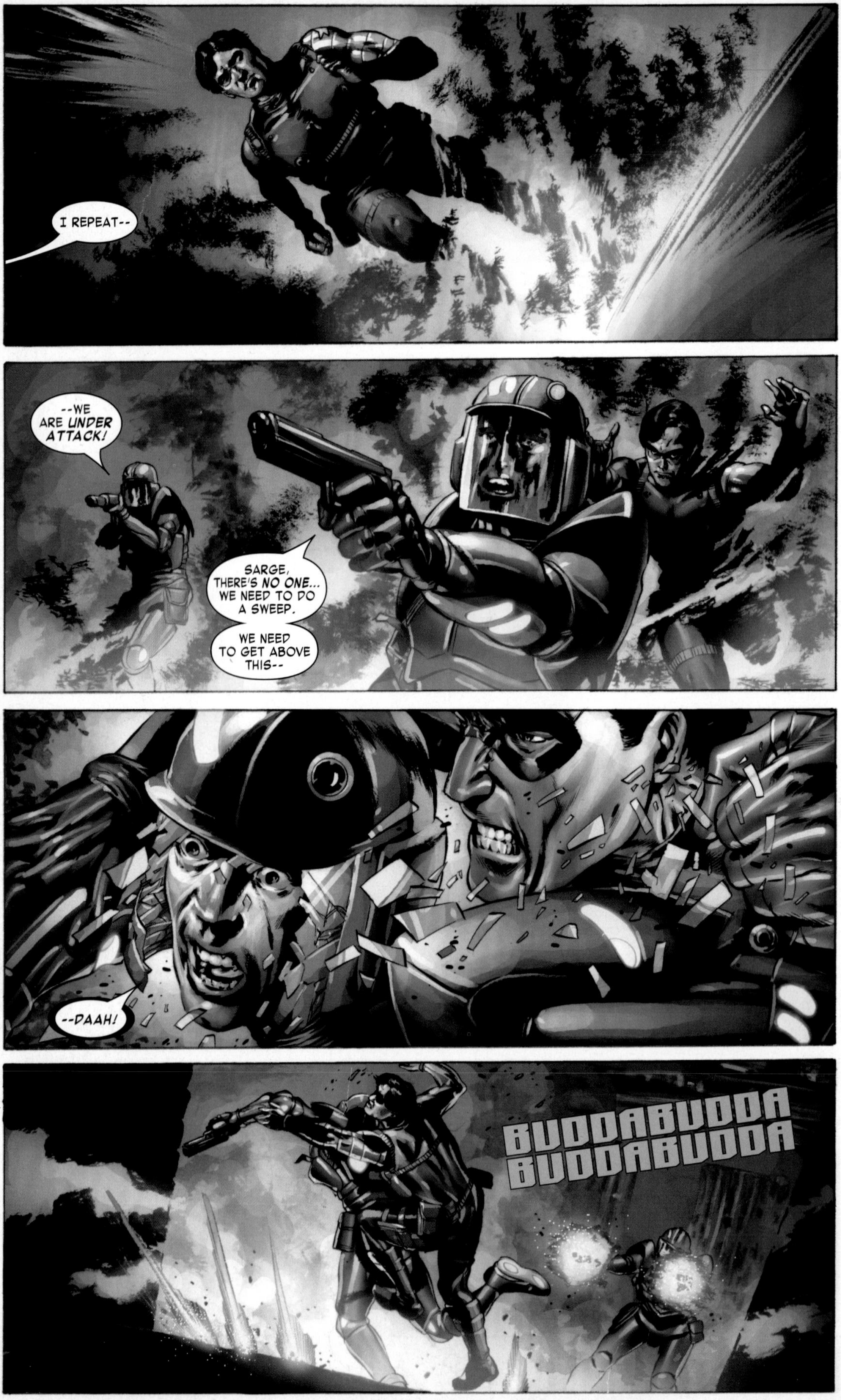
I REPEAT--
--WE ARE UNDER ATTACK!
SARGE, THERE'S NO ONE... WE NEED TO DO A SWEEP.
WE NEED TO GET ABOVE THIS--
--DAAH!
BUDDABUDDA BUDDABUDDA

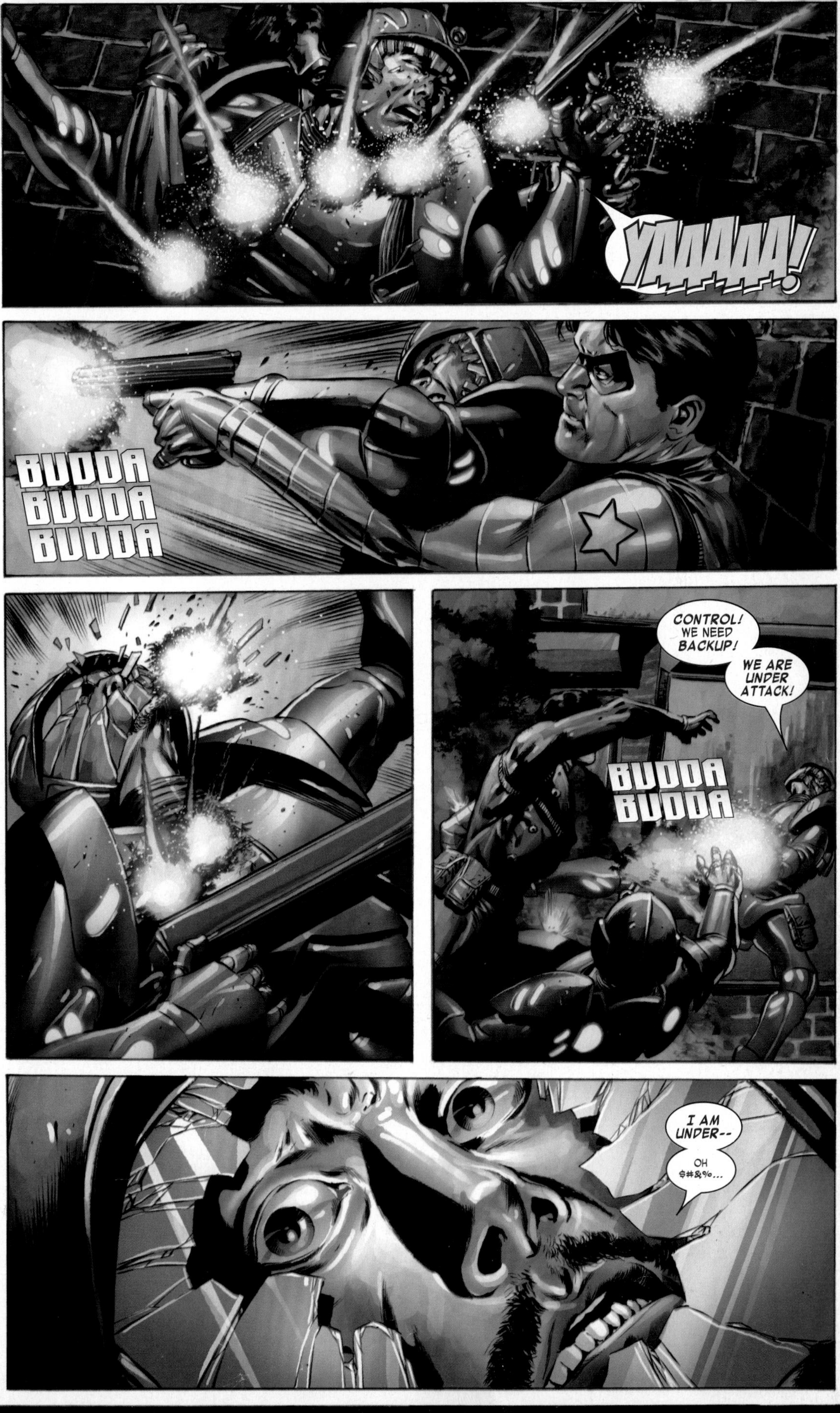
YAAAAA!
BUDDA
BUDDA
BUDDA
CONTROL! WE NEED BACKUP!
WE ARE UNDER ATTACK!
BUDDA
BUDDA
I AM UNDER--
OH $#&%...

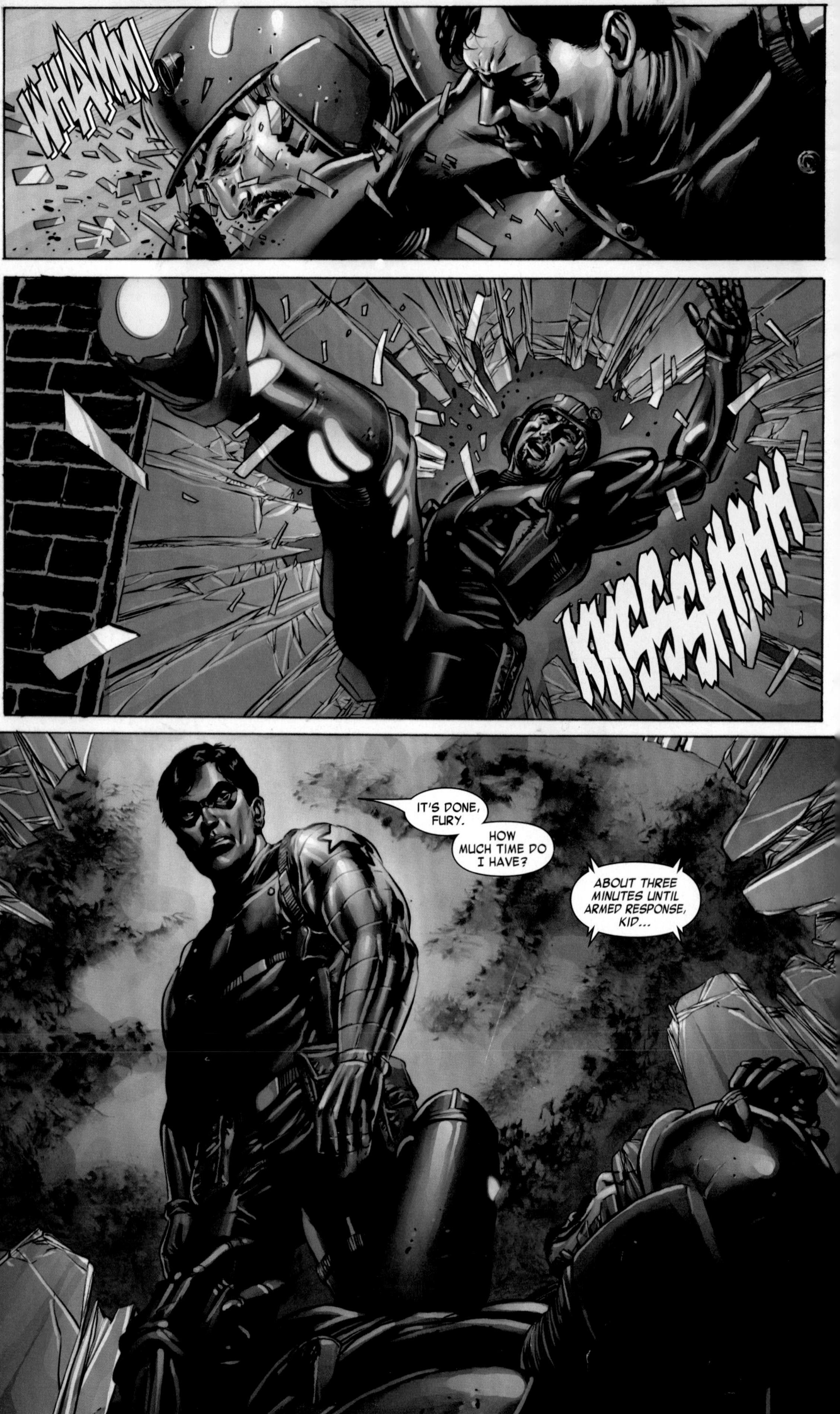
WHAMM
KKSSHHH
IT'S DONE, FURY.
HOW MUCH TIME DO I HAVE?
ABOUT THREE MINUTES UNTIL ARMED RESPONSE, KID...

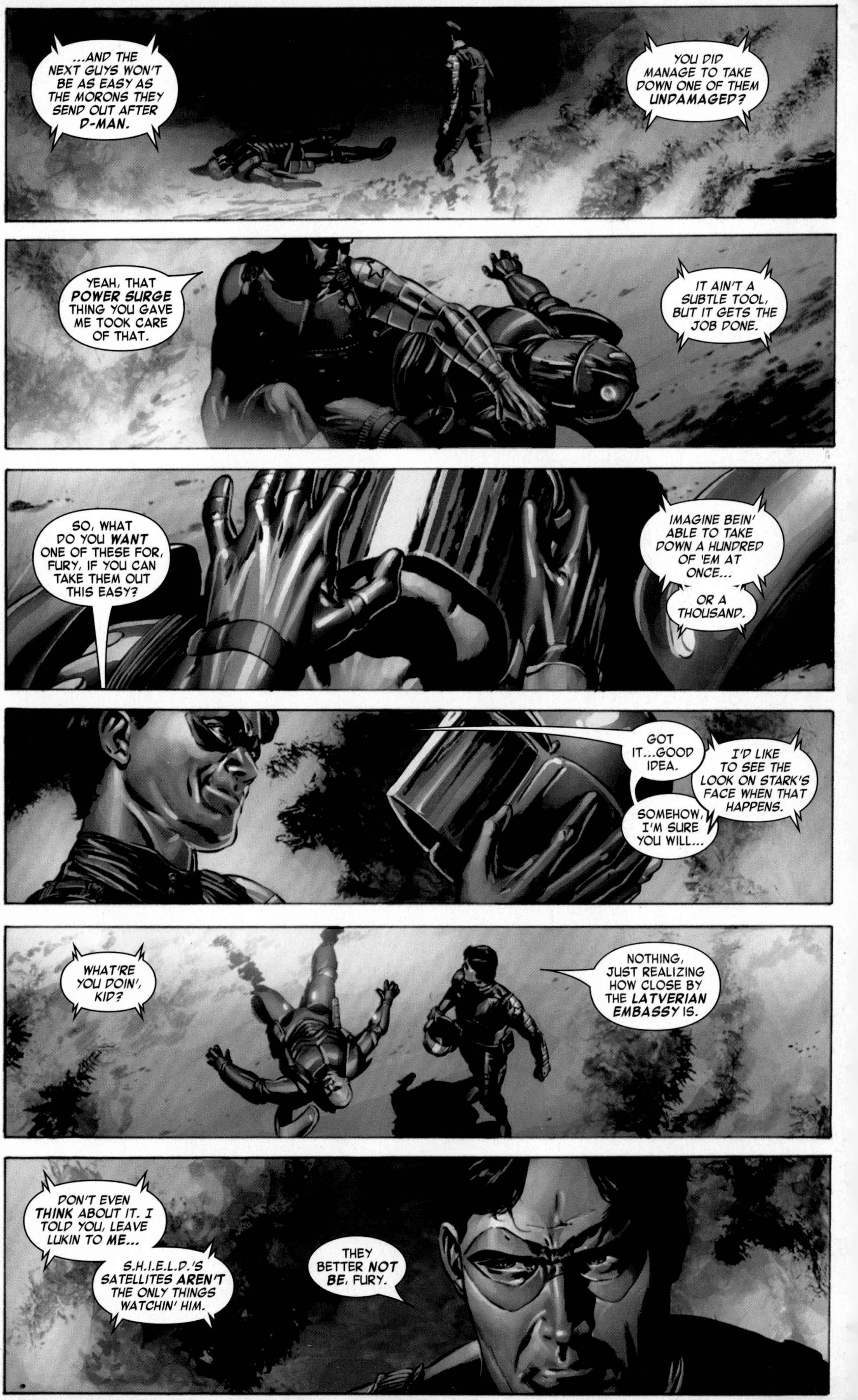
...AND THE NEXT GUYS WON'T BE AS EASY AS THE MORONS THEY SEND OUT AFTER D-MAN.
YOU DID MANAGE TO TAKE DOWN ONE OF THEM UNDAMAGED?
YEAH, THAT POWER SURGE THING YOU GAVE ME TOOK CARE OF THAT.
IT AIN'T A SUBTLE TOOL, BUT IT GETS THE JOB DONE.
SO, WHAT DO YOU WANT ONE OF THESE FOR, FURY, IF YOU CAN TAKE THEM OUT THIS EASY?
IMAGINE BEIN' ABLE TO TAKE DOWN A HUNDRED OF 'EM AT ONCE...
OR A THOUSAND.
GOT IT...GOOD IDEA.
I'D LIKE TO SEE THE LOOK ON STARK'S FACE WHEN THAT HAPPENS.
SOMEHOW, I'M SURE YOU WILL...
WHAT'RE YOU DOIN', KID?
NOTHING, JUST REALIZING HOW CLOSE BY THE LATVERIAN EMBASSY IS.
DON'T EVEN THINK ABOUT IT. I TOLD YOU, LEAVE LUKIN TO ME...
S.H.I.E.L.D.'S SATELLITES AREN'T THE ONLY THINGS WATCHIN' HIM.
THEY BETTER NOT BE, FURY.

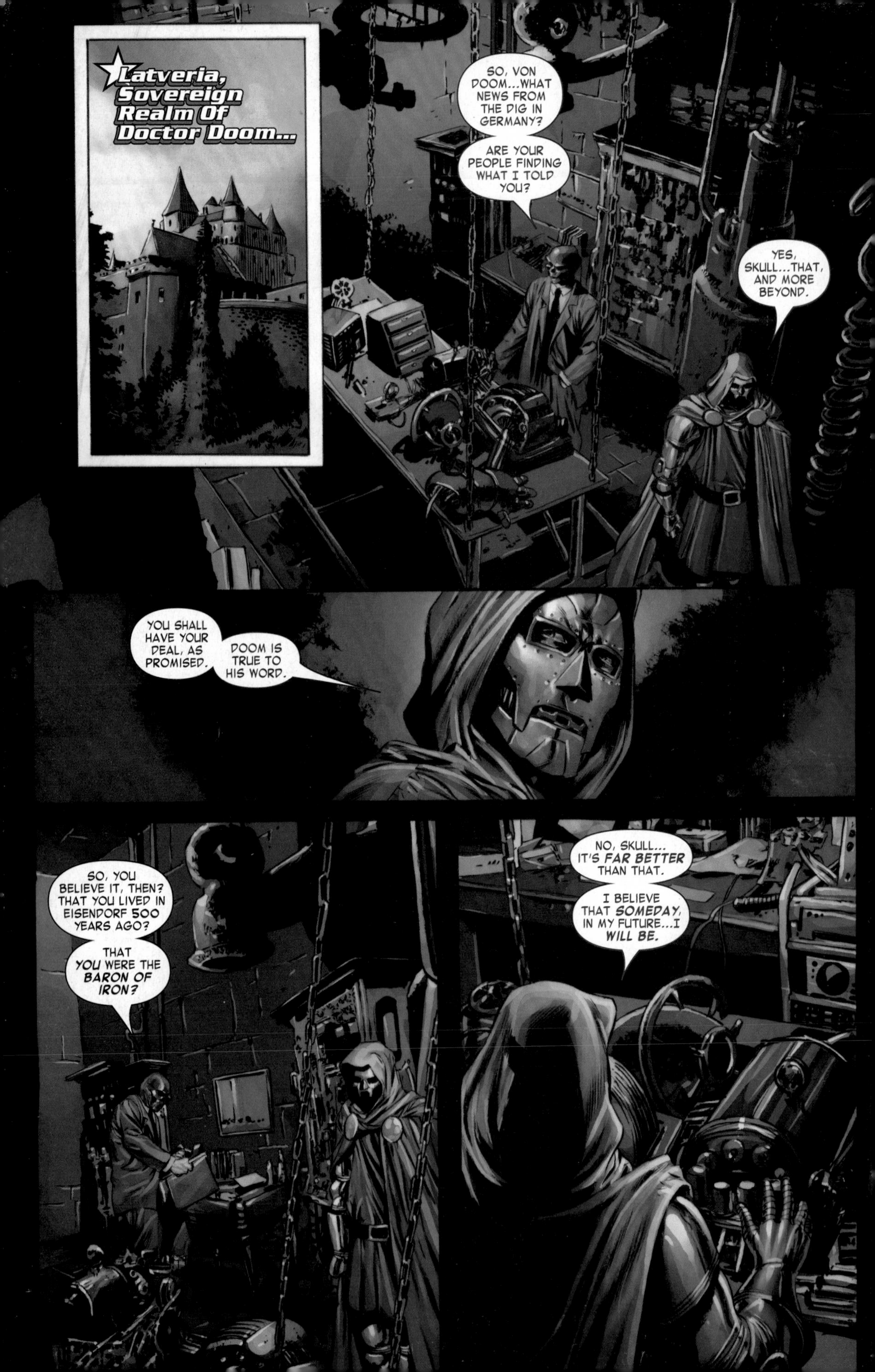
Latveria, Sovereign Realm Of Doctor Doom...
SO, VON DOOM...WHAT NEWS FROM THE DIG IN GERMANY?
ARE YOUR PEOPLE FINDING WHAT I TOLD YOU?
YES, SKULL...THAT, AND MORE BEYOND.
YOU SHALL HAVE YOUR DEAL, AS PROMISED.
DOOM IS TRUE TO HIS WORD.
SO, YOU BELIEVE IT, THEN? THAT YOU LIVED IN EISENDORF 500 YEARS AGO?
THAT YOU WERE THE BARON OF IRON?
NO, SKULL... IT'S FAR BETTER THAN THAT.
I BELIEVE THAT SOMEDAY, IN MY FUTURE...I WILL BE.

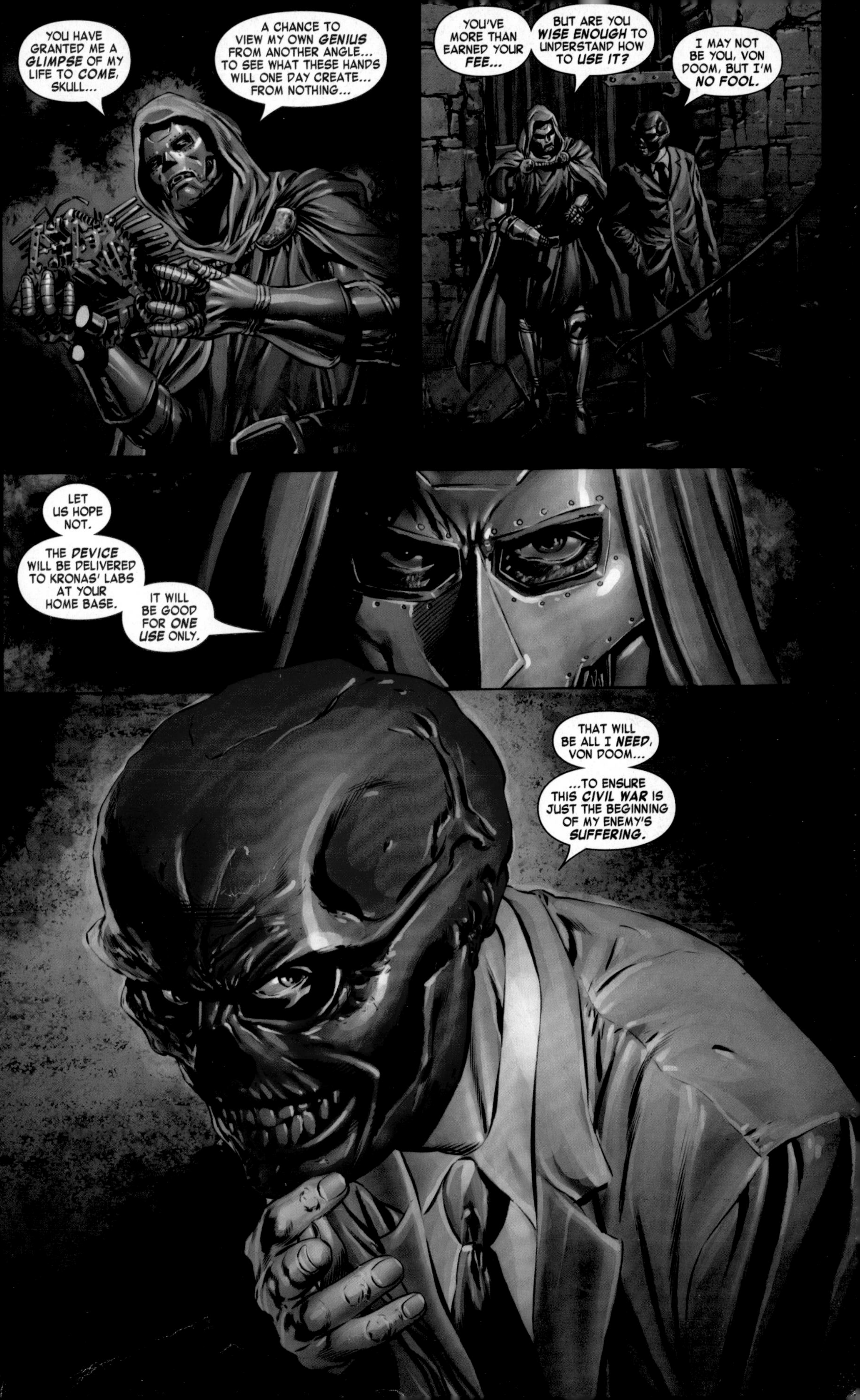
YOU HAVE GRANTED ME A GLIMPSE OF MY LIFE TO COME, SKULL...
A CHANCE TO VIEW MY OWN GENIUS FROM ANOTHER ANGLE... TO SEE WHAT THESE HANDS WILL ONE DAY CREATE... FROM NOTHING...
YOU'VE MORE THAN EARNED YOUR FEE...
BUT ARE YOU WISE ENOUGH TO UNDERSTAND HOW TO USE IT?
I MAY NOT BE YOU, VON DOOM, BUT I'M NO FOOL.
LET US HOPE NOT.
THE DEVICE WILL BE DELIVERED TO KRONAS' LABS AT YOUR HOME BASE.
IT WILL BE GOOD FOR ONE USE ONLY.
THAT WILL BE ALL I NEED, VON DOOM...
...TO ENSURE THIS CIVIL WAR IS JUST THE BEGINNING OF MY ENEMY'S SUFFERING.

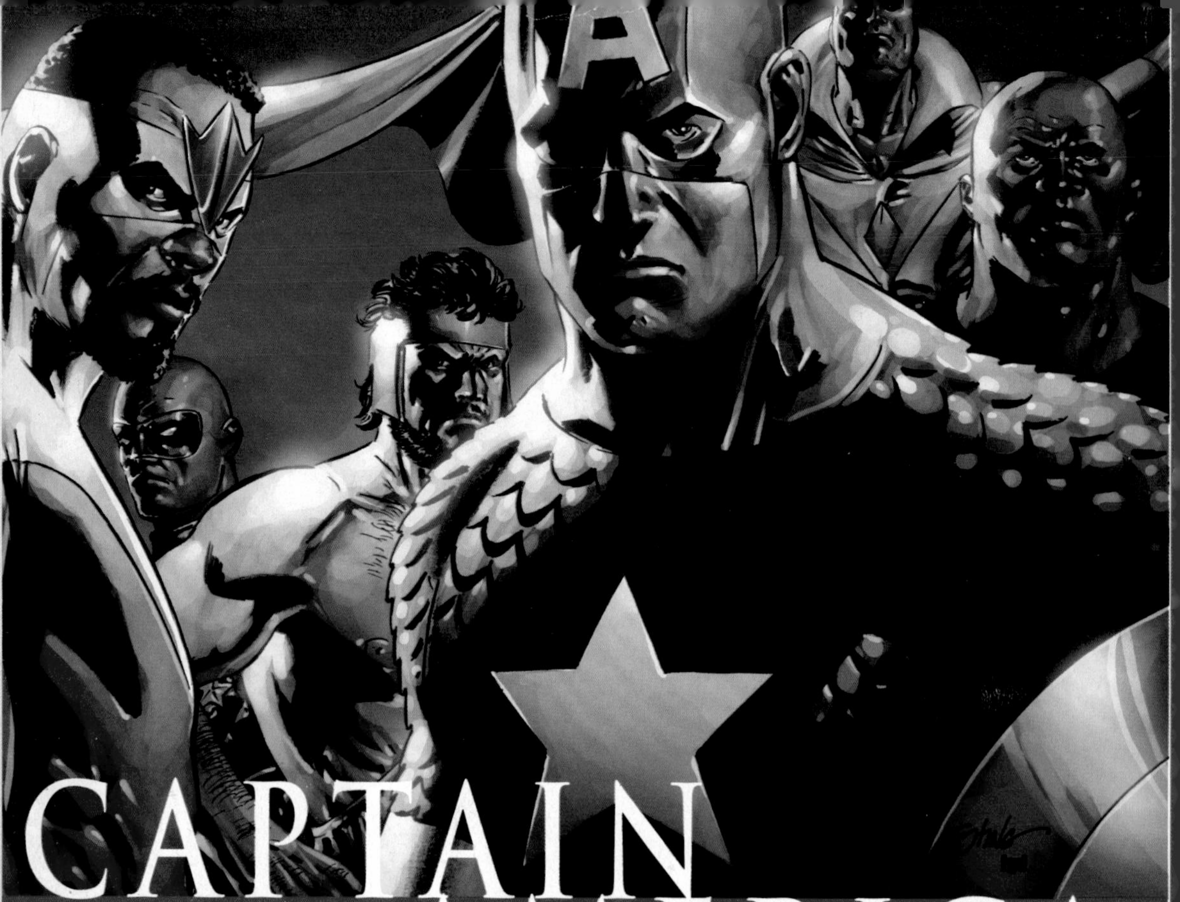

CAPTAIN AMERICA

A MARVEL COMICS EVENT

CIVIL WAR

CAPTAIN AMERICA #24

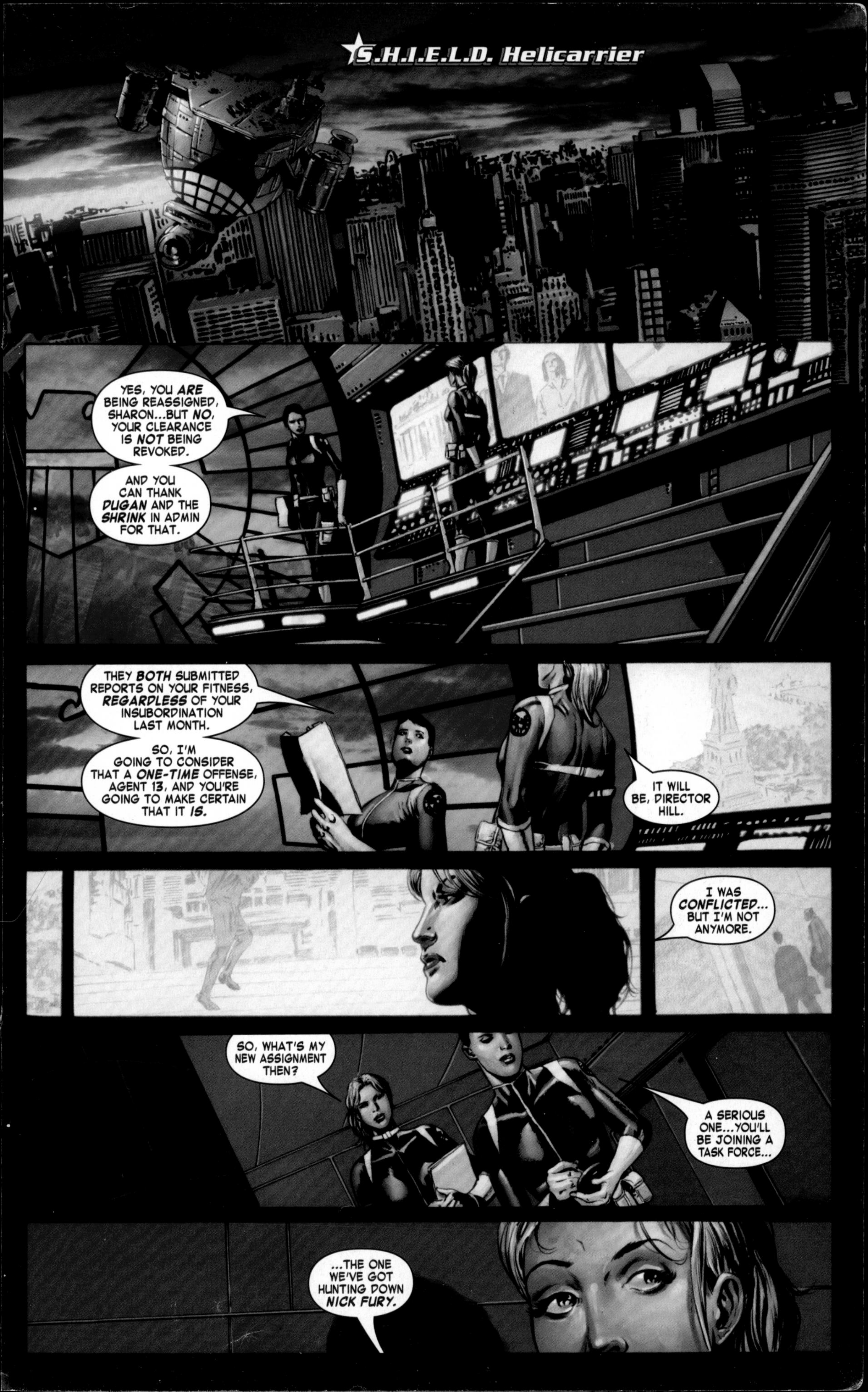
S.H.I.E.L.D. Helicarrier
YES, YOU ARE BEING REASSIGNED, SHARON...BUT NO, YOUR CLEARANCE IS NOT BEING REVOKED.
AND YOU CAN THANK DUGAN AND THE SHRINK IN ADMIN FOR THAT.
THEY BOTH SUBMITTED REPORTS ON YOUR FITNESS, REGARDLESS OF YOUR INSUBORDINATION LAST MONTH.
SO, I'M GOING TO CONSIDER THAT A ONE-TIME OFFENSE, AGENT 13, AND YOU'RE GOING TO MAKE CERTAIN THAT IT IS.
IT WILL BE, DIRECTOR HILL.
I WAS CONFLICTED... BUT I'M NOT ANYMORE.
SO, WHAT'S MY NEW ASSIGNMENT THEN?
A SERIOUS ONE...YOU'LL BE JOINING A TASK FORCE...
...THE ONE WE'VE GOT HUNTING DOWN NICK FURY.

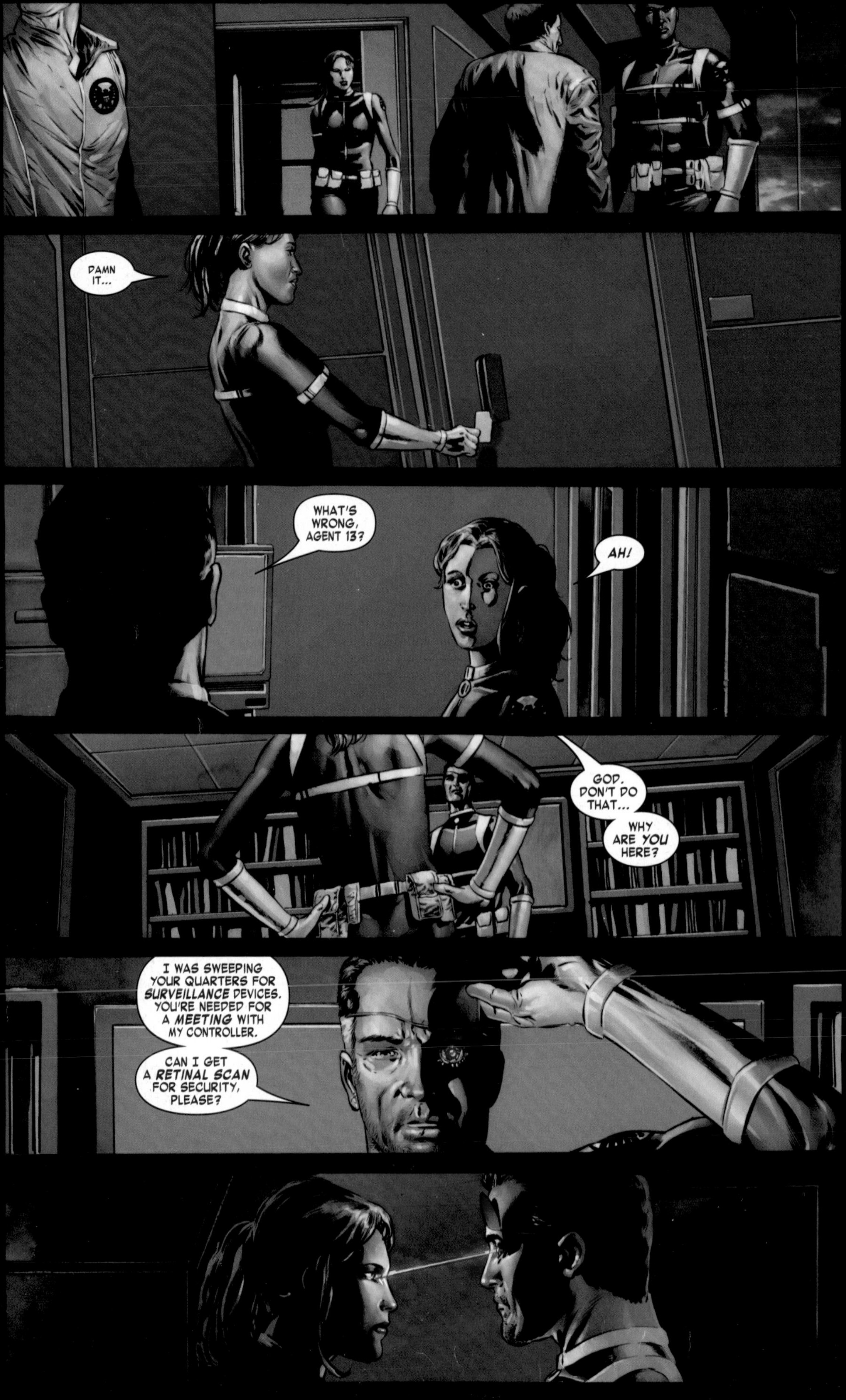
DAMN IT...
WHAT'S WRONG, AGENT 13?
AH!
GOD. DON'T DO THAT...
WHY ARE YOU HERE?
I WAS SWEEPING YOUR QUARTERS FOR SURVEILLANCE DEVICES. YOU'RE NEEDED FOR A MEETING WITH MY CONTROLLER.
CAN I GET A RETINAL SCAN FOR SECURITY, PLEASE?

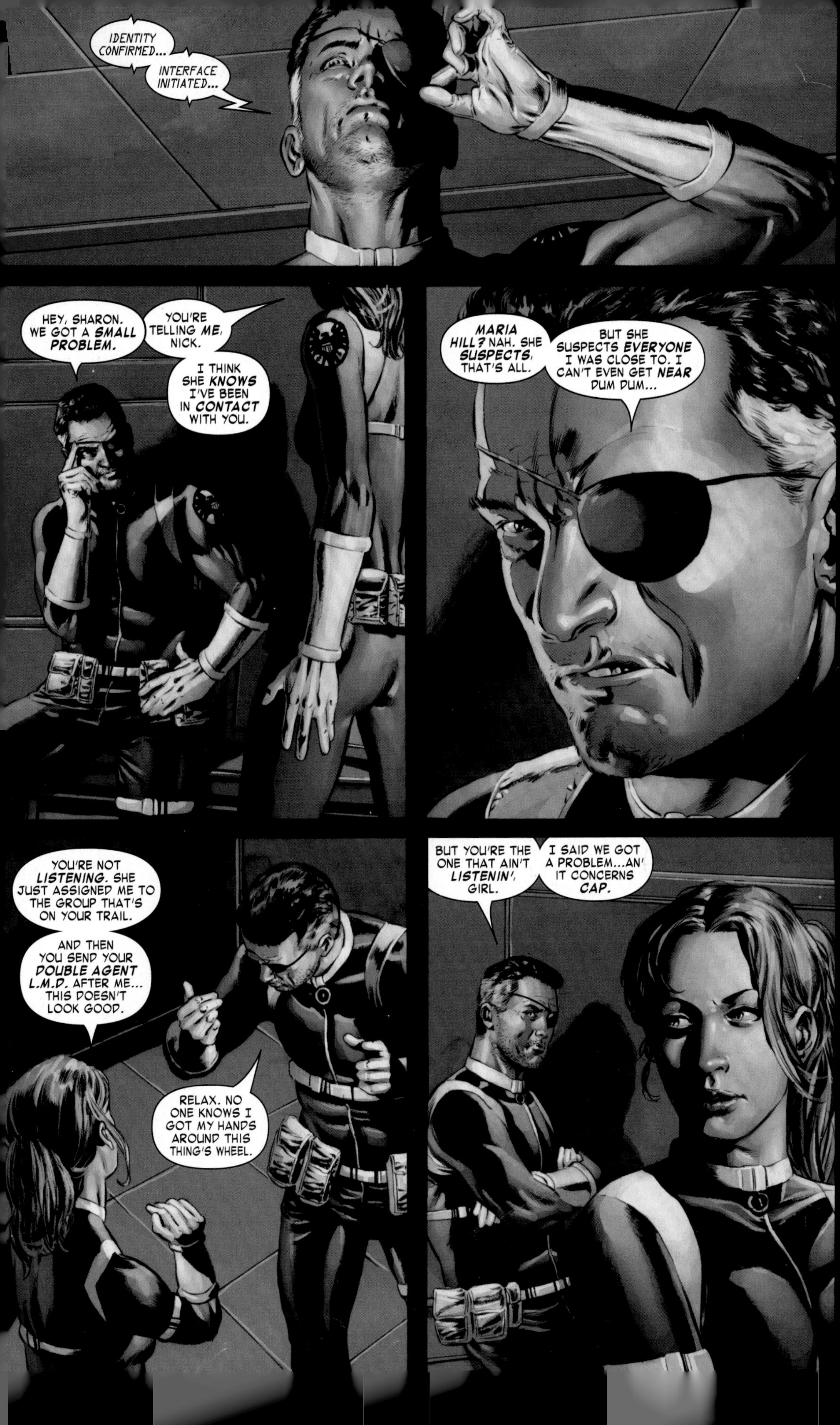
IDENTITY CONFIRMED...
INTERFACE INITIATED...
HEY, SHARON. WE GOT A SMALL PROBLEM.
YOU'RE TELLING ME, NICK.
I THINK SHE KNOWS I'VE BEEN IN CONTACT WITH YOU.
MARIA HILL? NAH. SHE SUSPECTS, THAT'S ALL.
BUT SHE SUSPECTS EVERYONE I WAS CLOSE TO. I CAN'T EVEN GET NEAR DUM DUM...
YOU'RE NOT LISTENING. SHE JUST ASSIGNED ME TO THE GROUP THAT'S ON YOUR TRAIL.
AND THEN YOU SEND YOUR DOUBLE AGENT L.M.D. AFTER ME... THIS DOESN'T LOOK GOOD.
RELAX. NO ONE KNOWS I GOT MY HANDS AROUND THIS THING'S WHEEL.
BUT YOU'RE THE ONE THAT AIN'T LISTENIN', GIRL.
I SAID WE GOT A PROBLEM...AN' IT CONCERNS CAP.

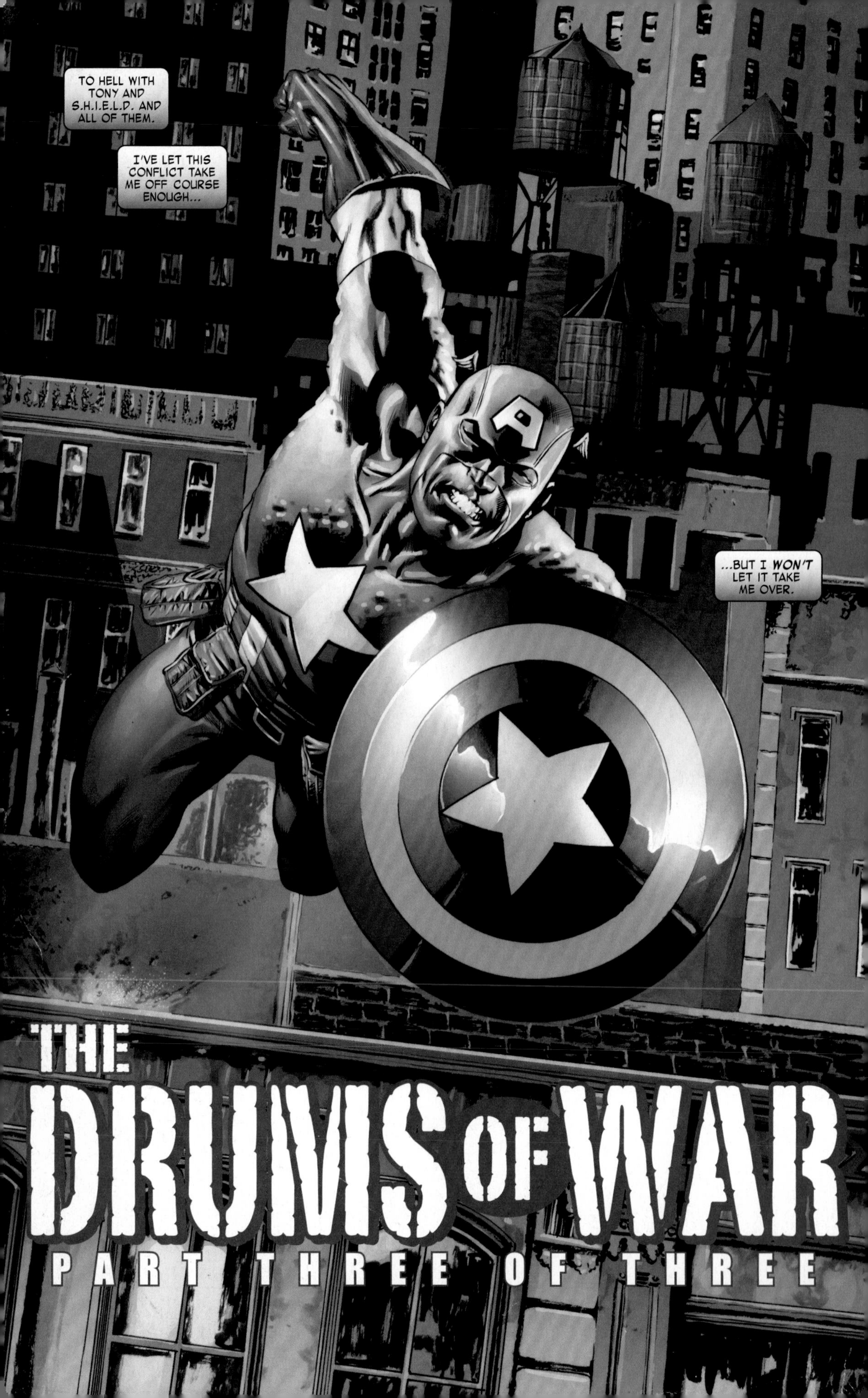
TO HELL WITH TONY AND S.H.I.E.L.D. AND ALL OF THEM.
I'VE LET THIS CONFLICT TAKE ME OFF COURSE ENOUGH...
...BUT I WON'T LET IT TAKE ME OVER.
THE DRUMS OF WAR
PART THREE OF THREE

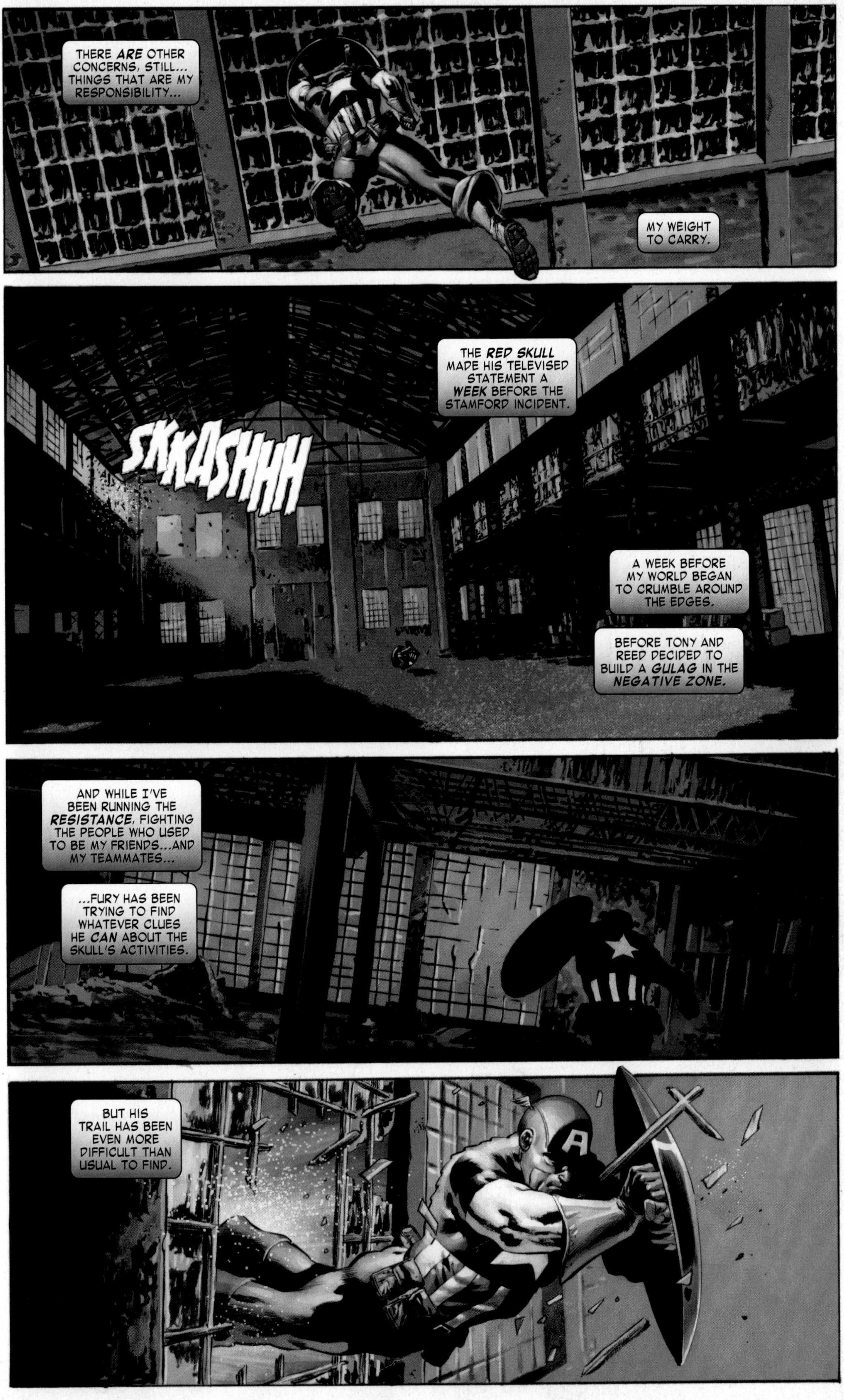
THERE ARE OTHER CONCERNS, STILL... THINGS THAT ARE MY RESPONSIBILITY...
MY WEIGHT TO CARRY.
THE RED SKULL MADE HIS TELEVISED STATEMENT A WEEK BEFORE THE STAMFORD INCIDENT.
SKKASHHH
A WEEK BEFORE MY WORLD BEGAN TO CRUMBLE AROUND THE EDGES.
BEFORE TONY AND REED DECIDED TO BUILD A GULAG IN THE NEGATIVE ZONE.
AND WHILE I'VE BEEN RUNNING THE RESISTANCE, FIGHTING THE PEOPLE WHO USED TO BE MY FRIENDS...AND MY TEAMMATES...
...FURY HAS BEEN TRYING TO FIND WHATEVER CLUES HE CAN ABOUT THE SKULL'S ACTIVITIES.
BUT HIS TRAIL HAS BEEN EVEN MORE DIFFICULT THAN USUAL TO FIND.

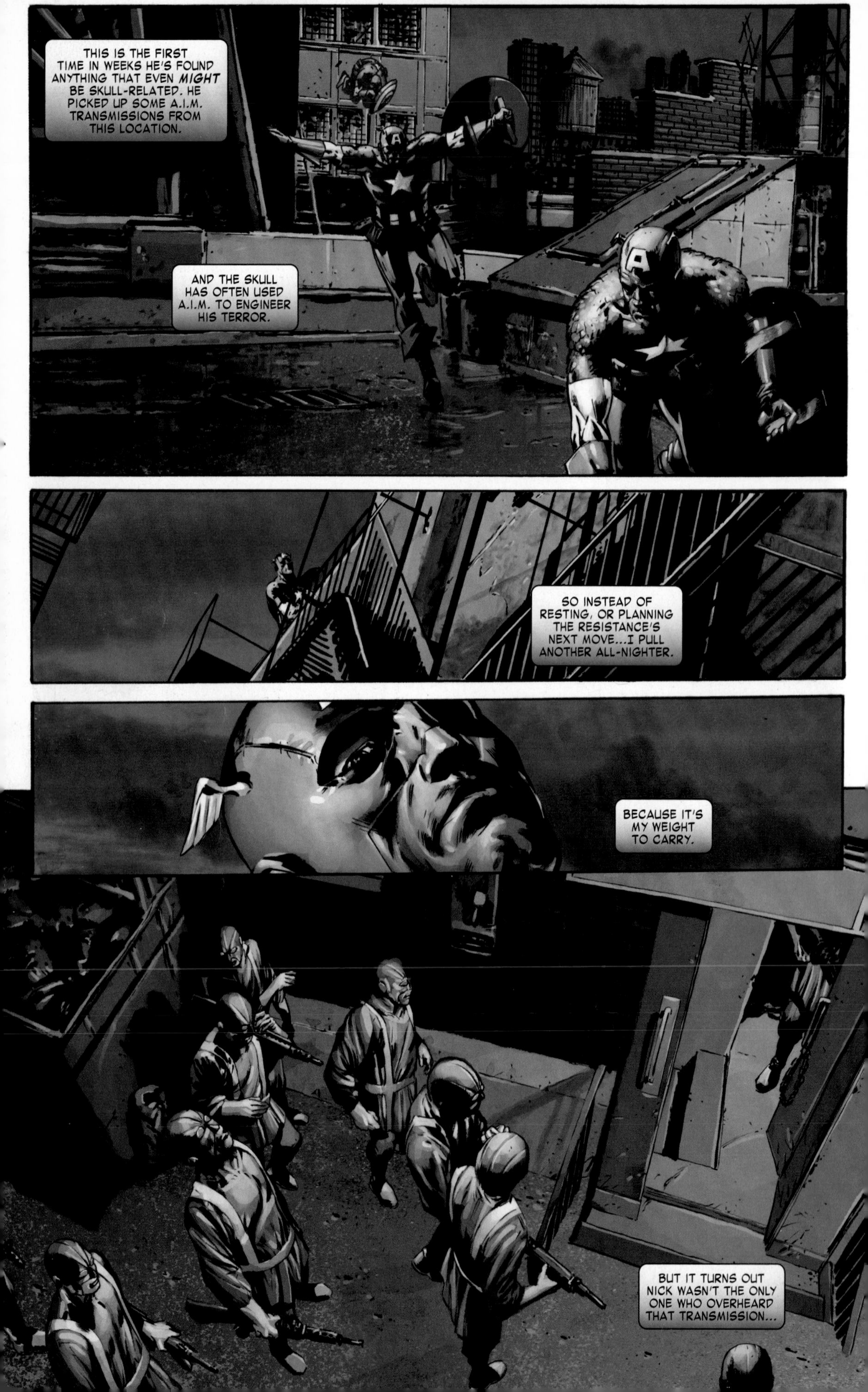
THIS IS THE FIRST TIME IN WEEKS HE'S FOUND ANYTHING THAT EVEN *MIGHT* BE SKULL-RELATED. HE PICKED UP SOME A.I.M. TRANSMISSIONS FROM THIS LOCATION.
AND THE SKULL HAS OFTEN USED A.I.M. TO ENGINEER HIS TERROR.
SO INSTEAD OF RESTING, OR PLANNING THE RESISTANCE'S NEXT MOVE...I PULL ANOTHER ALL-NIGHTER.
BECAUSE IT'S MY WEIGHT TO CARRY.
BUT IT TURNS OUT NICK WASN'T THE ONLY ONE WHO OVERHEARD THAT TRANSMISSION...

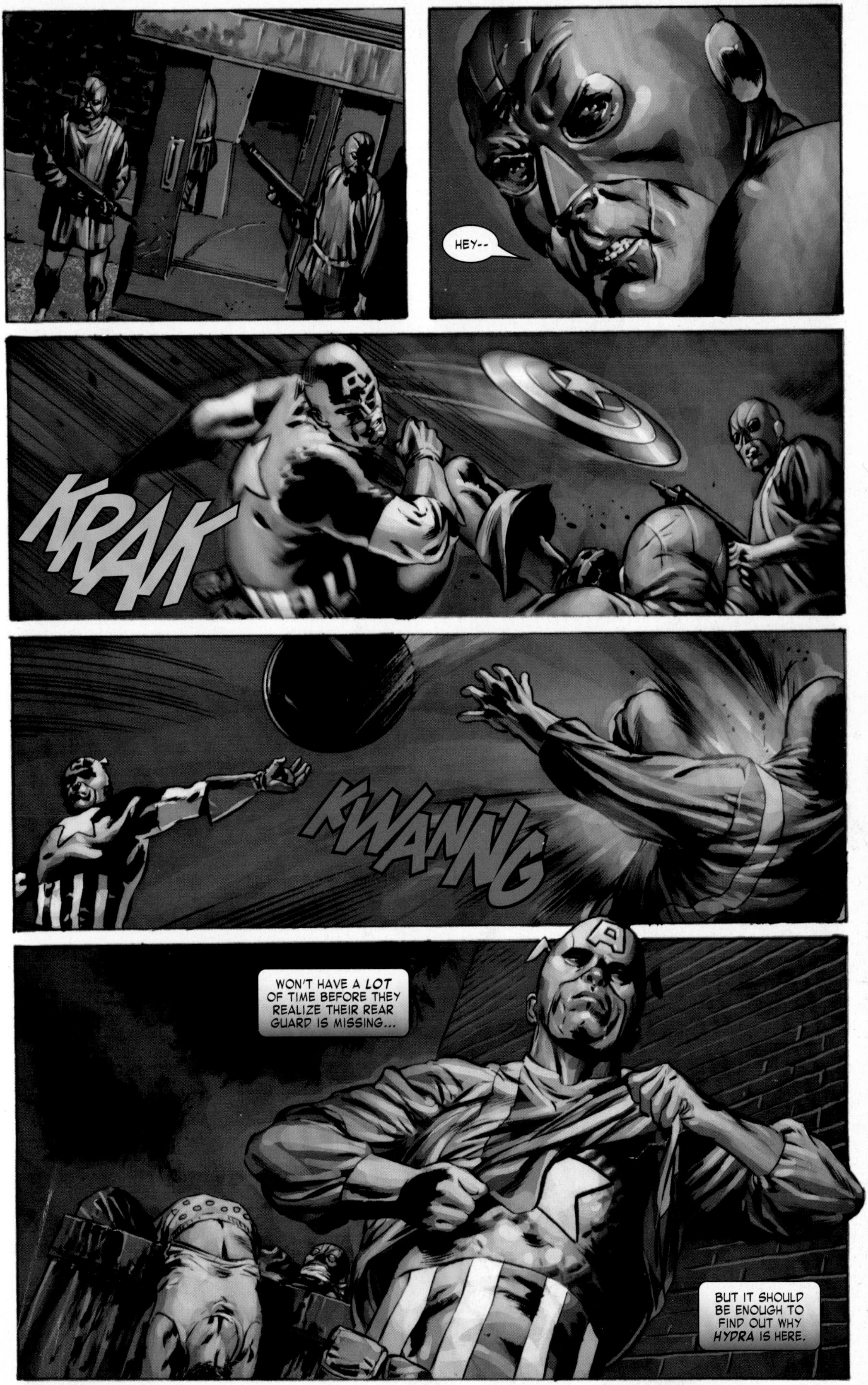
HEY--
KRAK
KWANNG
WON'T HAVE A LOT OF TIME BEFORE THEY REALIZE THEIR REAR GUARD IS MISSING...
BUT IT SHOULD BE ENOUGH TO FIND OUT WHY HYDRA IS HERE.

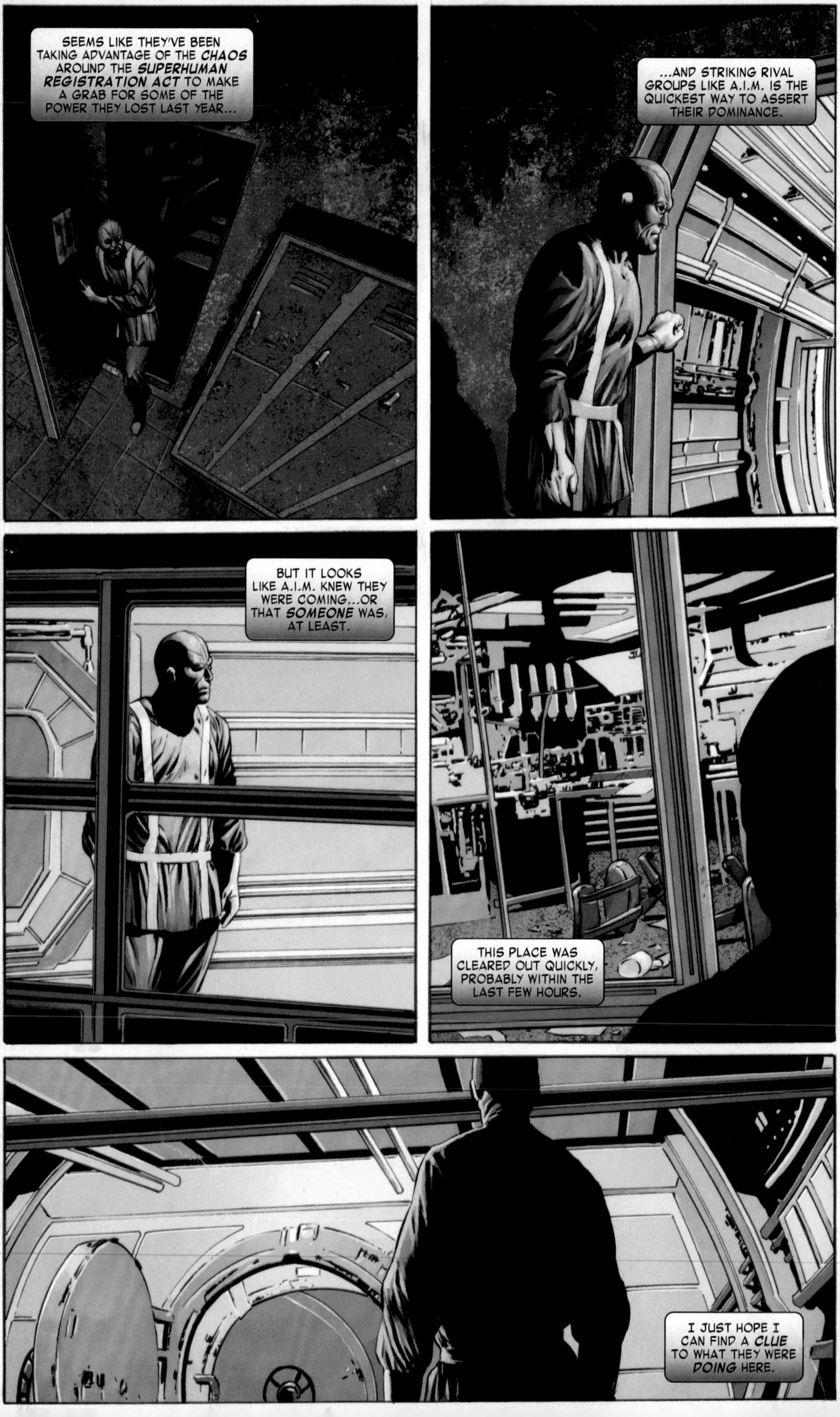
SEEMS LIKE THEY'VE BEEN TAKING ADVANTAGE OF THE CHAOS AROUND THE SUPERHUMAN REGISTRATION ACT TO MAKE A GRAB FOR SOME OF THE POWER THEY LOST LAST YEAR...
...AND STRIKING RIVAL GROUPS LIKE A.I.M. IS THE QUICKEST WAY TO ASSERT THEIR DOMINANCE.
BUT IT LOOKS LIKE A.I.M. KNEW THEY WERE COMING...OR THAT SOMEONE WAS, AT LEAST.
THIS PLACE WAS CLEARED OUT QUICKLY, PROBABLY WITHIN THE LAST FEW HOURS.
I JUST HOPE I CAN FIND A CLUE TO WHAT THEY WERE DOING HERE.

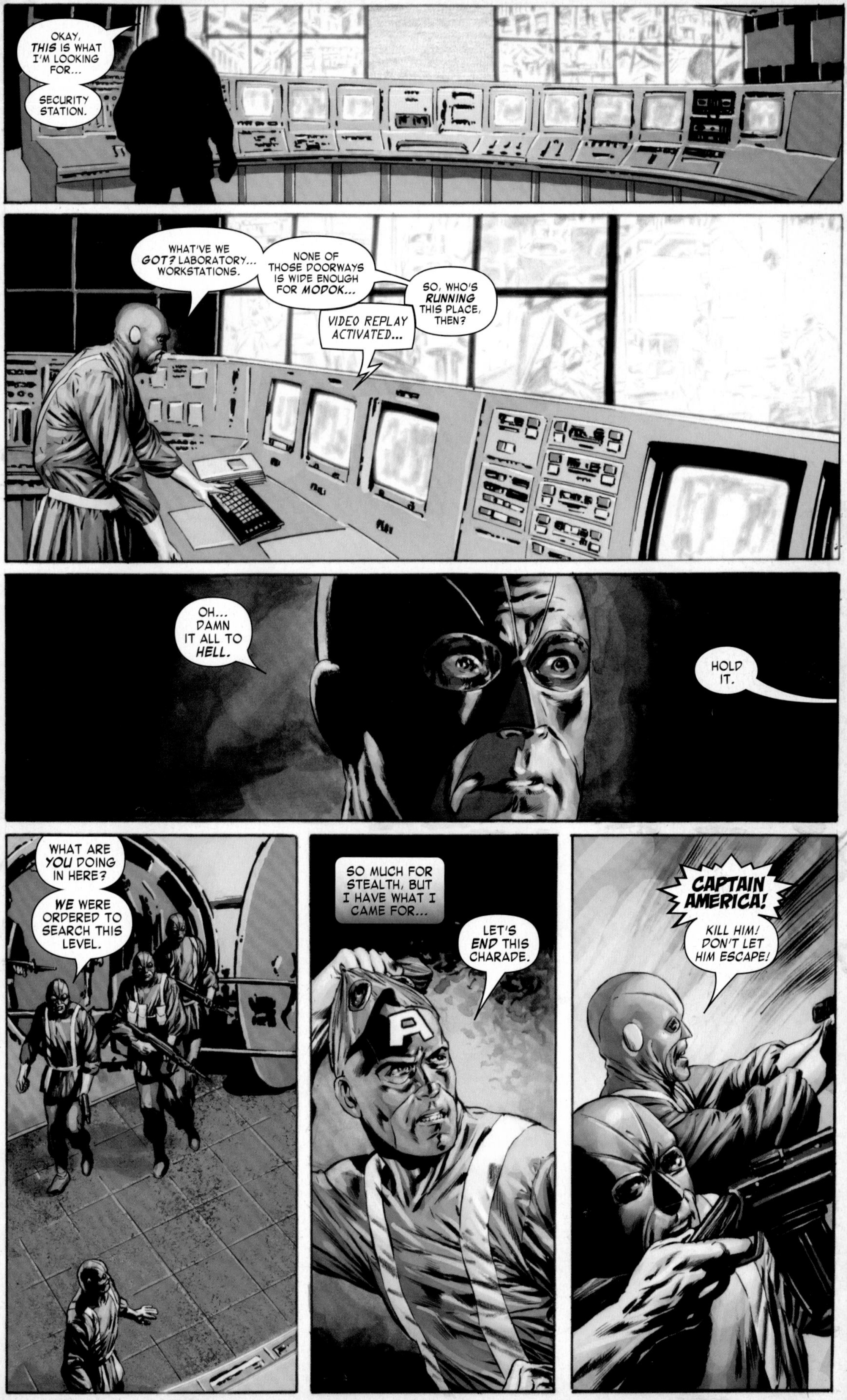

OKAY, THIS IS WHAT I'M LOOKING FOR...
SECURITY STATION.
WHAT'VE WE GOT? LABORATORY... WORKSTATIONS.
NONE OF THOSE DOORWAYS IS WIDE ENOUGH FOR MODOK...
SO, WHO'S RUNNING THIS PLACE, THEN?
VIDEO REPLAY ACTIVATED...
OH... DAMN IT ALL TO HELL.
HOLD IT.
WHAT ARE YOU DOING IN HERE?
WE WERE ORDERED TO SEARCH THIS LEVEL.
SO MUCH FOR STEALTH, BUT I HAVE WHAT I CAME FOR...
LET'S END THIS CHARADE.
CAPTAIN AMERICA!
KILL HIM! DON'T LET HIM ESCAPE!

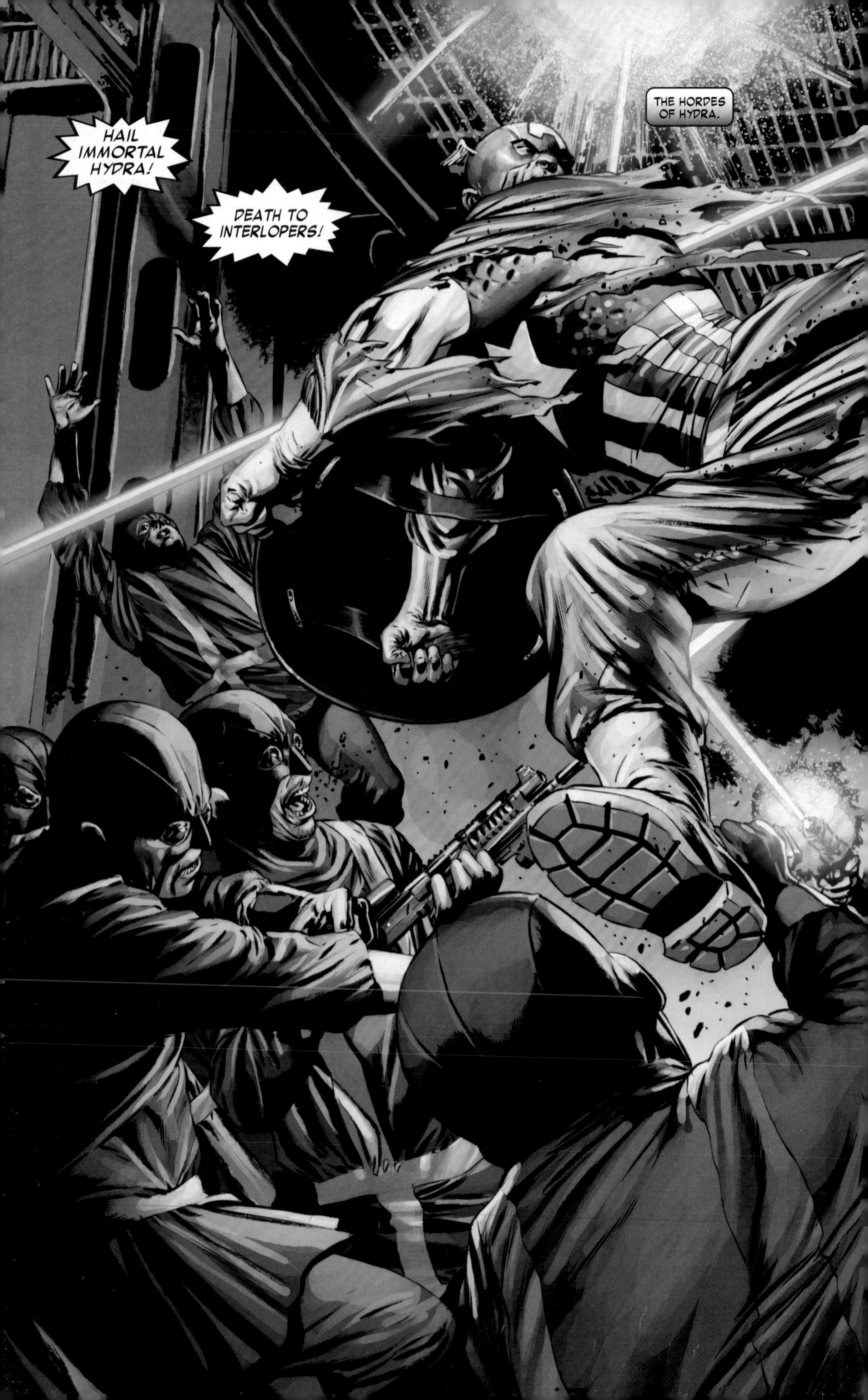
THE HORDES OF HYDRA.
HAIL IMMORTAL HYDRA!
DEATH TO INTERLOPERS!

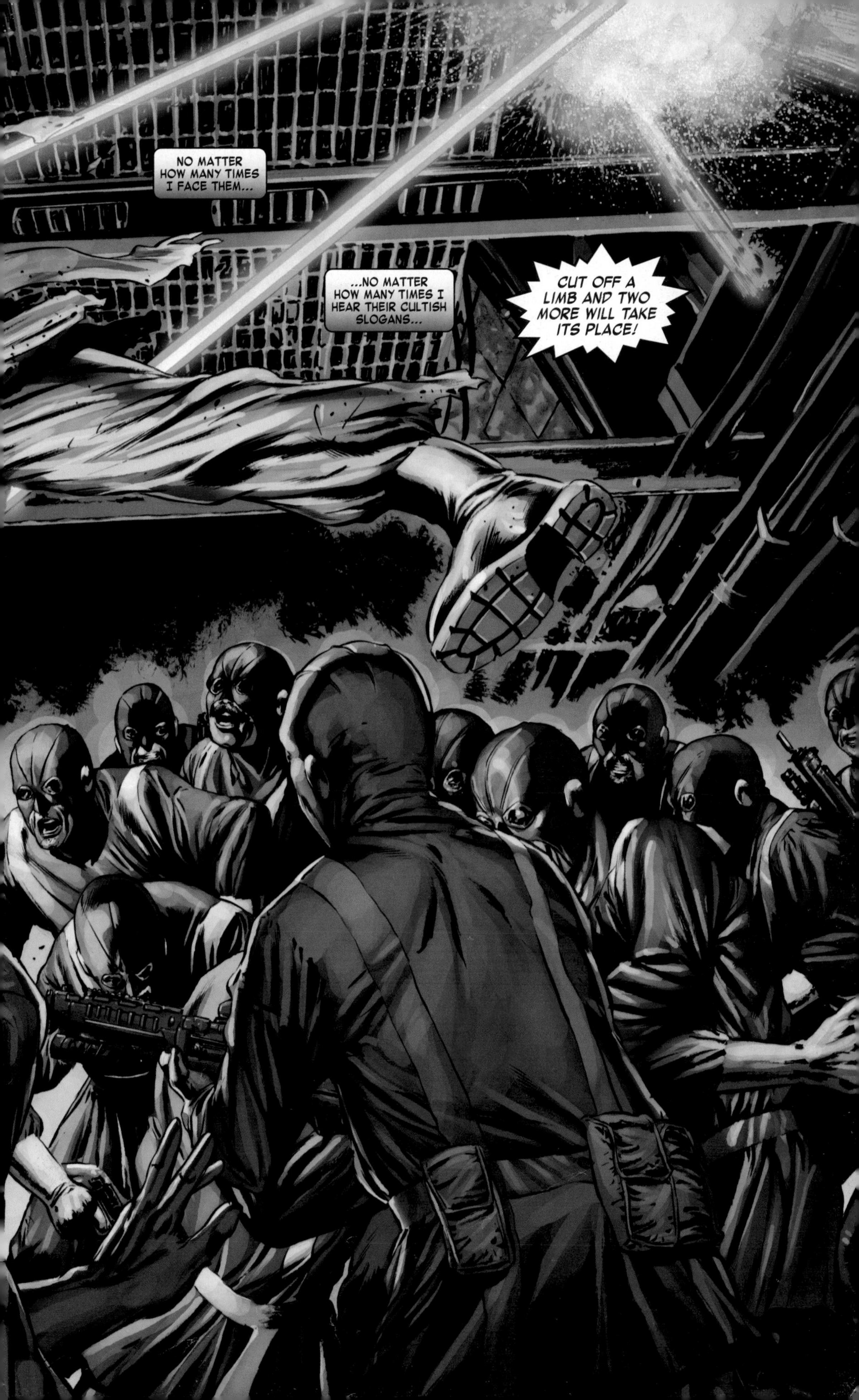
NO MATTER HOW MANY TIMES I FACE THEM...
...NO MATTER HOW MANY TIMES I HEAR THEIR CULTISH SLOGANS...
CUT OFF A LIMB AND TWO MORE WILL TAKE ITS PLACE!

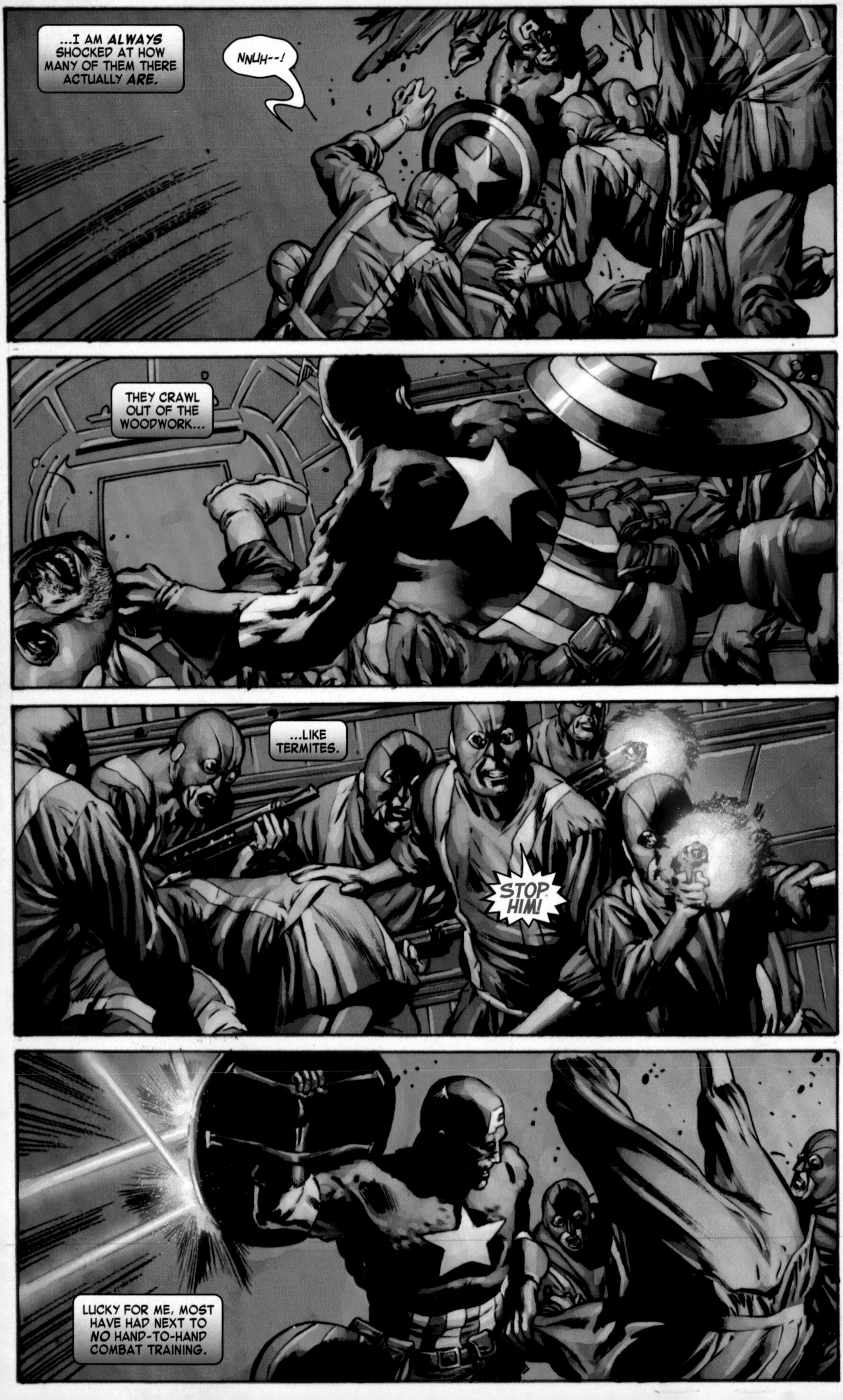
...I AM ALWAYS SHOCKED AT HOW MANY OF THEM THERE ACTUALLY ARE.
NNUH--!
THEY CRAWL OUT OF THE WOODWORK...
...LIKE TERMITES.
STOP HIM!
LUCKY FOR ME, MOST HAVE HAD NEXT TO NO HAND-TO-HAND COMBAT TRAINING.

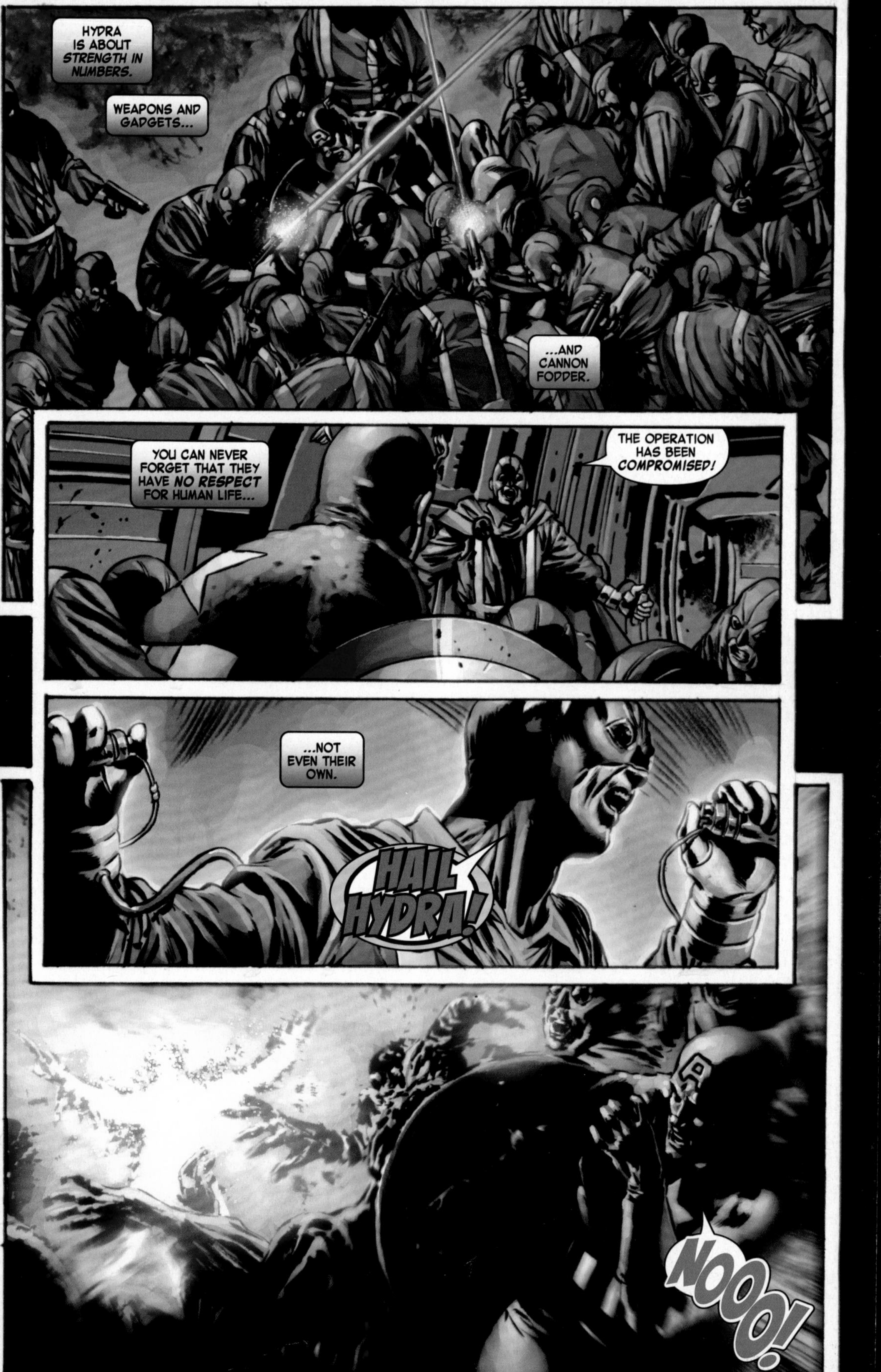
HYDRA IS ABOUT STRENGTH IN NUMBERS.
WEAPONS AND GADGETS...
...AND CANNON FODDER.
YOU CAN NEVER FORGET THAT THEY HAVE NO RESPECT FOR HUMAN LIFE...
THE OPERATION HAS BEEN COMPROMISED!
...NOT EVEN THEIR OWN.
HAIL HYDRA!
NOOO!

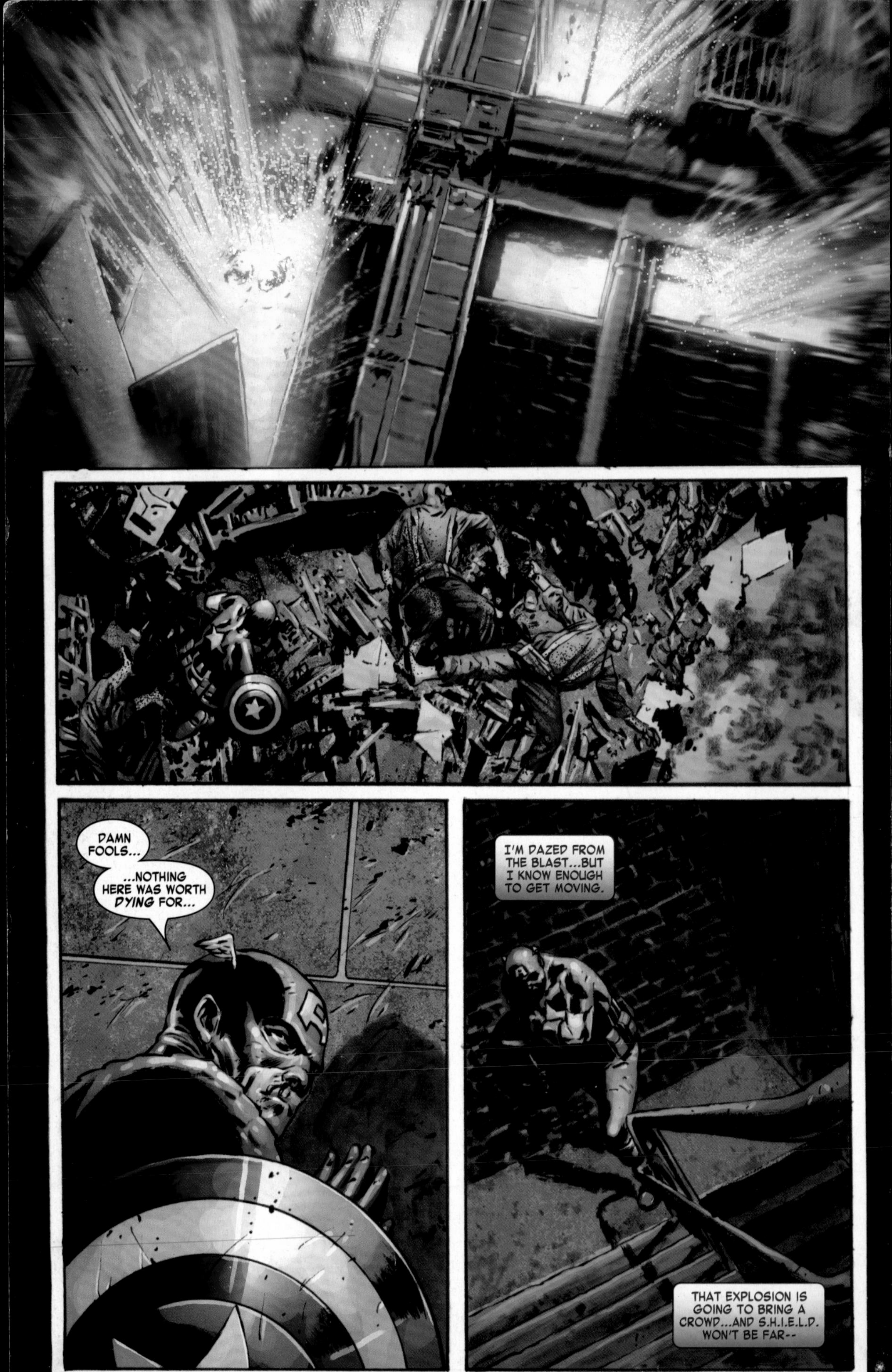
DAMN FOOLS...
...NOTHING HERE WAS WORTH DYING FOR...
I'M DAZED FROM THE BLAST...BUT I KNOW ENOUGH TO GET MOVING.
THAT EXPLOSION IS GOING TO BRING A CROWD...AND S.H.I.E.L.D. WON'T BE FAR--

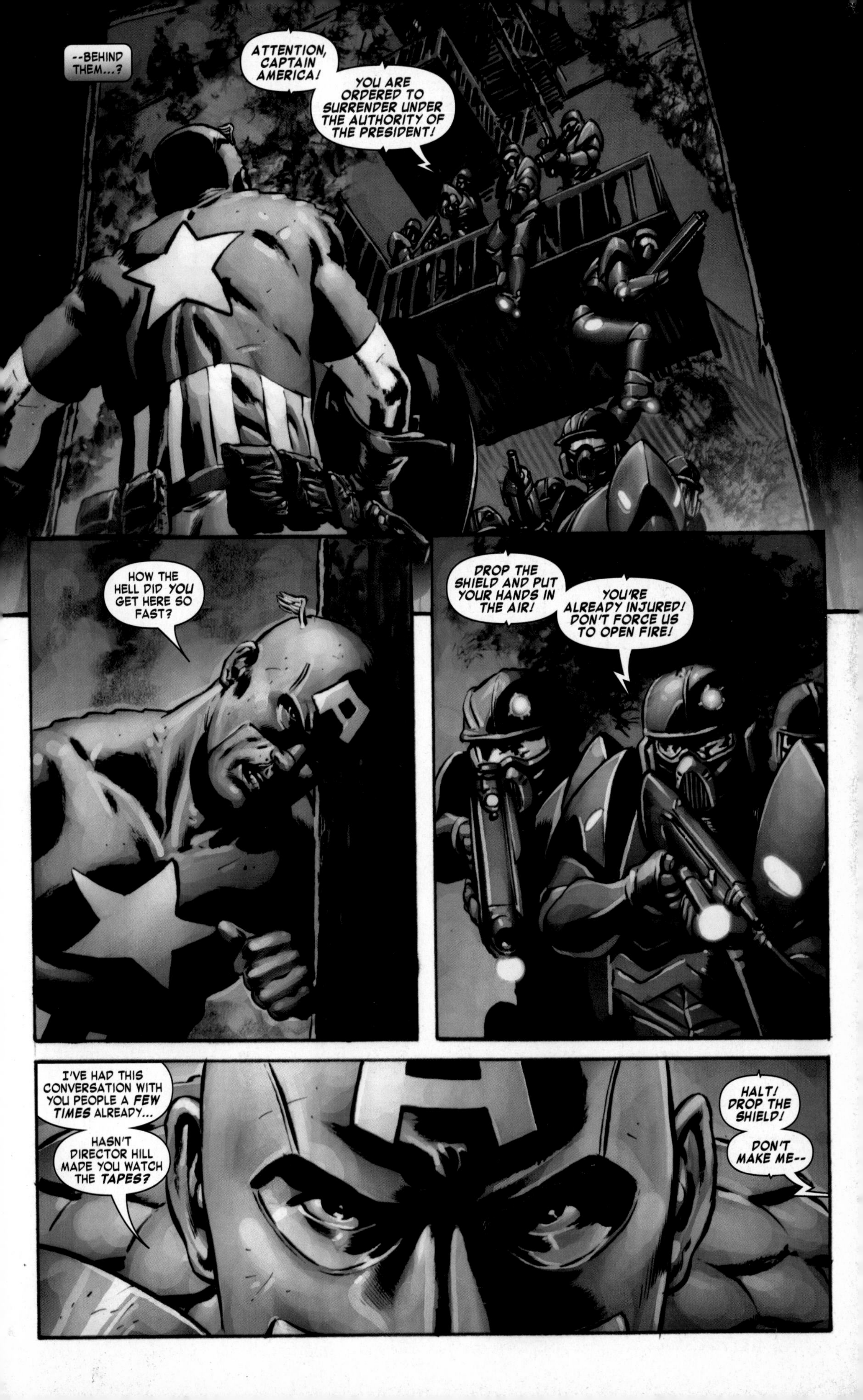
--BEHIND THEM...?
ATTENTION, CAPTAIN AMERICA!
YOU ARE ORDERED TO SURRENDER UNDER THE AUTHORITY OF THE PRESIDENT!
HOW THE HELL DID YOU GET HERE SO FAST?
DROP THE SHIELD AND PUT YOUR HANDS IN THE AIR!
YOU'RE ALREADY INJURED! DON'T FORCE US TO OPEN FIRE!
I'VE HAD THIS CONVERSATION WITH YOU PEOPLE A FEW TIMES ALREADY...
HASN'T DIRECTOR HILL MADE YOU WATCH THE TAPES?
HALT! DROP THE SHIELD!
DON'T MAKE ME--

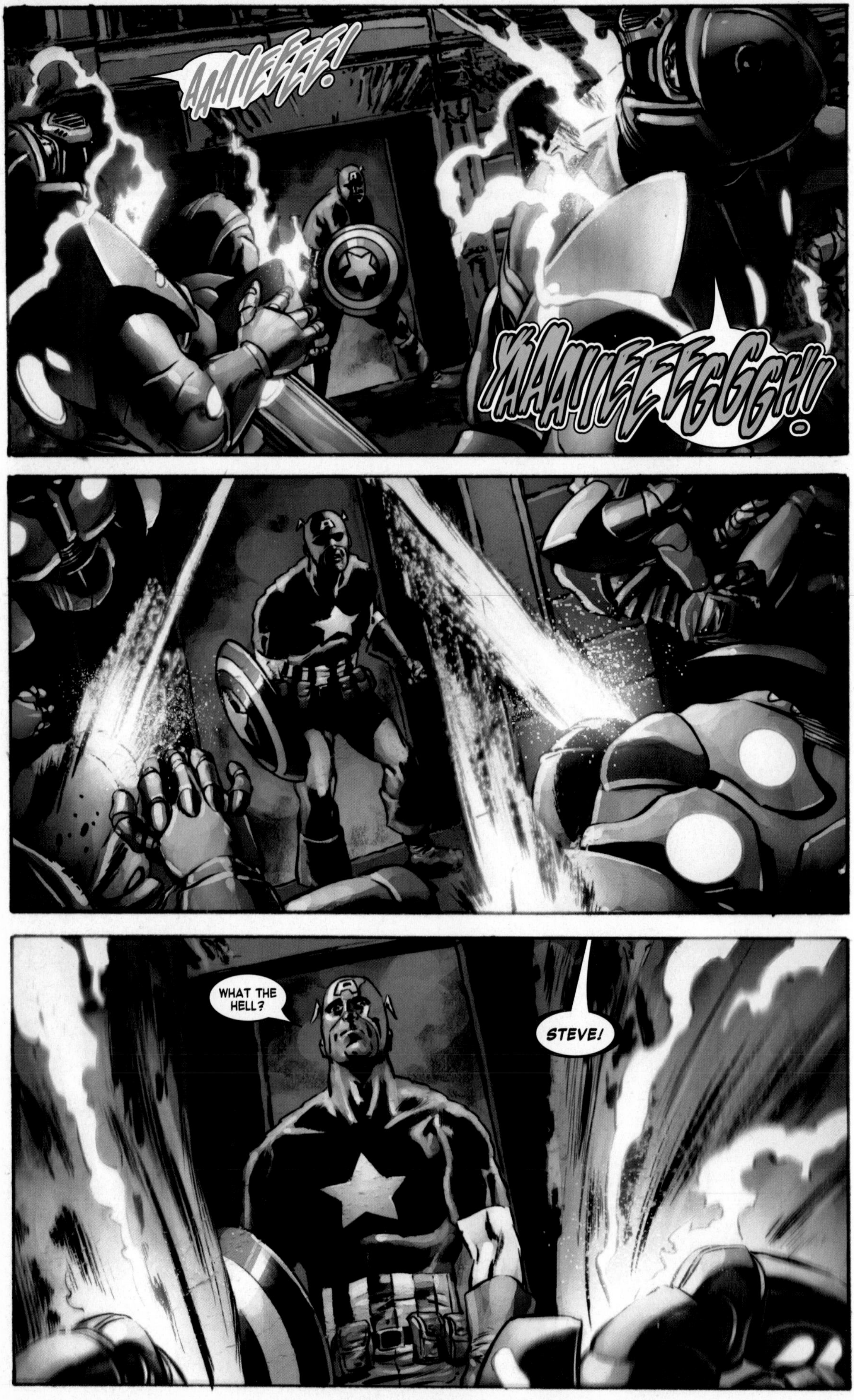
AAAIIEEEE!
YAAAIIEEEGGGH!
WHAT THE HELL?
STEVE!

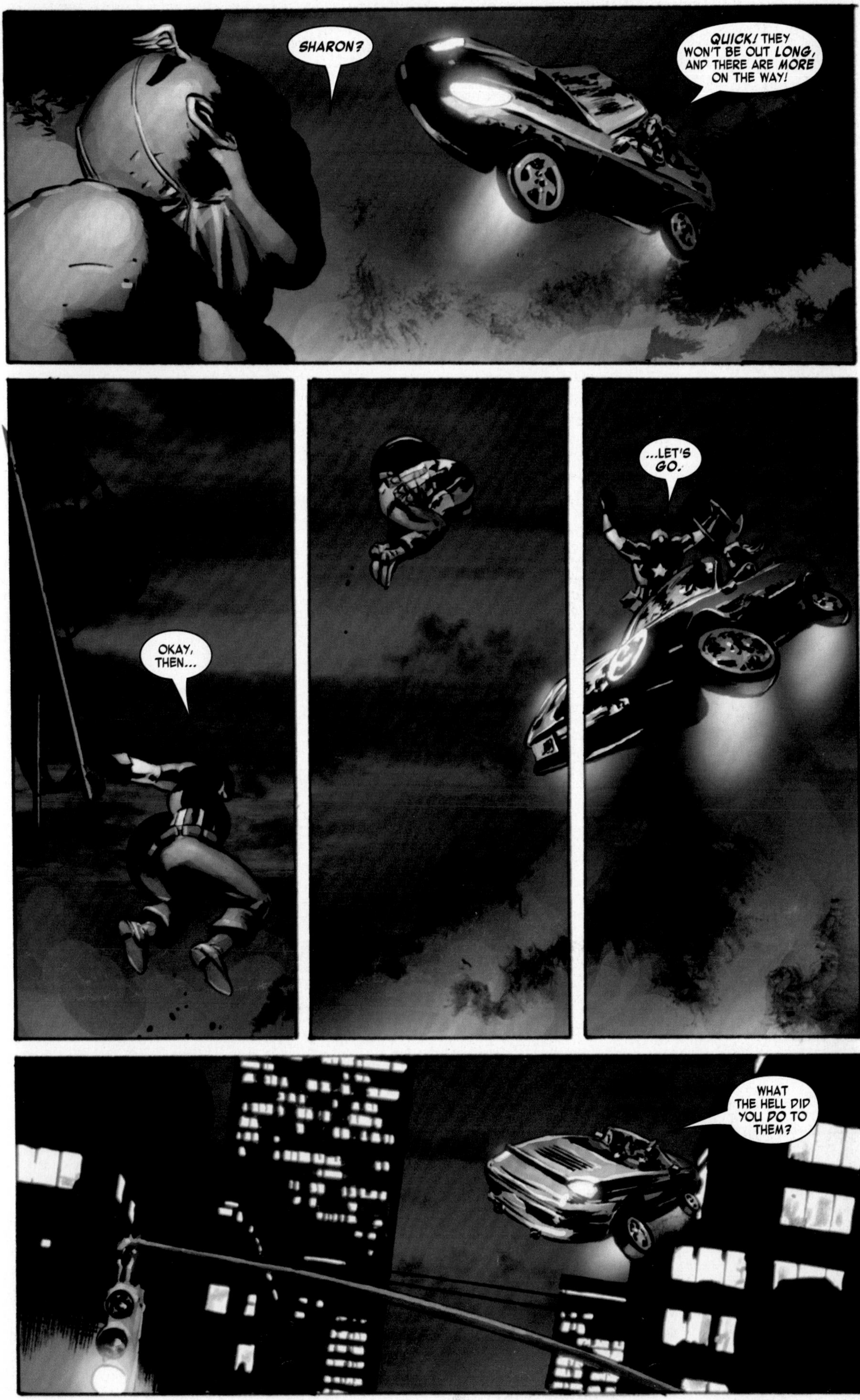
SHARON?
QUICK! THEY WON'T BE OUT LONG, AND THERE ARE MORE ON THE WAY!
OKAY, THEN...
...LET'S GO.
WHAT THE HELL DID YOU DO TO THEM?

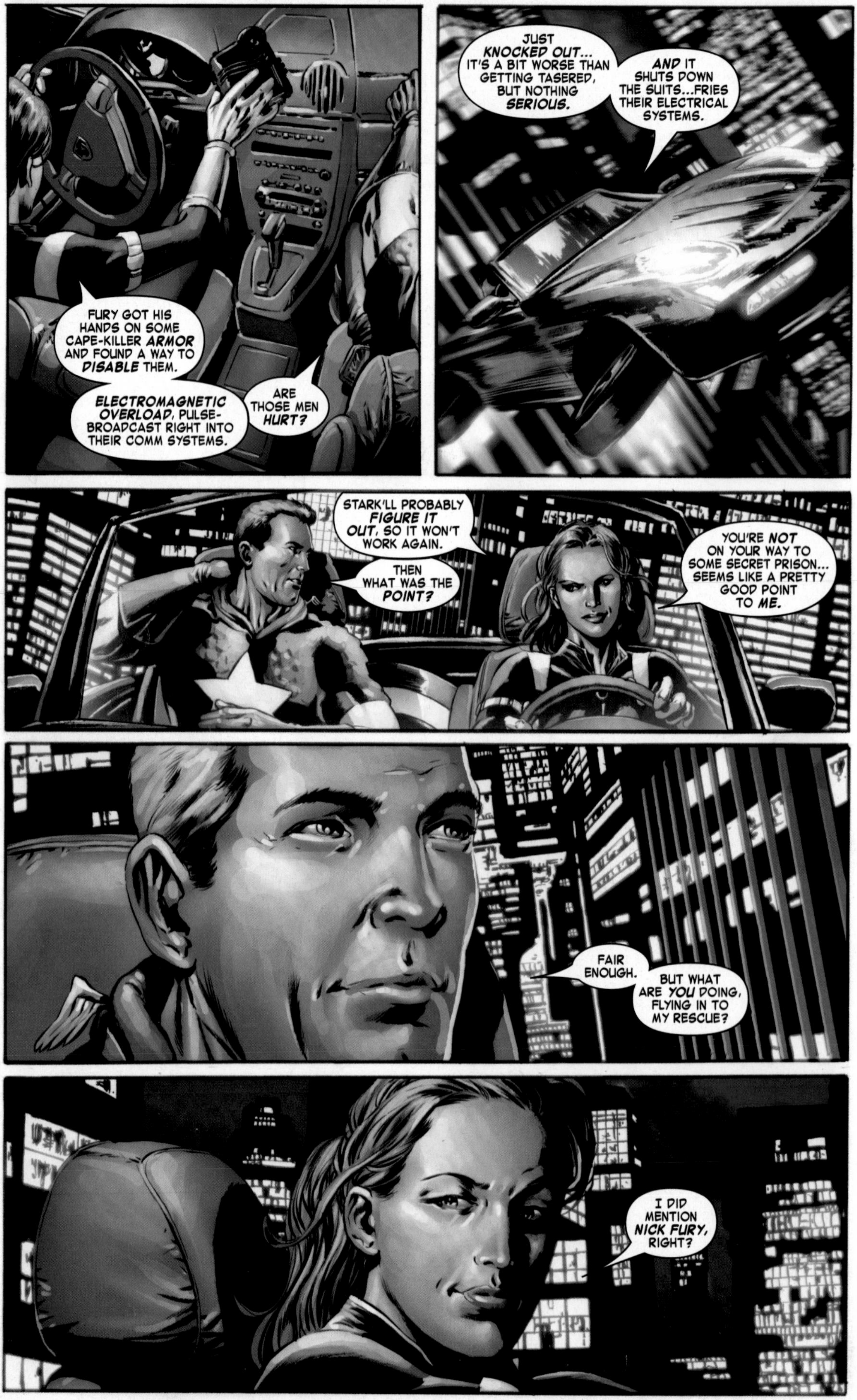
FURY GOT HIS HANDS ON SOME CAPE-KILLER ARMOR AND FOUND A WAY TO DISABLE THEM.
ELECTROMAGNETIC OVERLOAD, PULSE-BROADCAST RIGHT INTO THEIR COMM SYSTEMS.
ARE THOSE MEN HURT?
JUST KNOCKED OUT... IT'S A BIT WORSE THAN GETTING TASERED, BUT NOTHING SERIOUS.
AND IT SHUTS DOWN THE SUITS...FRIES THEIR ELECTRICAL SYSTEMS.
STARK'LL PROBABLY FIGURE IT OUT, SO IT WON'T WORK AGAIN.
THEN WHAT WAS THE POINT?
YOU'RE NOT ON YOUR WAY TO SOME SECRET PRISON... SEEMS LIKE A PRETTY GOOD POINT TO ME.
FAIR ENOUGH.
BUT WHAT ARE YOU DOING, FLYING IN TO MY RESCUE?
I DID MENTION NICK FURY, RIGHT?

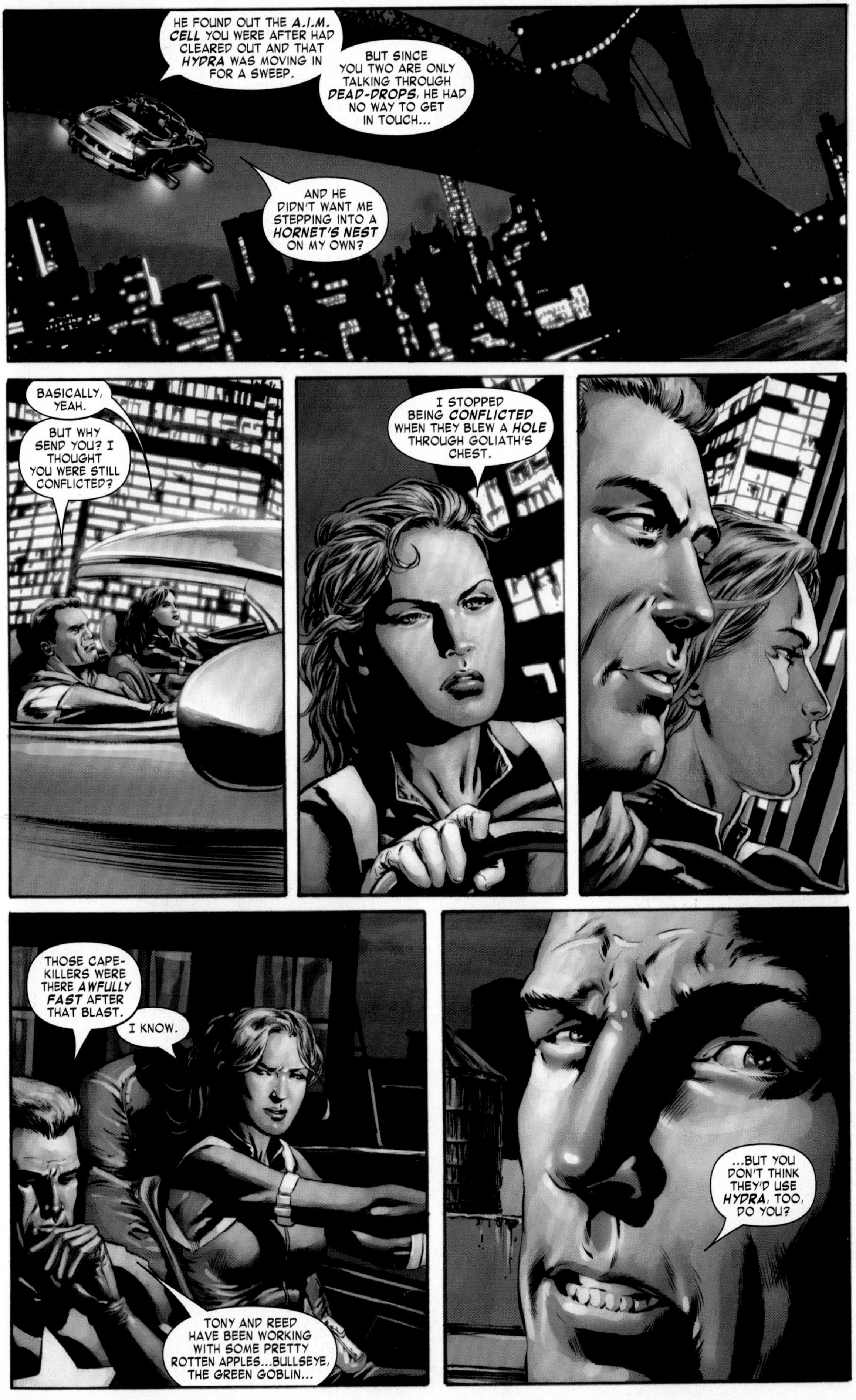
HE FOUND OUT THE A.I.M. CELL YOU WERE AFTER HAD CLEARED OUT AND THAT HYDRA WAS MOVING IN FOR A SWEEP.
BUT SINCE YOU TWO ARE ONLY TALKING THROUGH DEAD-DROPS, HE HAD NO WAY TO GET IN TOUCH...
AND HE DIDN'T WANT ME STEPPING INTO A HORNET'S NEST ON MY OWN?
BASICALLY, YEAH.
BUT WHY SEND YOU? I THOUGHT YOU WERE STILL CONFLICTED?
I STOPPED BEING CONFLICTED WHEN THEY BLEW A HOLE THROUGH GOLIATH'S CHEST.
THOSE CAPE-KILLERS WERE THERE AWFULLY FAST AFTER THAT BLAST.
I KNOW.
TONY AND REED HAVE BEEN WORKING WITH SOME PRETTY ROTTEN APPLES...BULLSEYE, THE GREEN GOBLIN...
...BUT YOU DON'T THINK THEY'D USE HYDRA, TOO, DO YOU?

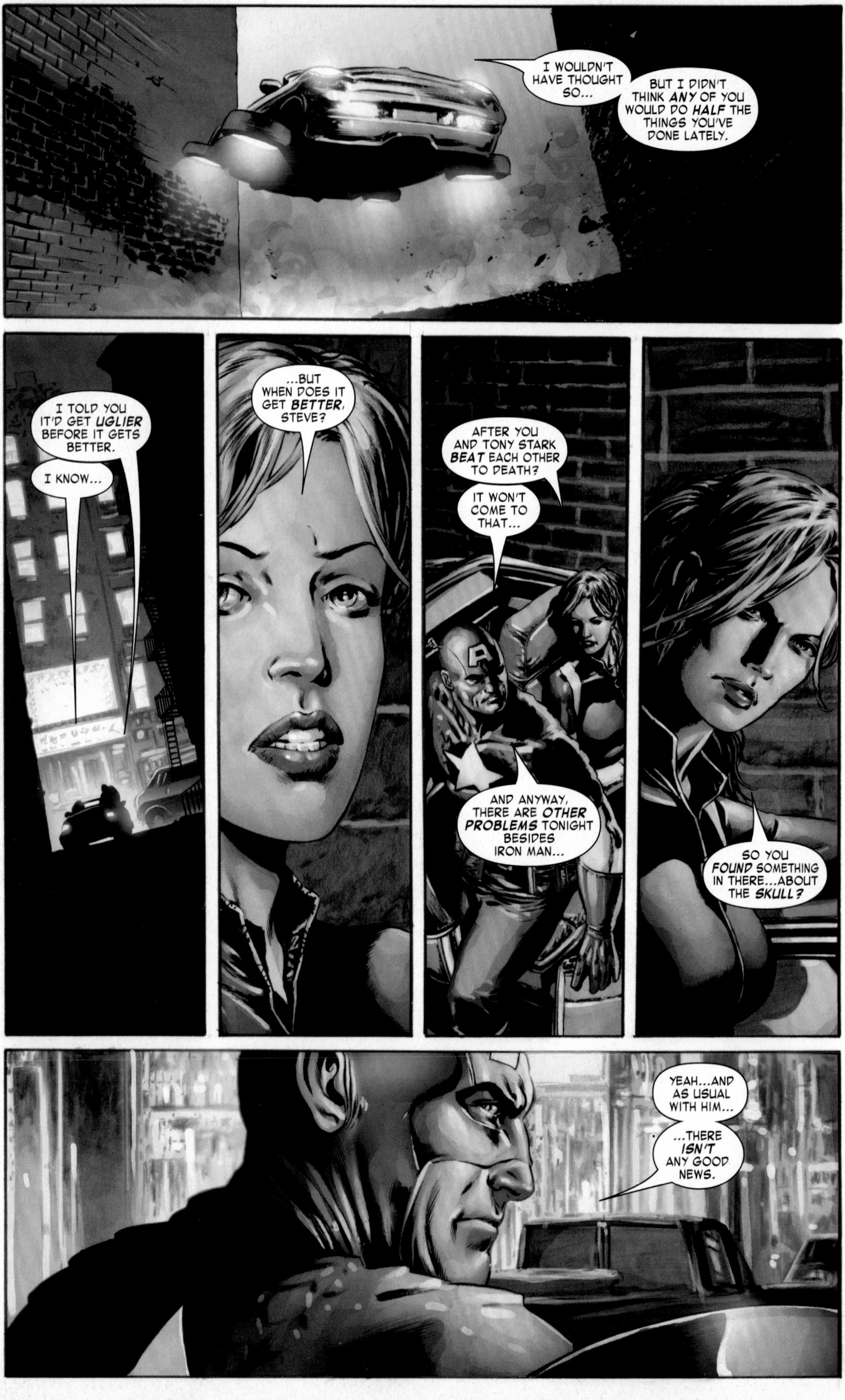
I WOULDN'T HAVE THOUGHT SO...
BUT I DIDN'T THINK ANY OF YOU WOULD DO HALF THE THINGS YOU'VE DONE LATELY.
I TOLD YOU IT'D GET UGLIER BEFORE IT GETS BETTER.
I KNOW...
...BUT WHEN DOES IT GET BETTER, STEVE?
AFTER YOU AND TONY STARK BEAT EACH OTHER TO DEATH?
IT WON'T COME TO THAT...
AND ANYWAY, THERE ARE OTHER PROBLEMS TONIGHT BESIDES IRON MAN...
SO YOU FOUND SOMETHING IN THERE...ABOUT THE SKULL?
YEAH...AND AS USUAL WITH HIM...
...THERE ISN'T ANY GOOD NEWS.

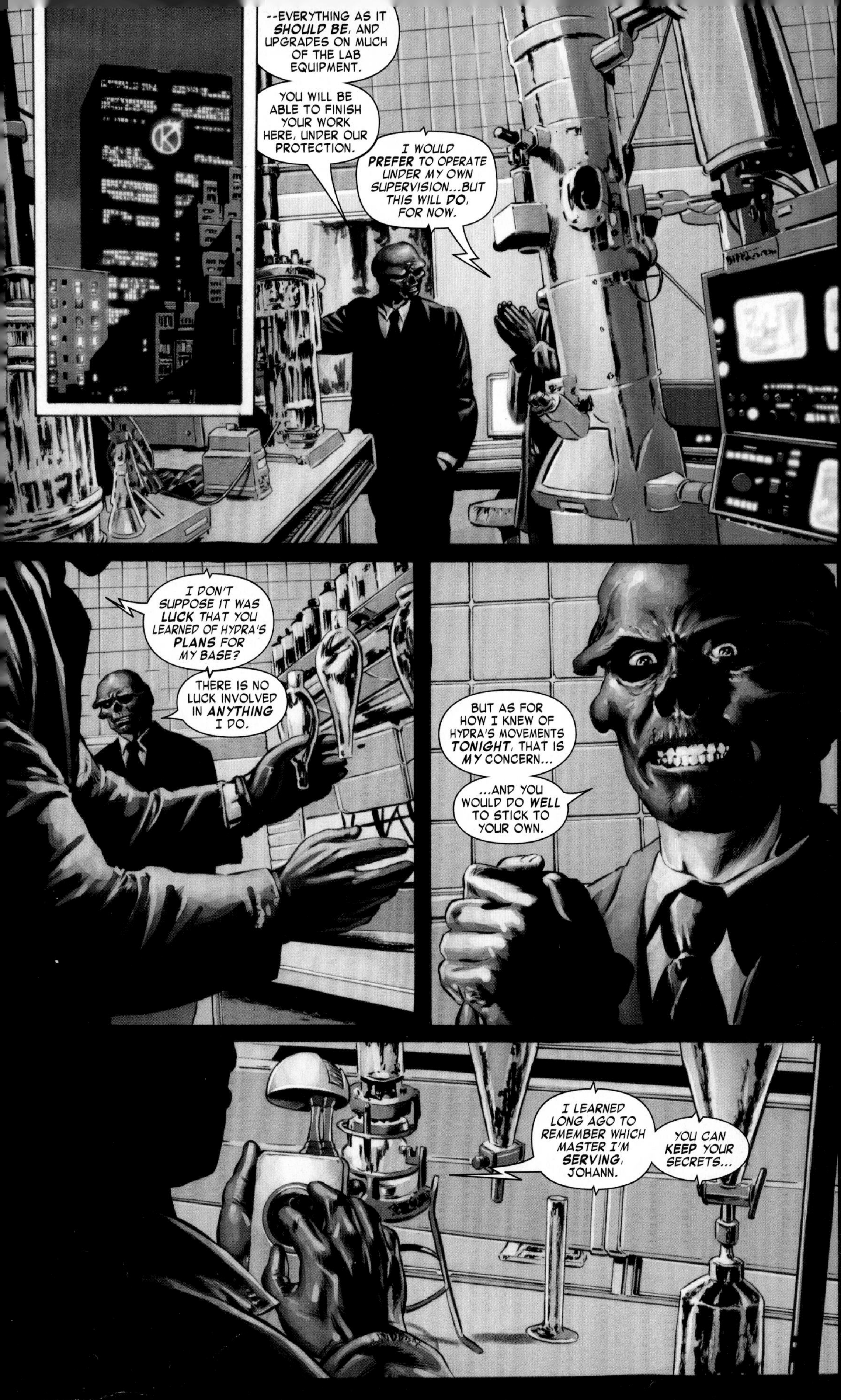
--EVERYTHING AS IT SHOULD BE, AND UPGRADES ON MUCH OF THE LAB EQUIPMENT.
YOU WILL BE ABLE TO FINISH YOUR WORK HERE, UNDER OUR PROTECTION.
I WOULD PREFER TO OPERATE UNDER MY OWN SUPERVISION...BUT THIS WILL DO, FOR NOW.
I DON'T SUPPOSE IT WAS LUCK THAT YOU LEARNED OF HYDRA'S PLANS FOR MY BASE?
THERE IS NO LUCK INVOLVED IN ANYTHING I DO.
BUT AS FOR HOW I KNEW OF HYDRA'S MOVEMENTS TONIGHT, THAT IS MY CONCERN...
...AND YOU WOULD DO WELL TO STICK TO YOUR OWN.
I LEARNED LONG AGO TO REMEMBER WHICH MASTER I'M SERVING, JOHANN.
YOU CAN KEEP YOUR SECRETS...

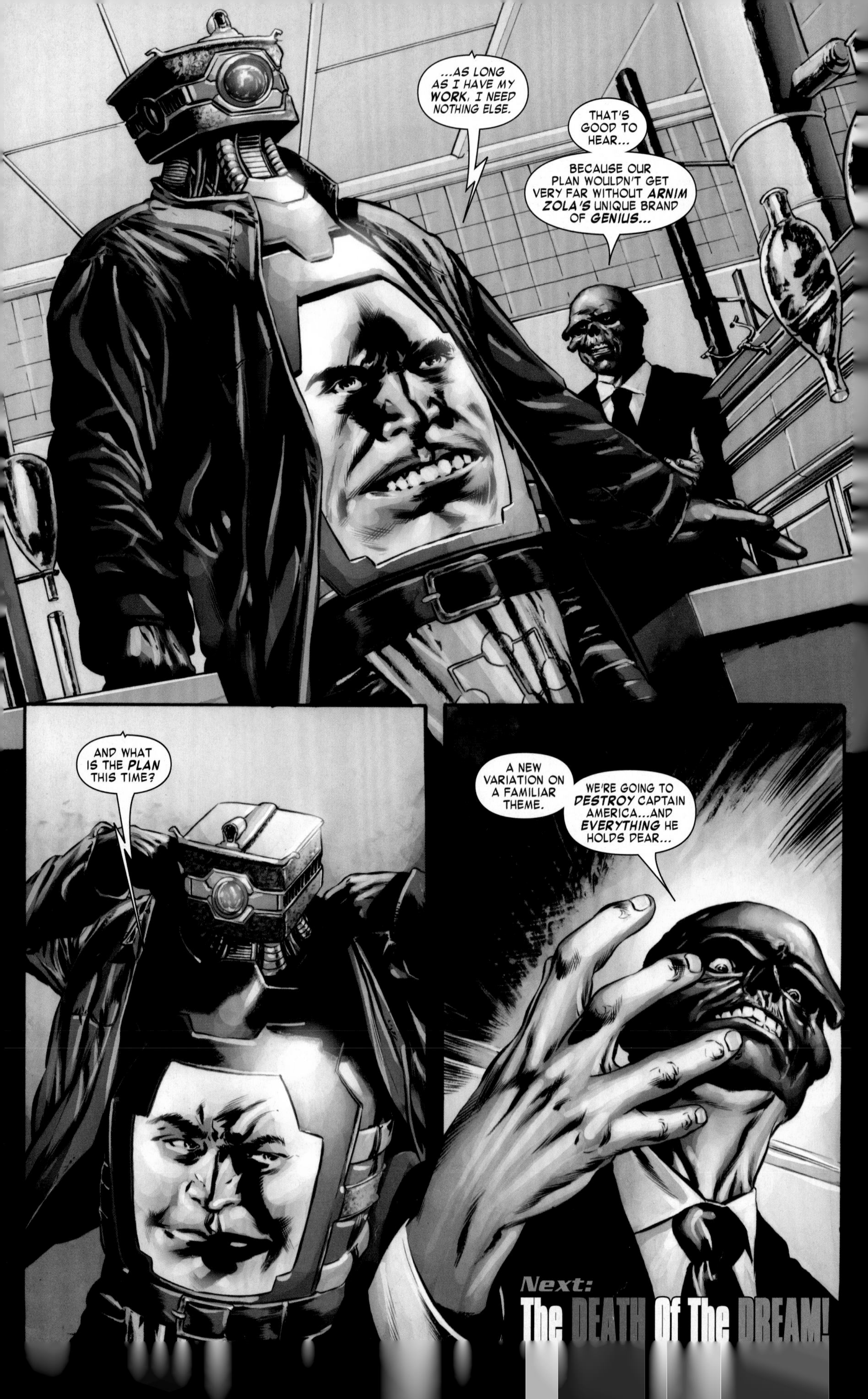
...AS LONG AS I HAVE MY WORK, I NEED NOTHING ELSE.
THAT'S GOOD TO HEAR...
BECAUSE OUR PLAN WOULDN'T GET VERY FAR WITHOUT ARNIM ZOLA'S UNIQUE BRAND OF GENIUS...
AND WHAT IS THE PLAN THIS TIME?
A NEW VARIATION ON A FAMILIAR THEME.
WE'RE GOING TO DESTROY CAPTAIN AMERICA...AND EVERYTHING HE HOLDS DEAR...
Next:
The DEATH Of The DREAM!

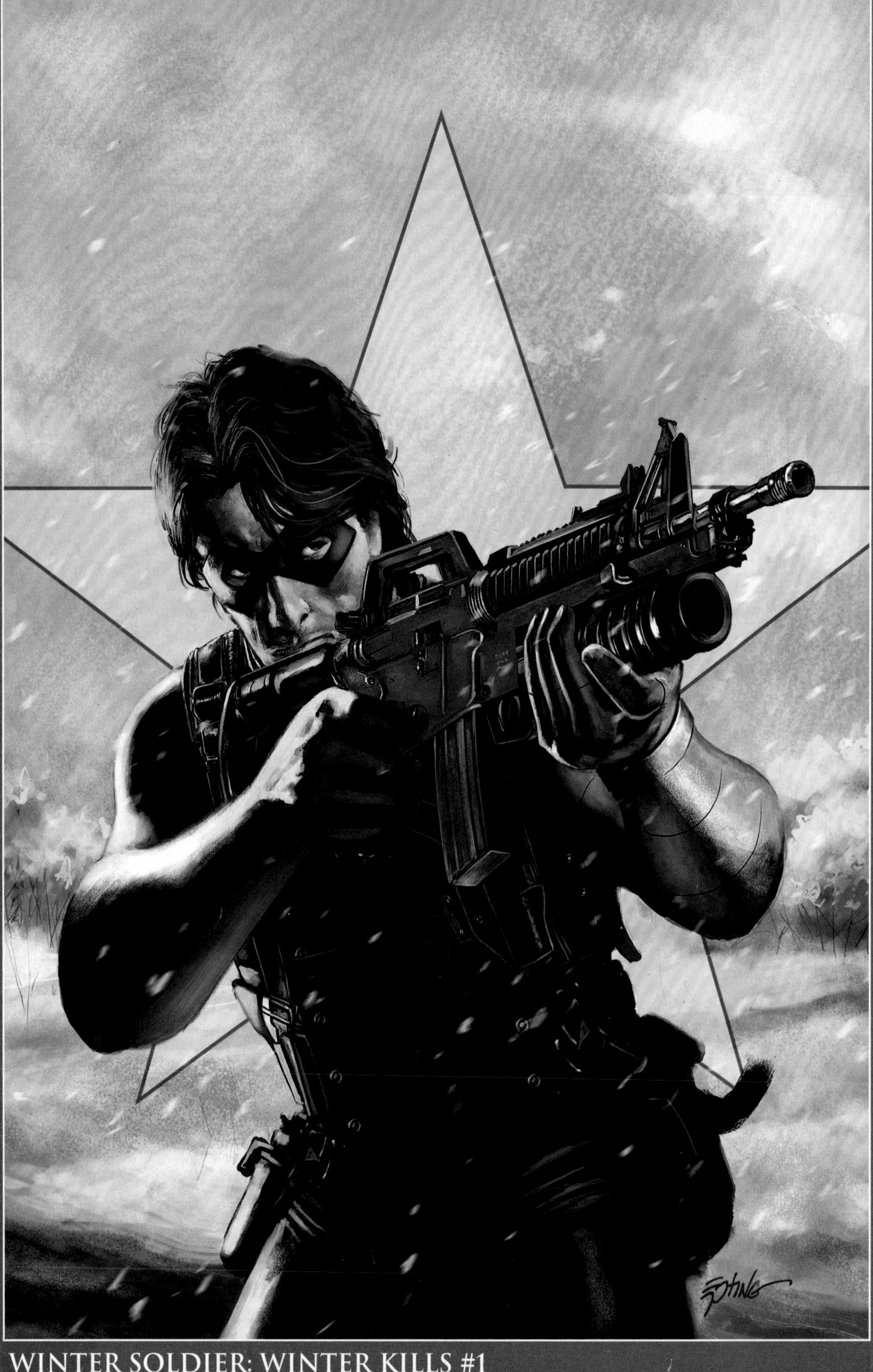

WINTER SOLDIER: WINTER KILLS #1

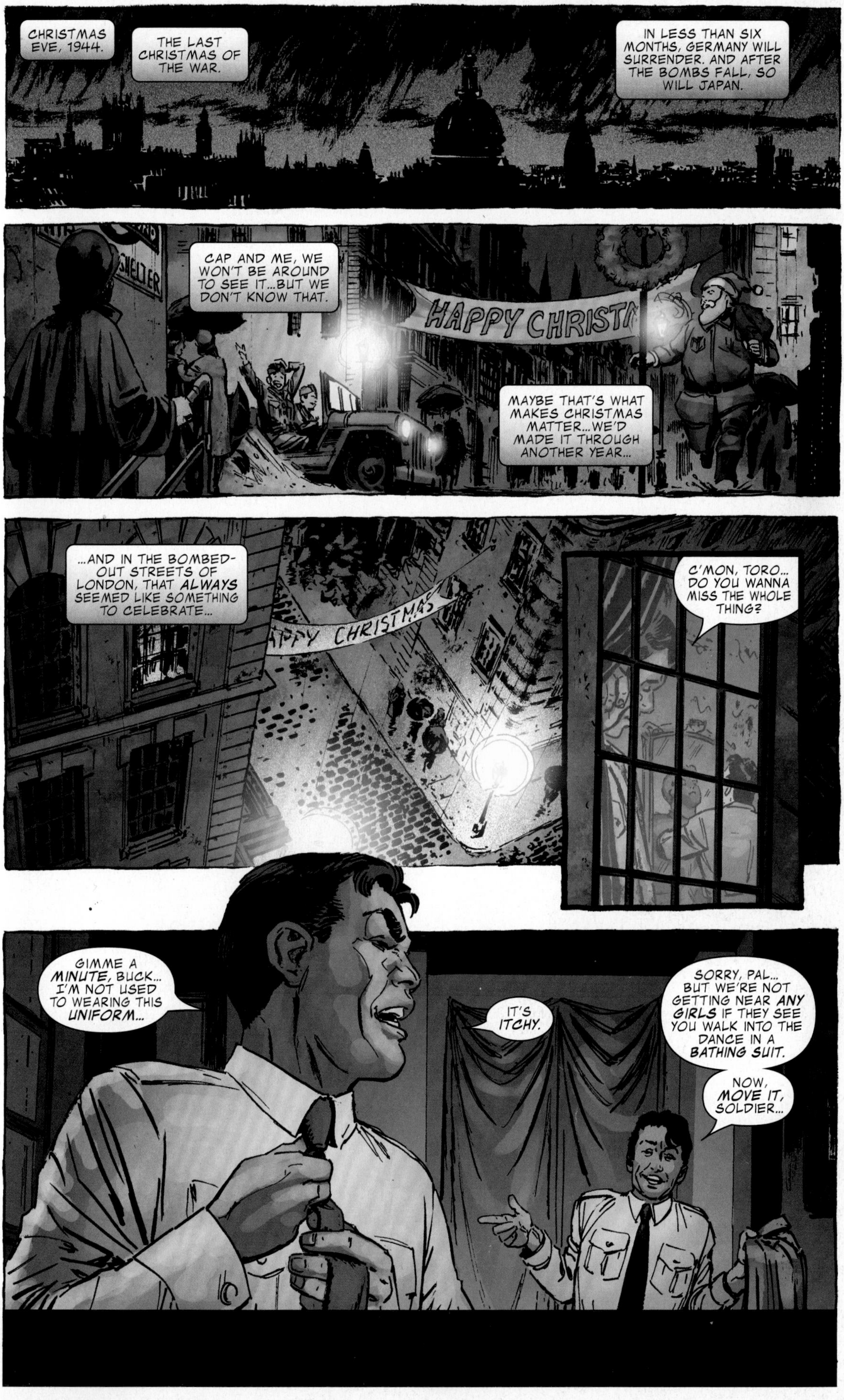
CHRISTMAS EVE, 1944.
THE LAST CHRISTMAS OF THE WAR.
IN LESS THAN SIX MONTHS, GERMANY WILL SURRENDER. AND AFTER THE BOMBS FALL, SO WILL JAPAN.
SHELTER
CAP AND ME, WE WON'T BE AROUND TO SEE IT...BUT WE DON'T KNOW THAT.
HAPPY CHRIST
MAYBE THAT'S WHAT MAKES CHRISTMAS MATTER...WE'D MADE IT THROUGH ANOTHER YEAR...
...AND IN THE BOMBED-OUT STREETS OF LONDON, THAT ALWAYS SEEMED LIKE SOMETHING TO CELEBRATE...
APPY CHRISTMAS
C'MON, TORO... DO YOU WANNA MISS THE WHOLE THING?
GIMME A MINUTE, BUCK... I'M NOT USED TO WEARING THIS UNIFORM...
IT'S ITCHY.
SORRY, PAL... BUT WE'RE NOT GETTING NEAR ANY GIRLS IF THEY SEE YOU WALK INTO THE DANCE IN A BATHING SUIT.
NOW, MOVE IT, SOLDIER...

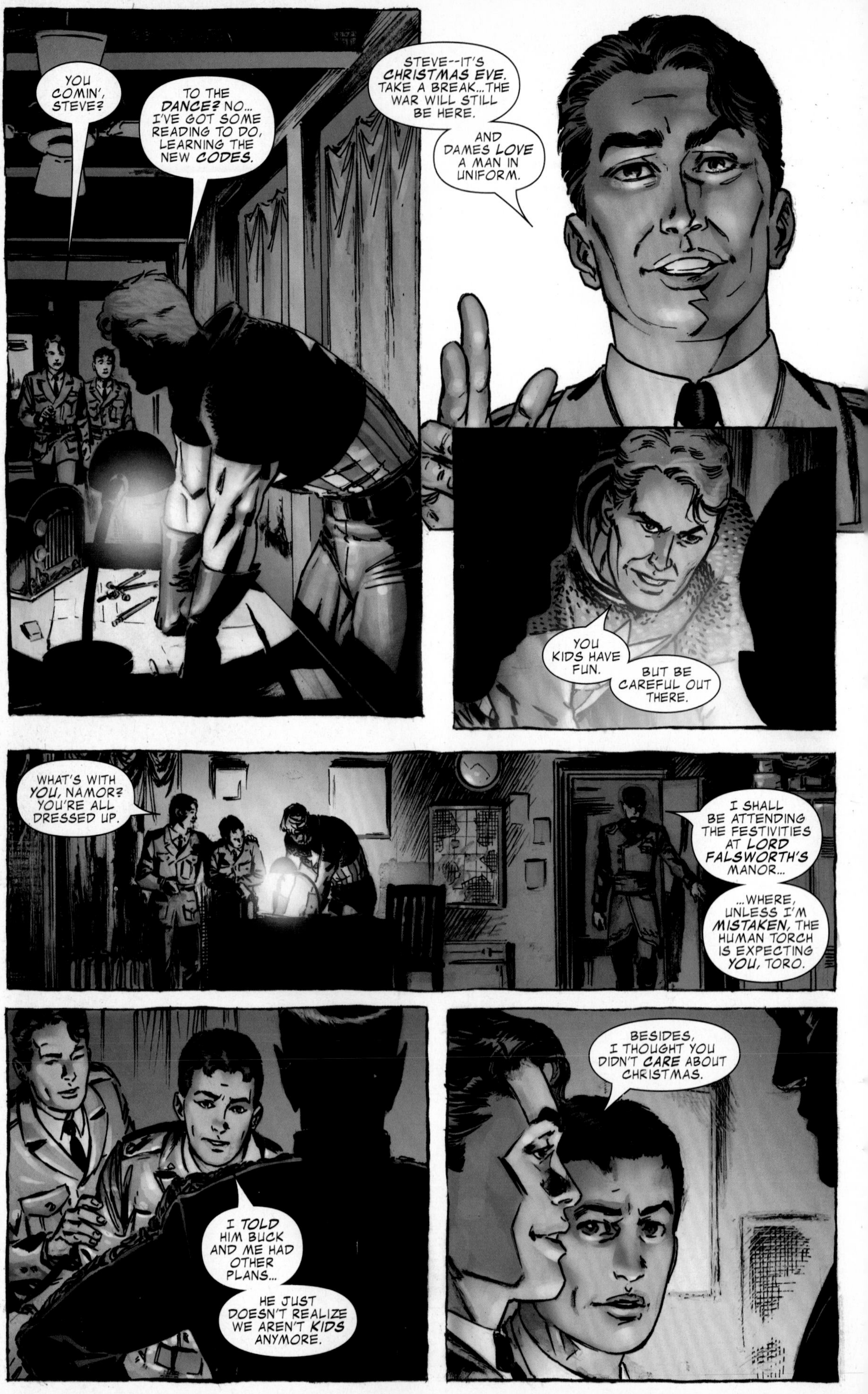
YOU COMIN', STEVE?
TO THE DANCE? NO... I'VE GOT SOME READING TO DO, LEARNING THE NEW CODES.
STEVE--IT'S CHRISTMAS EVE. TAKE A BREAK...THE WAR WILL STILL BE HERE.
AND DAMES LOVE A MAN IN UNIFORM.
YOU KIDS HAVE FUN.
BUT BE CAREFUL OUT THERE.
WHAT'S WITH YOU, NAMOR? YOU'RE ALL DRESSED UP.
I SHALL BE ATTENDING THE FESTIVITIES AT LORD FALSWORTH'S MANOR...
...WHERE, UNLESS I'M MISTAKEN, THE HUMAN TORCH IS EXPECTING YOU, TORO.
I TOLD HIM BUCK AND ME HAD OTHER PLANS...
HE JUST DOESN'T REALIZE WE AREN'T KIDS ANYMORE.
BESIDES, I THOUGHT YOU DIDN'T CARE ABOUT CHRISTMAS.

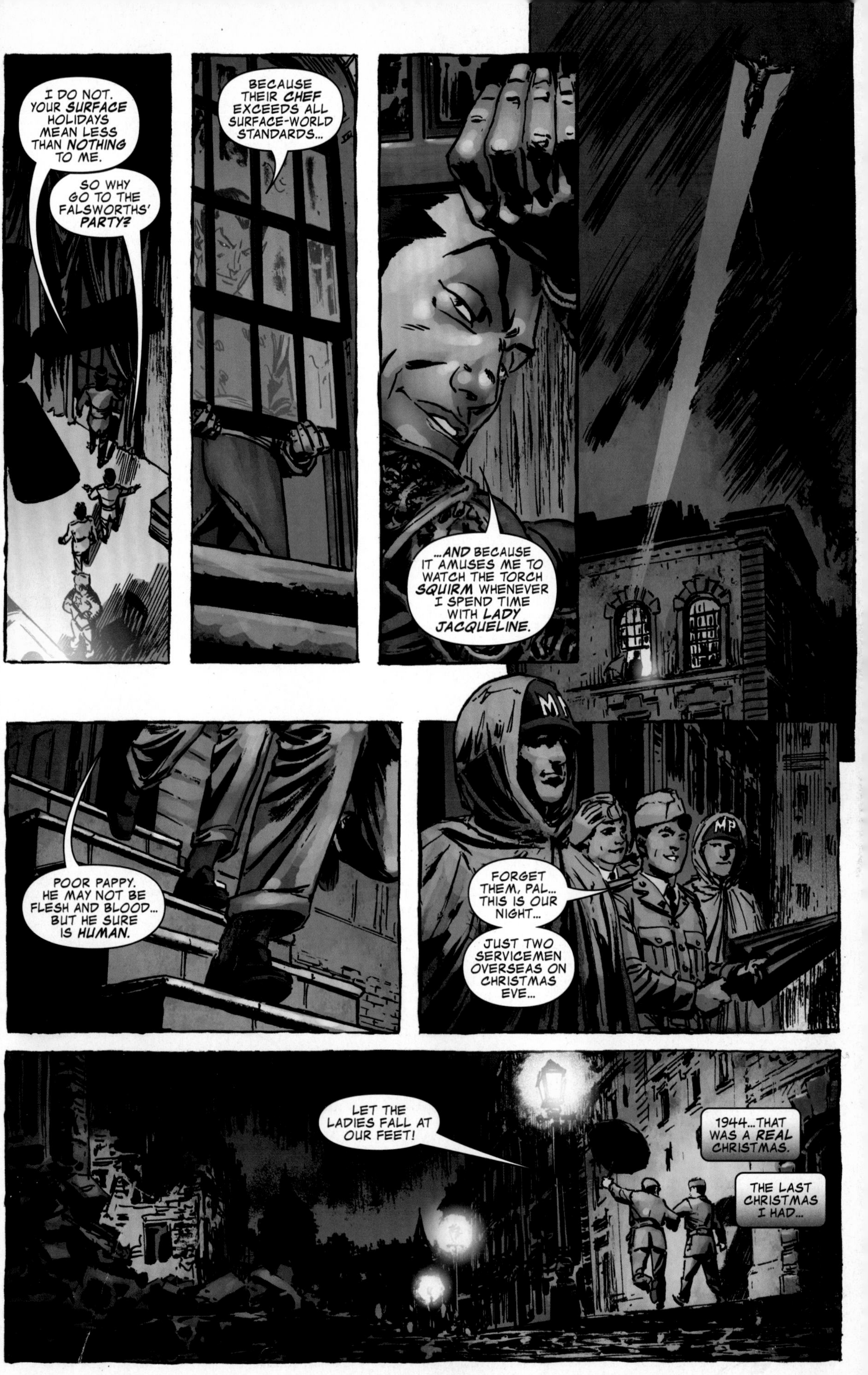
I DO NOT. YOUR SURFACE HOLIDAYS MEAN LESS THAN NOTHING TO ME.
SO WHY GO TO THE FALSWORTHS' PARTY?
BECAUSE THEIR CHEF EXCEEDS ALL SURFACE-WORLD STANDARDS...
...AND BECAUSE IT AMUSES ME TO WATCH THE TORCH SQUIRM WHENEVER I SPEND TIME WITH LADY JACQUELINE.
POOR PAPPY. HE MAY NOT BE FLESH AND BLOOD... BUT HE SURE IS HUMAN.
MP
FORGET THEM, PAL... THIS IS OUR NIGHT...
JUST TWO SERVICEMEN OVERSEAS ON CHRISTMAS EVE...
MP
LET THE LADIES FALL AT OUR FEET!
1944...THAT WAS A REAL CHRISTMAS.
THE LAST CHRISTMAS I HAD...

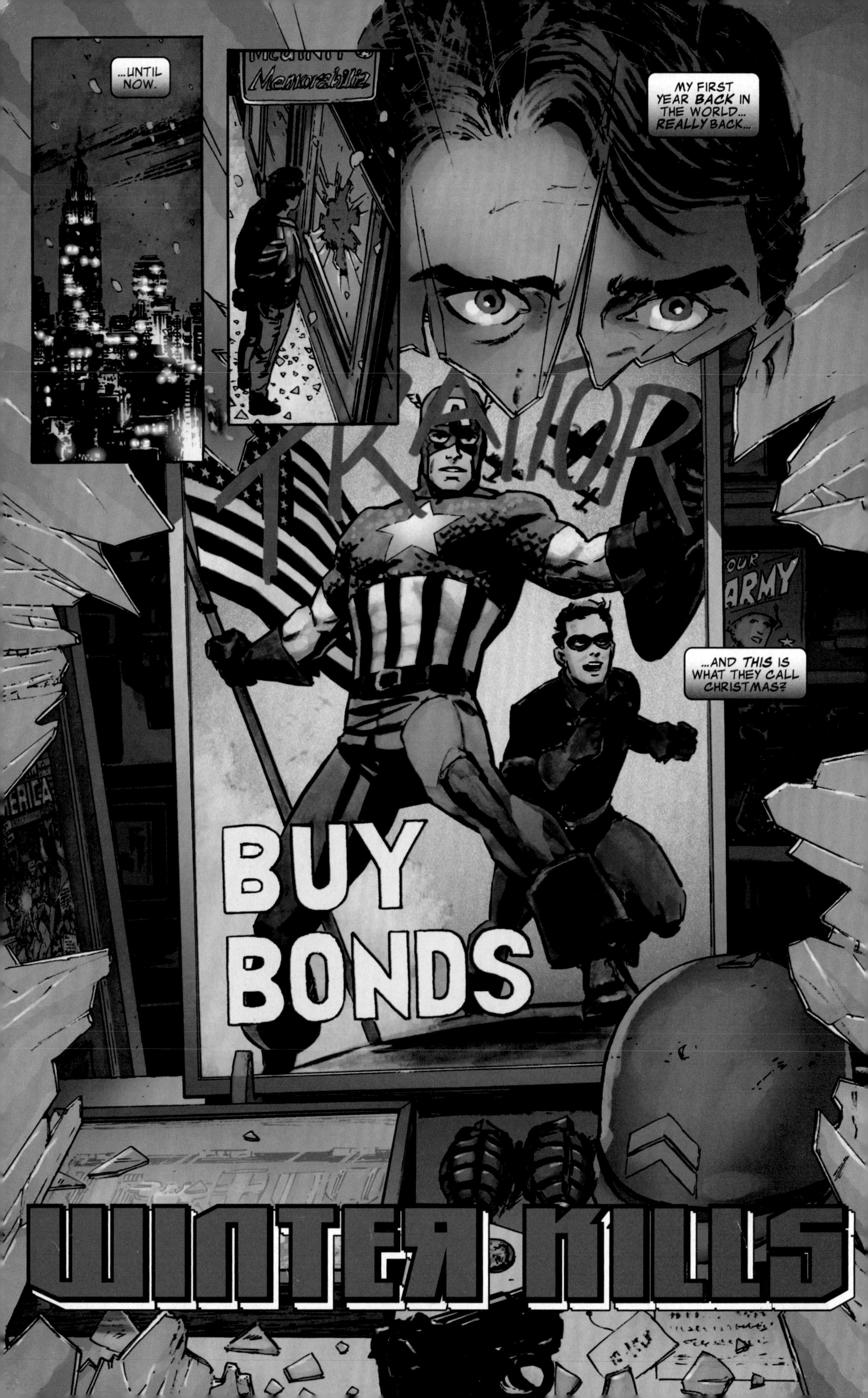
...UNTIL NOW.
Memorabilia
MY FIRST YEAR BACK IN THE WORLD... REALLY BACK...
TRAITOR
ARMY
...AND THIS IS WHAT THEY CALL CHRISTMAS?
BUY BONDS
WINTER KILLS

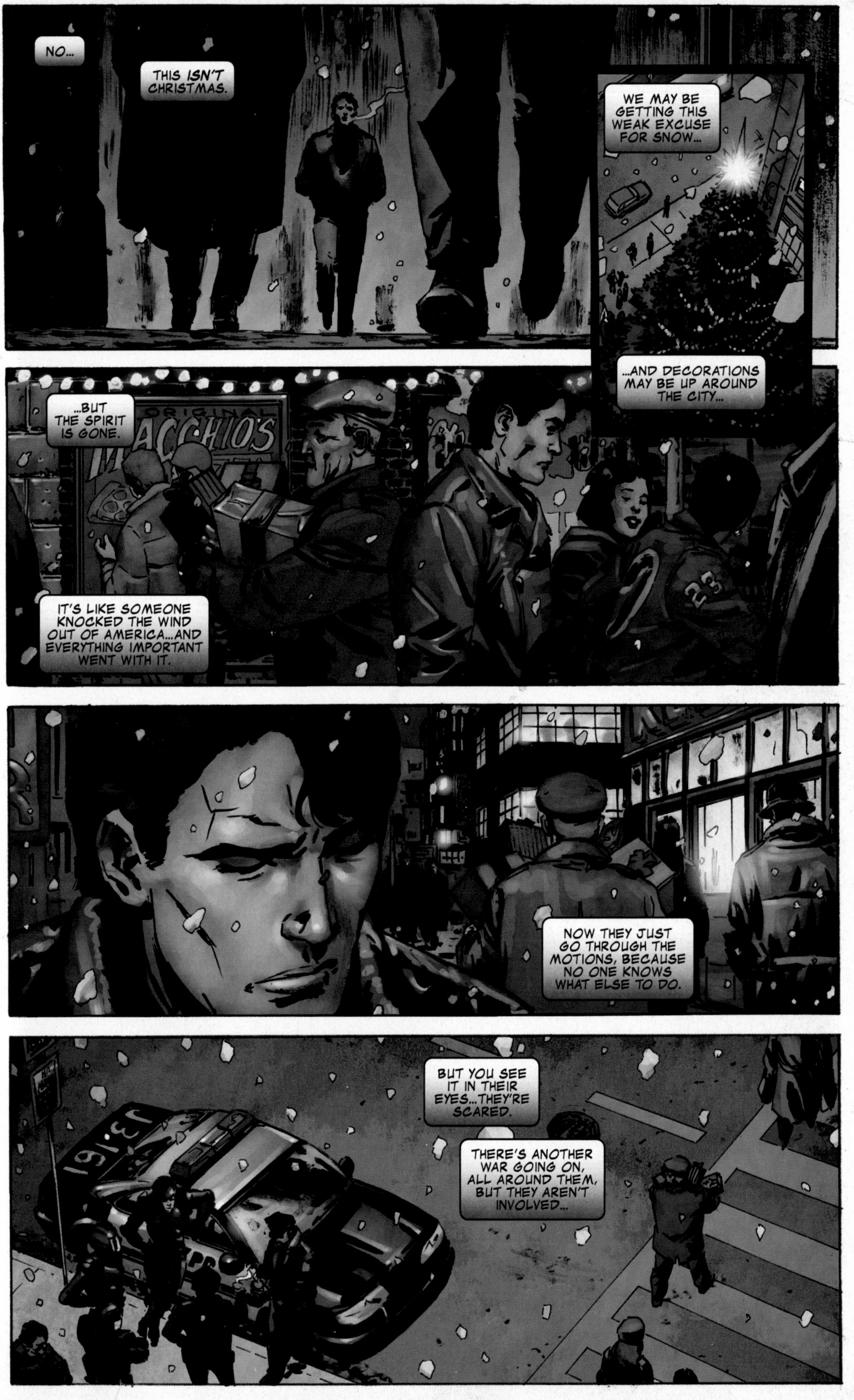
NO...
THIS ISN'T CHRISTMAS.
WE MAY BE GETTING THIS WEAK EXCUSE FOR SNOW...
...AND DECORATIONS MAY BE UP AROUND THE CITY...
...BUT THE SPIRIT IS GONE.
IT'S LIKE SOMEONE KNOCKED THE WIND OUT OF AMERICA...AND EVERYTHING IMPORTANT WENT WITH IT.
NOW THEY JUST GO THROUGH THE MOTIONS, BECAUSE NO ONE KNOWS WHAT ELSE TO DO.
BUT YOU SEE IT IN THEIR EYES...THEY'RE SCARED.
THERE'S ANOTHER WAR GOING ON, ALL AROUND THEM, BUT THEY AREN'T INVOLVED...

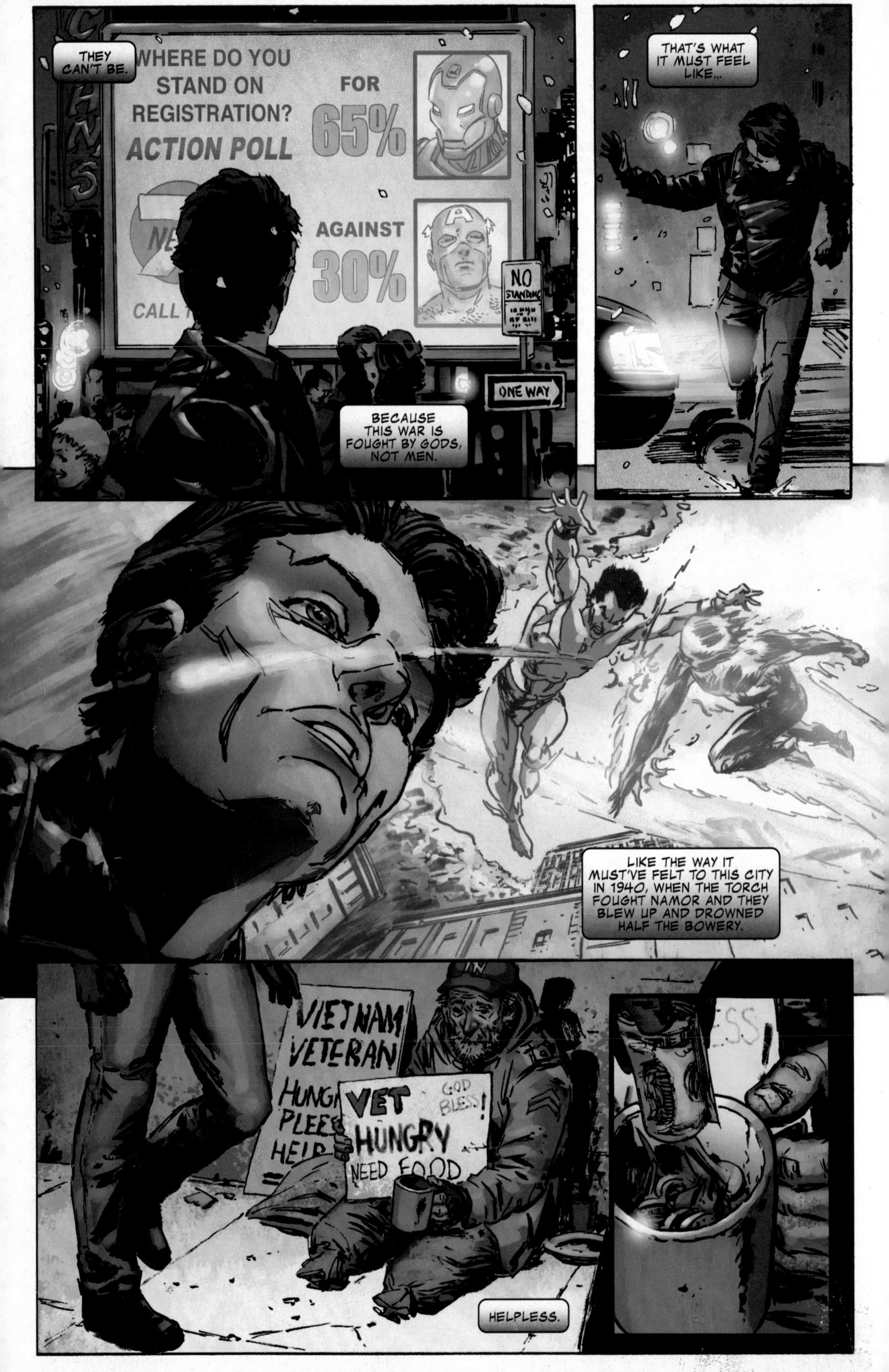
THEY CAN'T BE.
WHERE DO YOU STAND ON REGISTRATION?
ACTION POLL
FOR
65%
AGAINST
30%
CALL
NO STANDING
ONE WAY
BECAUSE THIS WAR IS FOUGHT BY GODS, NOT MEN.
THAT'S WHAT IT MUST FEEL LIKE...
LIKE THE WAY IT MUST'VE FELT TO THIS CITY IN 1940, WHEN THE TORCH FOUGHT NAMOR AND THEY BLEW UP AND DROWNED HALF THE BOWERY.
VIETNAM VETERAN
VET HUNGRY NEED FOOD
GOD BLESS!
HELPLESS.

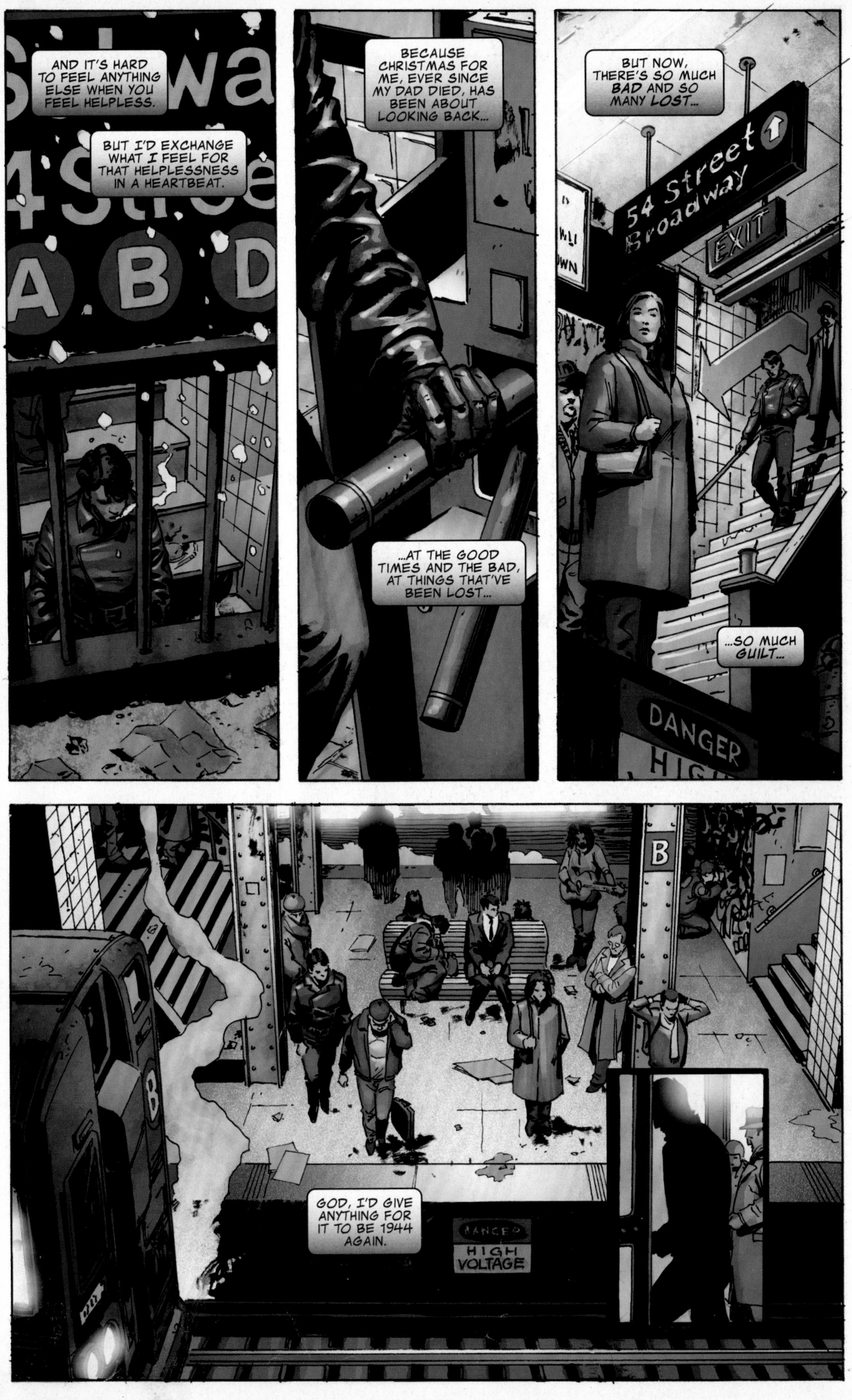
AND IT'S HARD TO FEEL ANYTHING ELSE WHEN YOU FEEL HELPLESS.
BUT I'D EXCHANGE WHAT I FEEL FOR THAT HELPLESSNESS IN A HEARTBEAT.
A B D
BECAUSE CHRISTMAS FOR ME, EVER SINCE MY DAD DIED, HAS BEEN ABOUT LOOKING BACK...
...AT THE GOOD TIMES AND THE BAD, AT THINGS THAT'VE BEEN LOST...
BUT NOW, THERE'S SO MUCH BAD AND SO MANY LOST...
54 Street Broadway
EXIT
...SO MUCH GUILT...
DANGER
B
GOD, I'D GIVE ANYTHING FOR IT TO BE 1944 AGAIN.
HIGH VOLTAGE

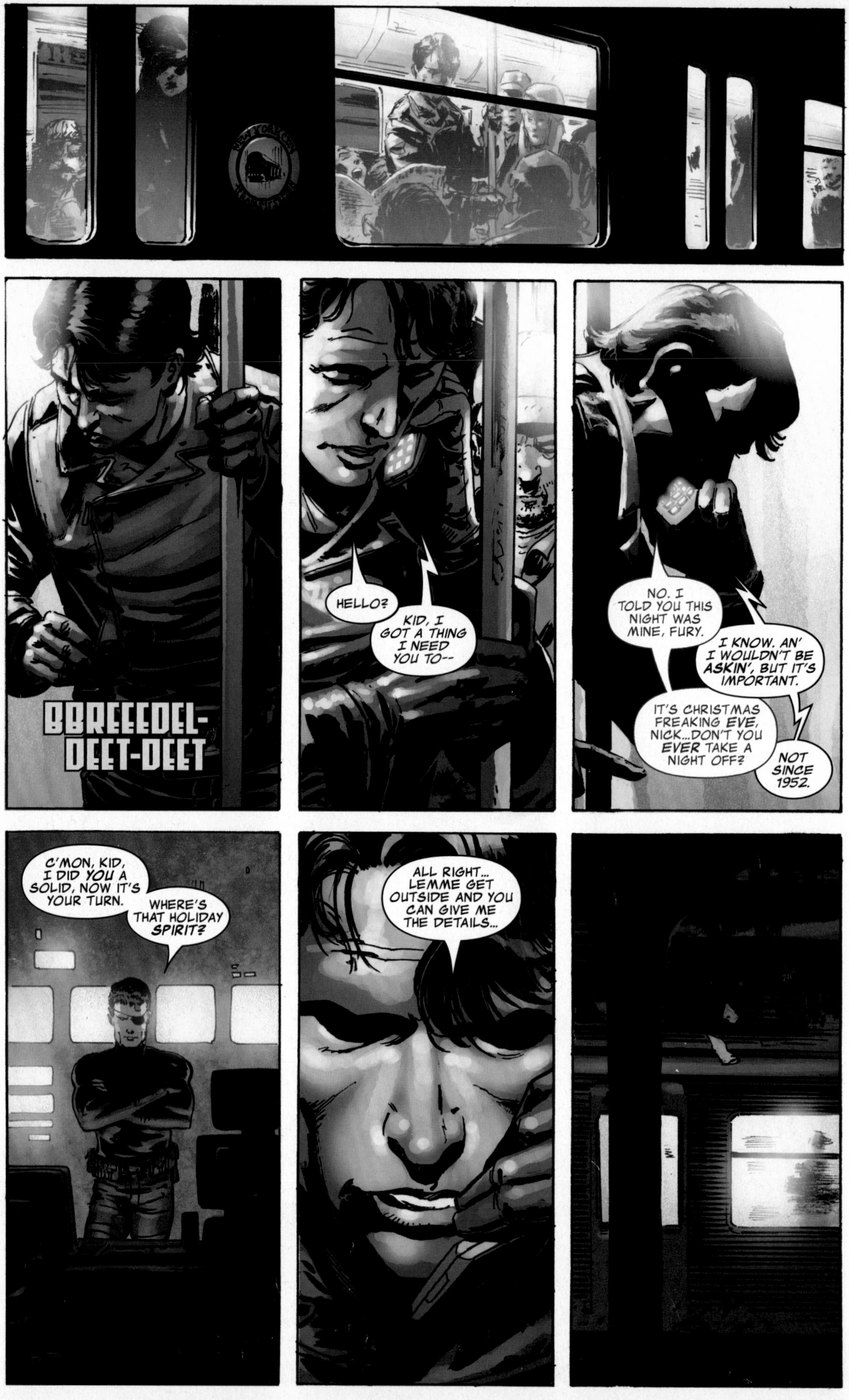
BBREEEDEL-DEET-DEET
HELLO?
KID, I GOT A THING I NEED YOU TO--
NO. I TOLD YOU THIS NIGHT WAS MINE, FURY.
I KNOW. AN' I WOULDN'T BE ASKIN', BUT IT'S IMPORTANT.
IT'S CHRISTMAS FREAKING EVE, NICK...DON'T YOU EVER TAKE A NIGHT OFF?
NOT SINCE 1952.
C'MON, KID, I DID YOU A SOLID, NOW IT'S YOUR TURN.
WHERE'S THAT HOLIDAY SPIRIT?
ALL RIGHT... LEMME GET OUTSIDE AND YOU CAN GIVE ME THE DETAILS...

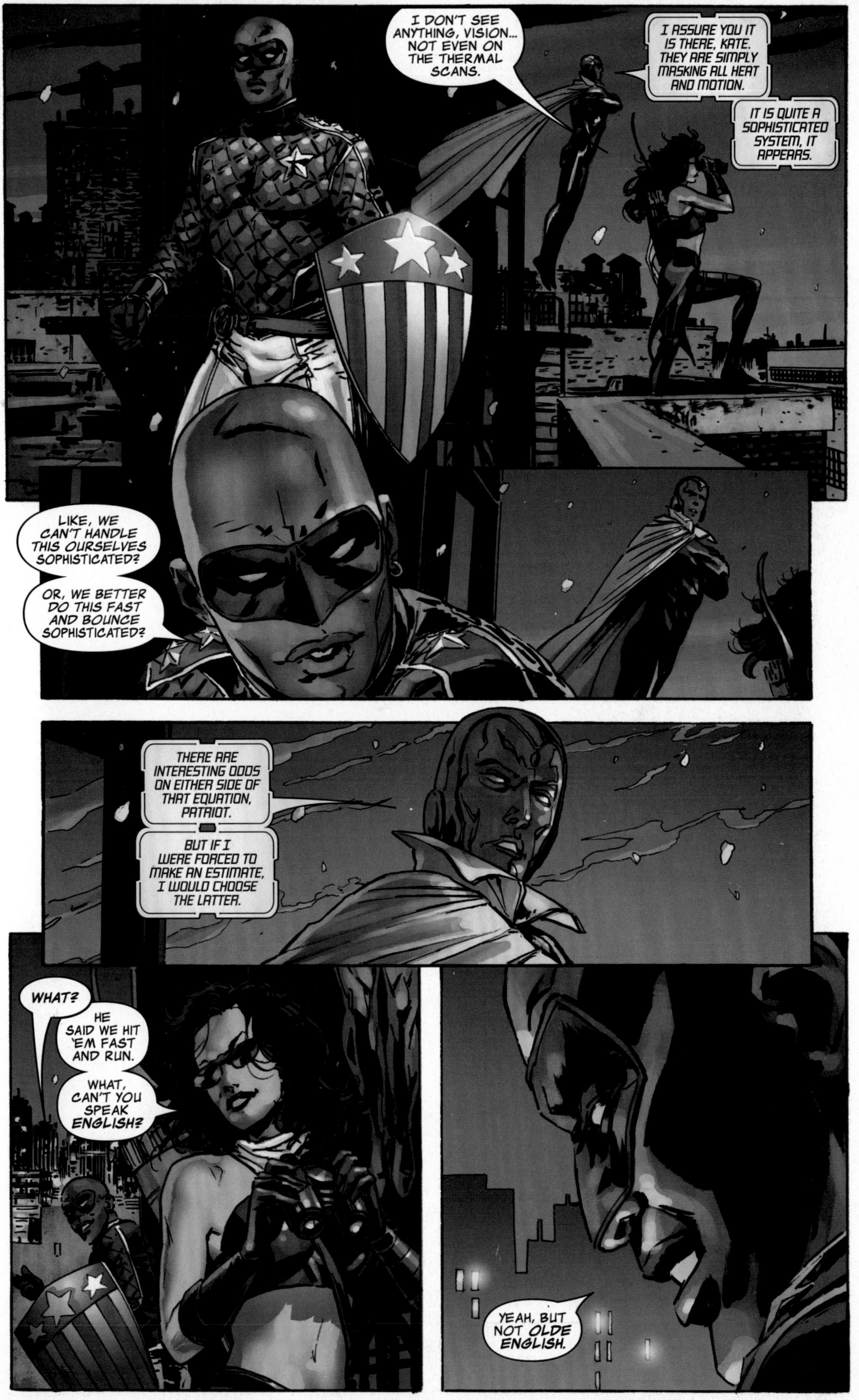

I DON'T SEE ANYTHING, VISION... NOT EVEN ON THE THERMAL SCANS.
I ASSURE YOU IT IS THERE, KATE. THEY ARE SIMPLY MASKING ALL HEAT AND MOTION.
IT IS QUITE A SOPHISTICATED SYSTEM, IT APPEARS.
LIKE, WE CAN'T HANDLE THIS OURSELVES SOPHISTICATED?
OR, WE BETTER DO THIS FAST AND BOUNCE SOPHISTICATED?
THERE ARE INTERESTING ODDS ON EITHER SIDE OF THAT EQUATION, PATRIOT.
BUT IF I WERE FORCED TO MAKE AN ESTIMATE, I WOULD CHOOSE THE LATTER.
WHAT?
HE SAID WE HIT 'EM FAST AND RUN.
WHAT, CAN'T YOU SPEAK ENGLISH?
YEAH, BUT NOT OLDE ENGLISH.

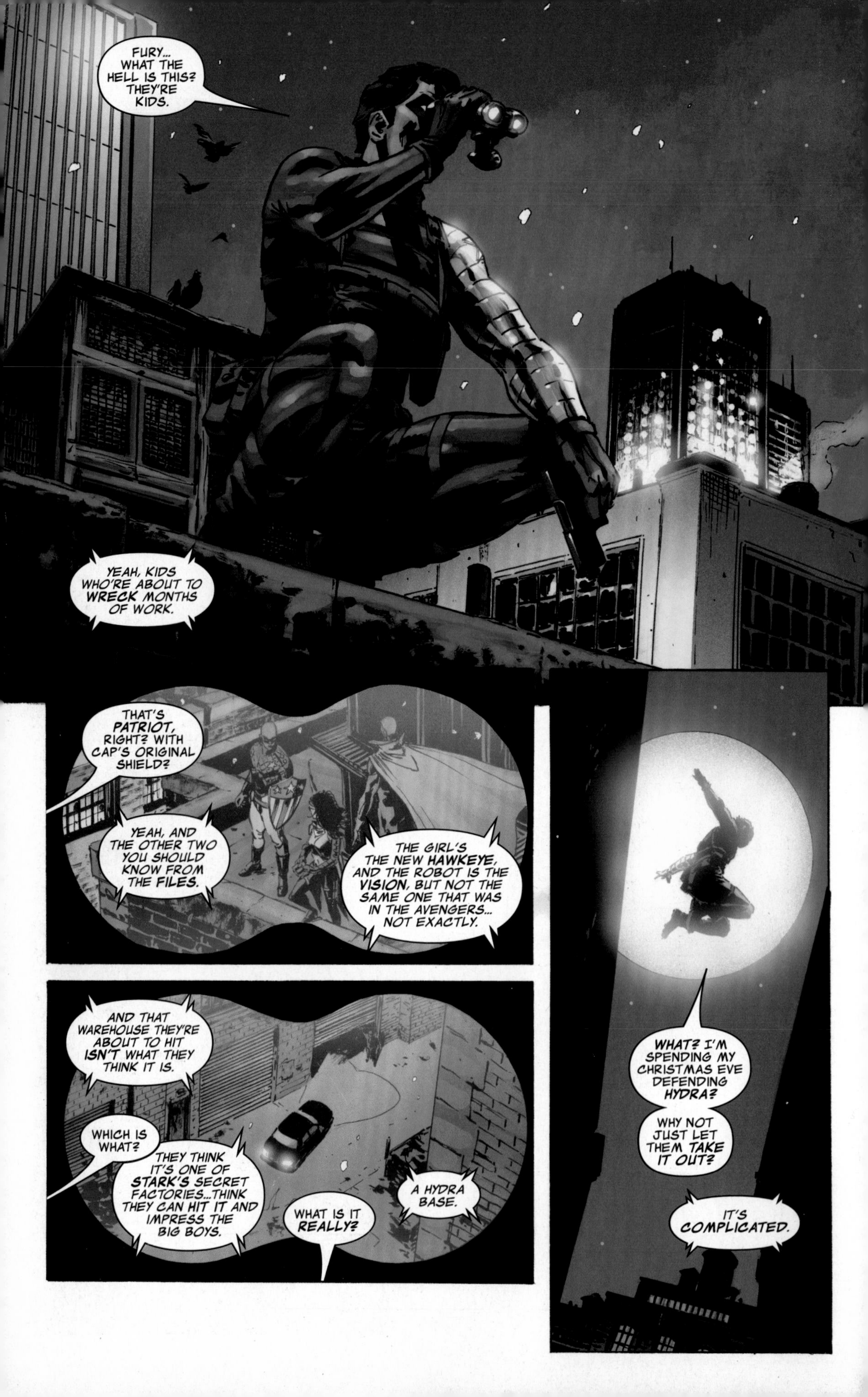
FURY... WHAT THE HELL IS THIS? THEY'RE KIDS.
YEAH, KIDS WHO'RE ABOUT TO WRECK MONTHS OF WORK.
THAT'S PATRIOT, RIGHT? WITH CAP'S ORIGINAL SHIELD?
YEAH, AND THE OTHER TWO YOU SHOULD KNOW FROM THE FILES.
THE GIRL'S THE NEW HAWKEYE, AND THE ROBOT IS THE VISION, BUT NOT THE SAME ONE THAT WAS IN THE AVENGERS... NOT EXACTLY.
AND THAT WAREHOUSE THEY'RE ABOUT TO HIT ISN'T WHAT THEY THINK IT IS.
WHICH IS WHAT?
THEY THINK IT'S ONE OF STARK'S SECRET FACTORIES...THINK THEY CAN HIT IT AND IMPRESS THE BIG BOYS.
WHAT IS IT REALLY?
A HYDRA BASE.
WHAT? I'M SPENDING MY CHRISTMAS EVE DEFENDING HYDRA?
WHY NOT JUST LET THEM TAKE IT OUT?
IT'S COMPLICATED.

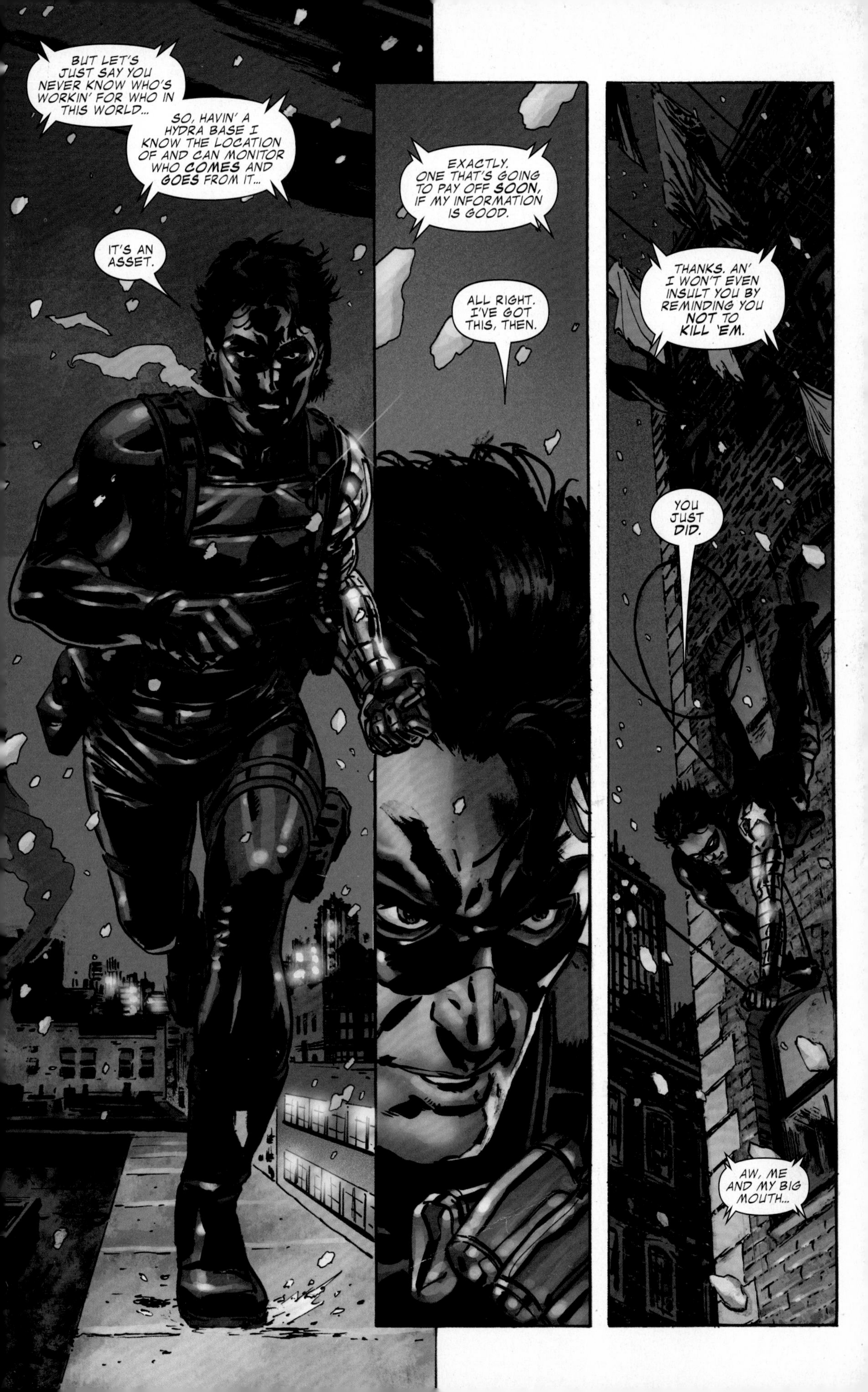
BUT LET'S JUST SAY YOU NEVER KNOW WHO'S WORKIN' FOR WHO IN THIS WORLD...
SO, HAVIN' A HYDRA BASE I KNOW THE LOCATION OF AND CAN MONITOR WHO COMES AND GOES FROM IT...
IT'S AN ASSET.
EXACTLY. ONE THAT'S GOING TO PAY OFF SOON, IF MY INFORMATION IS GOOD.
ALL RIGHT. I'VE GOT THIS, THEN.
THANKS. AN' I WON'T EVEN INSULT YOU BY REMINDING YOU NOT TO KILL 'EM.
YOU JUST DID.
AW, ME AND MY BIG MOUTH...

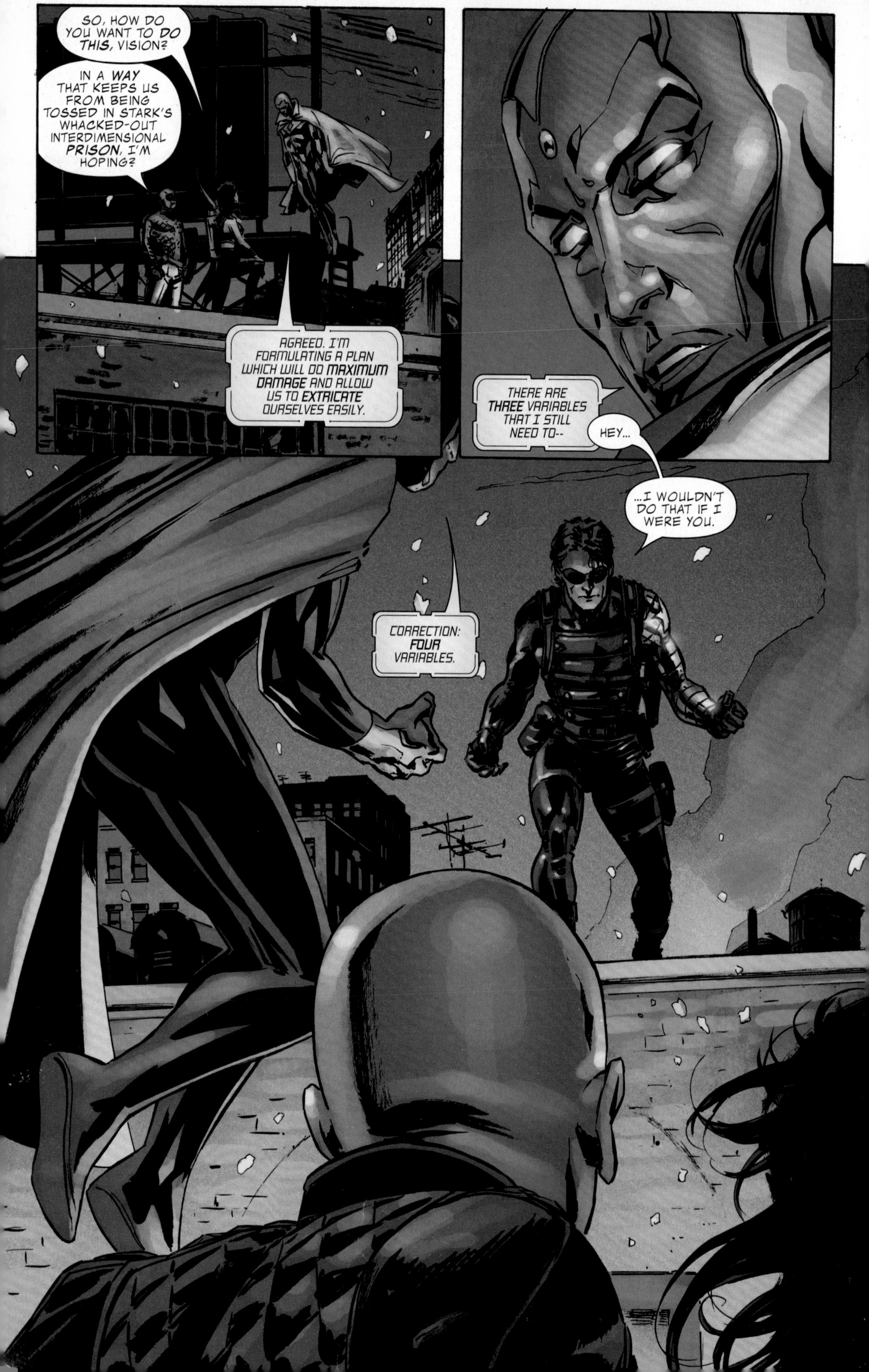
SO, HOW DO YOU WANT TO DO THIS, VISION?
IN A WAY THAT KEEPS US FROM BEING TOSSED IN STARK'S WHACKED-OUT INTERDIMENSIONAL PRISON, I'M HOPING?
AGREED. I'M FORMULATING A PLAN WHICH WILL DO MAXIMUM DAMAGE AND ALLOW US TO EXTRICATE OURSELVES EASILY.
THERE ARE THREE VARIABLES THAT I STILL NEED TO--
HEY...
...I WOULDN'T DO THAT IF I WERE YOU.
CORRECTION: FOUR VARIABLES.

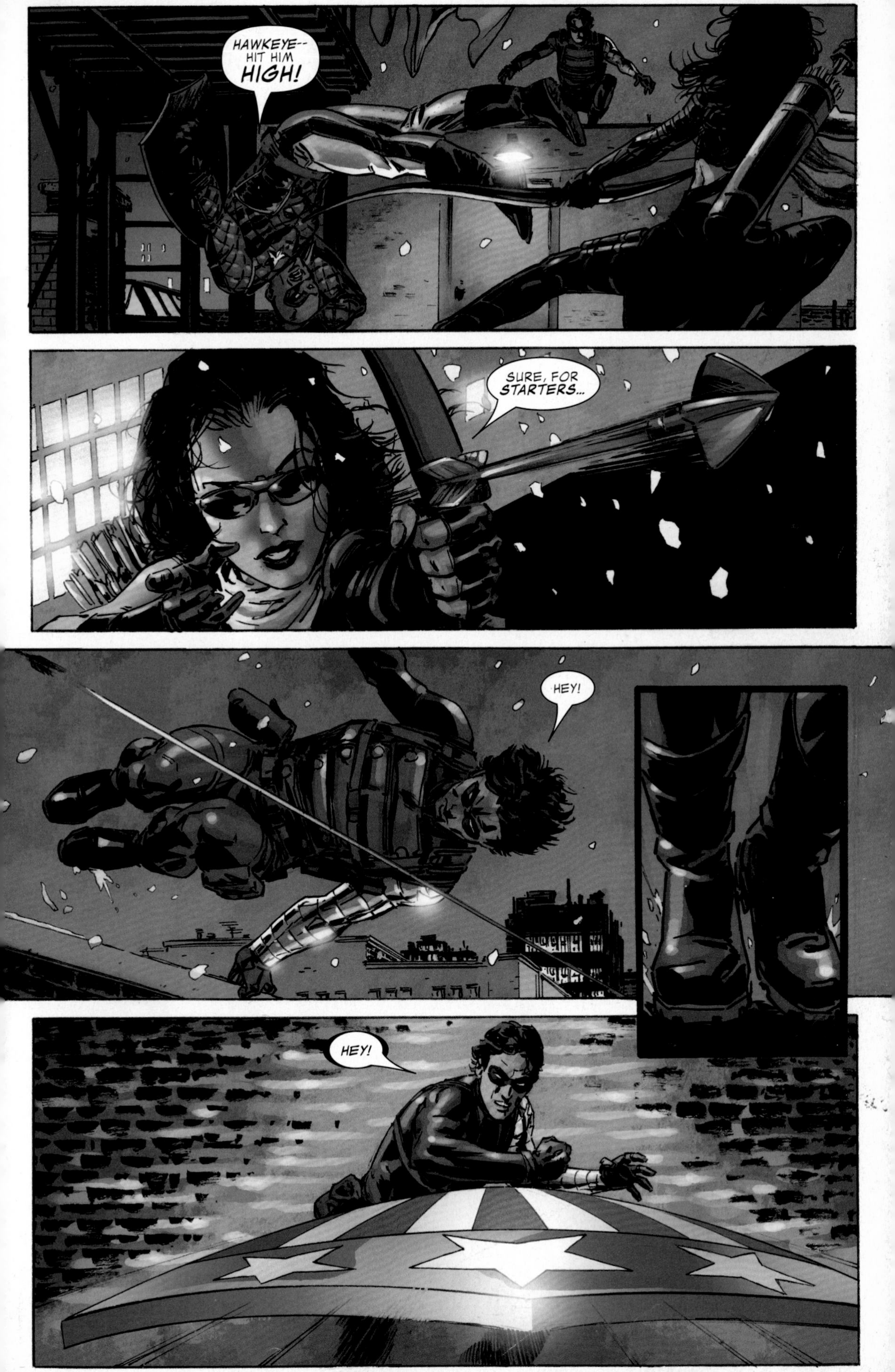
HAWKEYE-- HIT HIM HIGH!
SURE, FOR STARTERS...
HEY!
HEY!

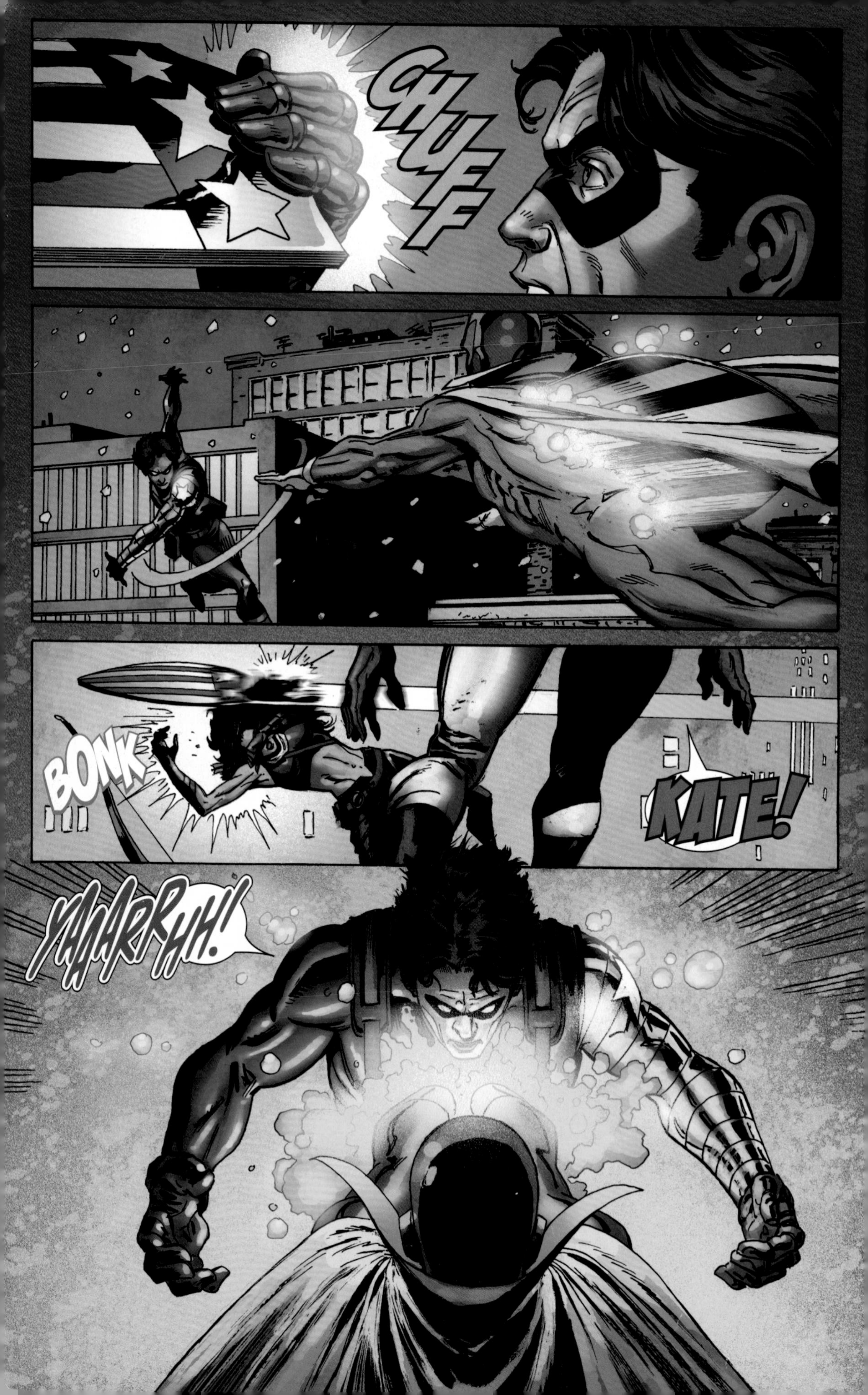
CHUFF
BONK
KATE!
YAAARRHH!

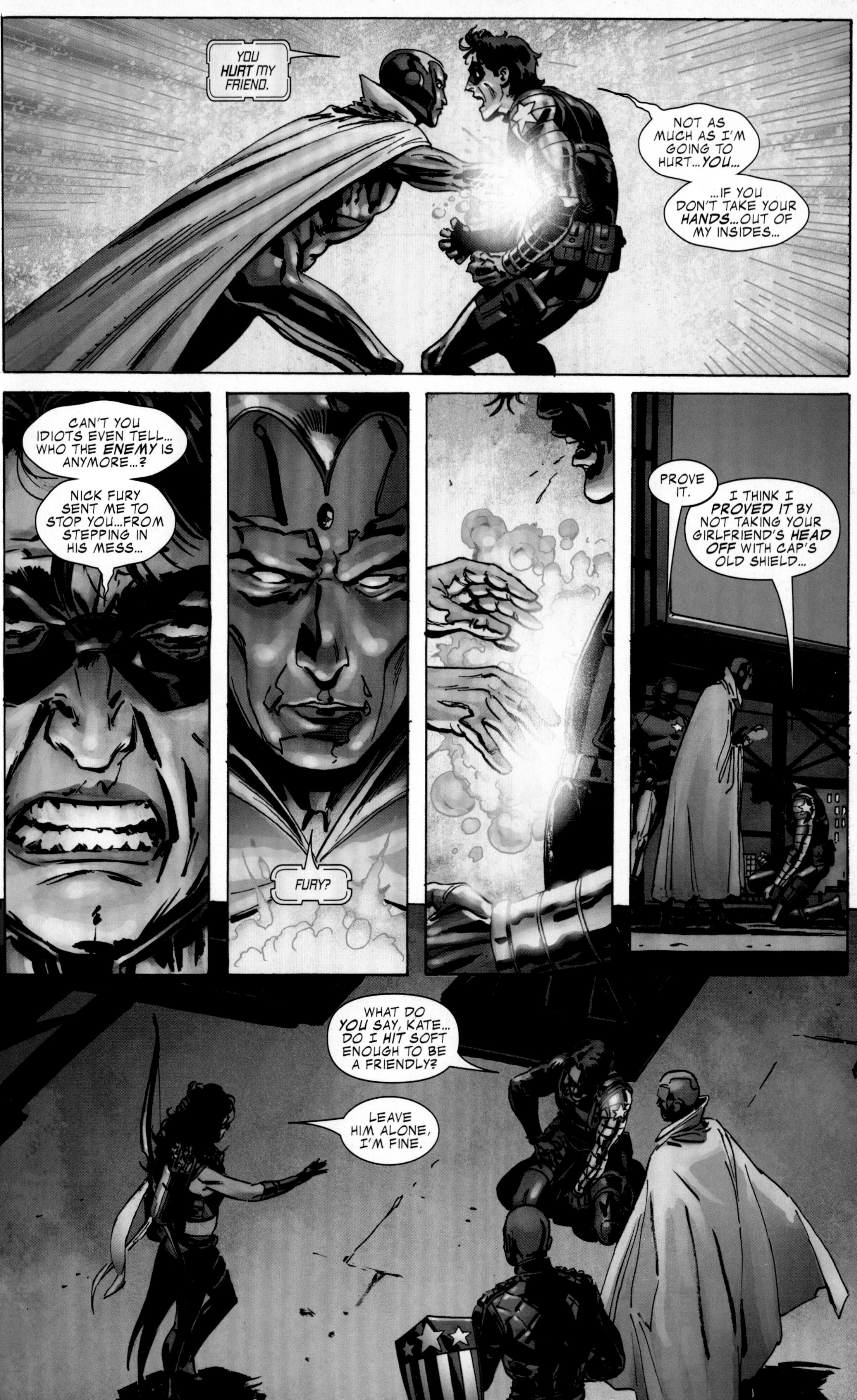
YOU HURT MY FRIEND.
NOT AS MUCH AS I'M GOING TO HURT...YOU...
...IF YOU DON'T TAKE YOUR HANDS...OUT OF MY INSIDES...
CAN'T YOU IDIOTS EVEN TELL... WHO THE ENEMY IS ANYMORE...?
NICK FURY SENT ME TO STOP YOU...FROM STEPPING IN HIS MESS...
FURY?
PROVE IT.
I THINK I PROVED IT BY NOT TAKING YOUR GIRLFRIEND'S HEAD OFF WITH CAP'S OLD SHIELD...
WHAT DO YOU SAY, KATE... DO I HIT SOFT ENOUGH TO BE A FRIENDLY?
LEAVE HIM ALONE, I'M FINE.

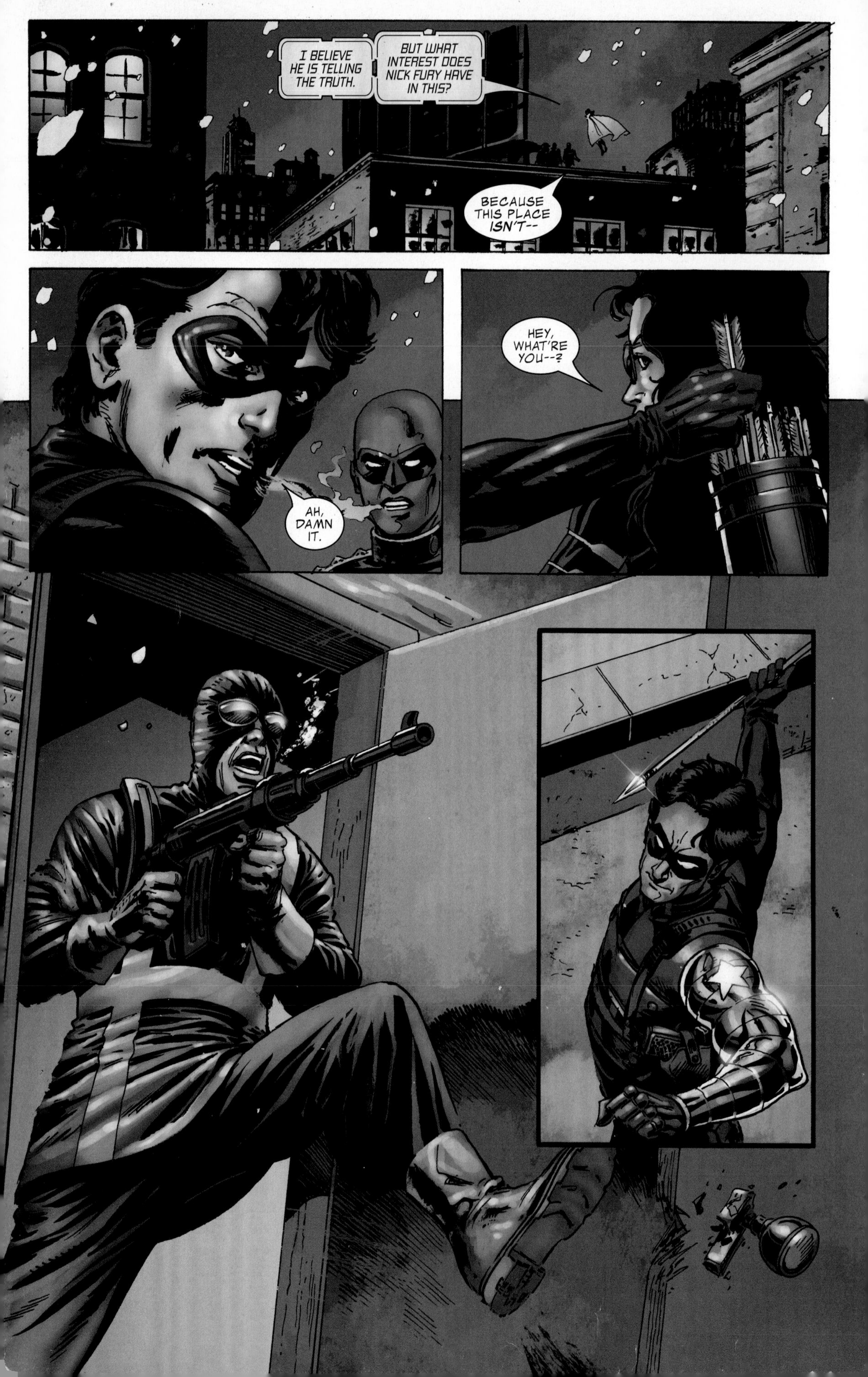
I BELIEVE HE IS TELLING THE TRUTH.
BUT WHAT INTEREST DOES NICK FURY HAVE IN THIS?
BECAUSE THIS PLACE ISN'T--
AH, DAMN IT.
HEY, WHAT'RE YOU--?

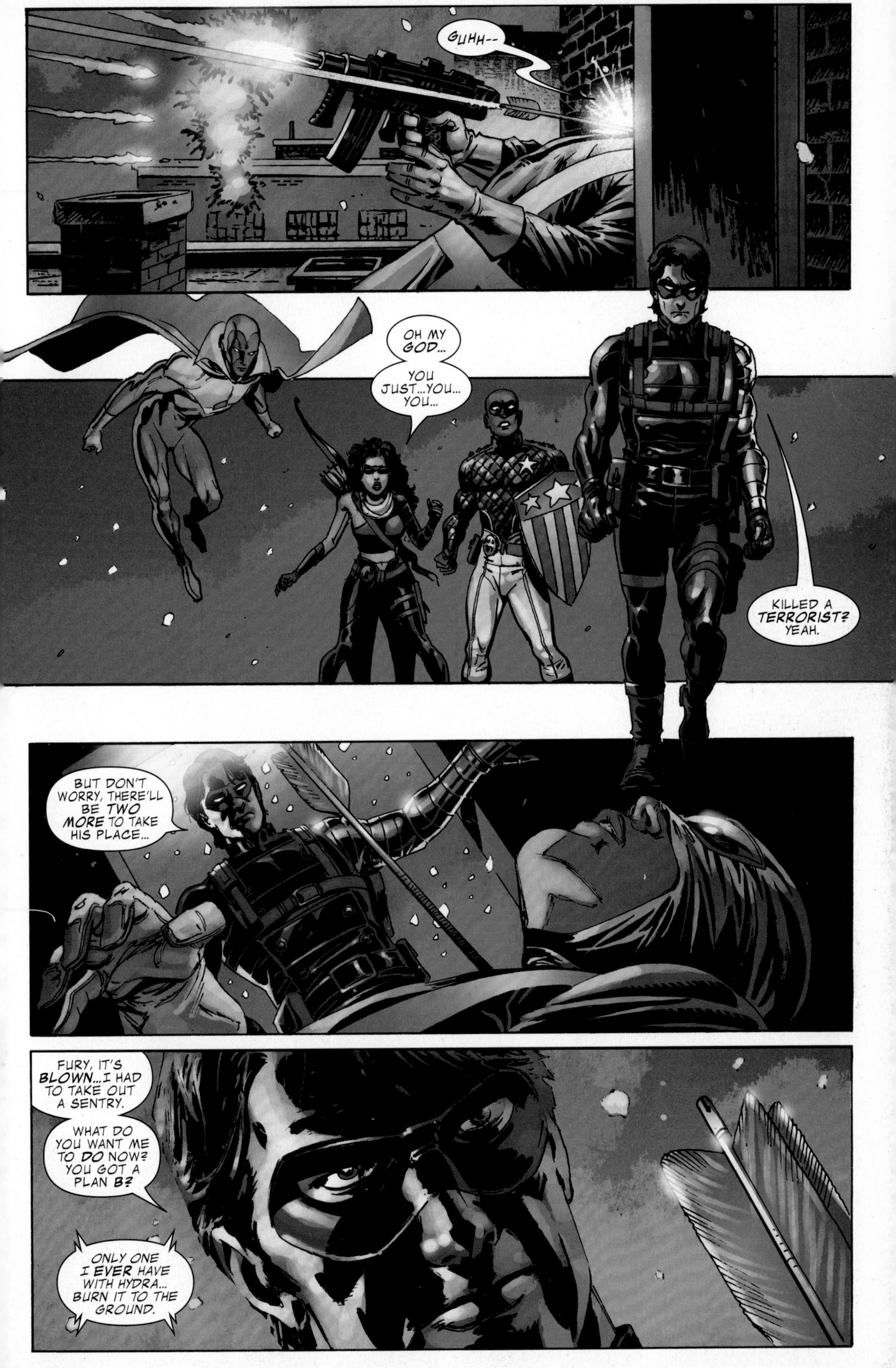
GUHH--
OH MY GOD...
YOU JUST...YOU... YOU...
KILLED A TERRORIST? YEAH.
BUT DON'T WORRY, THERE'LL BE TWO MORE TO TAKE HIS PLACE...
FURY, IT'S BLOWN...I HAD TO TAKE OUT A SENTRY.
WHAT DO YOU WANT ME TO DO NOW? YOU GOT A PLAN B?
ONLY ONE I EVER HAVE WITH HYDRA... BURN IT TO THE GROUND.

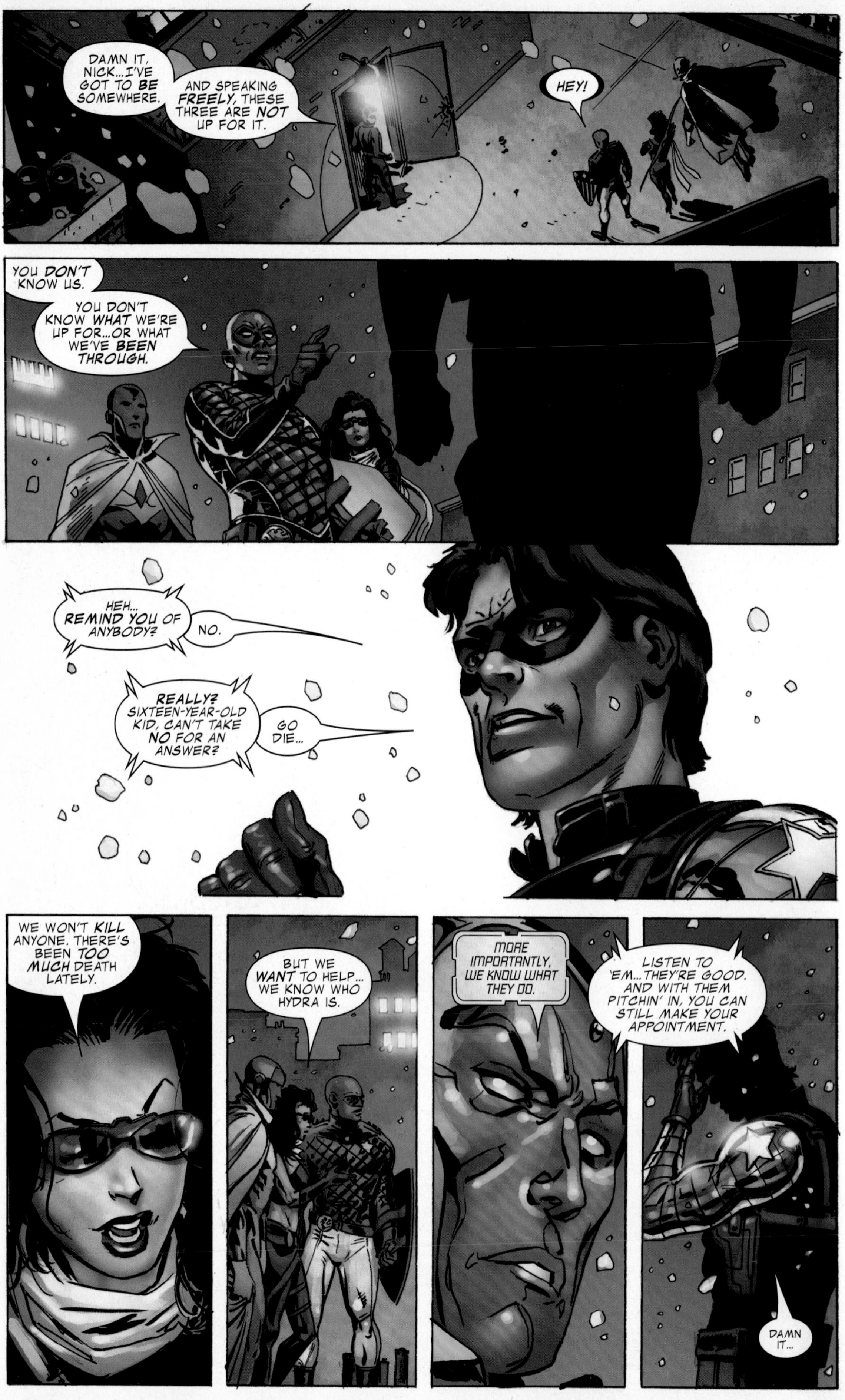
DAMN IT, NICK...I'VE GOT TO BE SOMEWHERE.
AND SPEAKING FREELY, THESE THREE ARE NOT UP FOR IT.
HEY!
YOU DON'T KNOW US.
YOU DON'T KNOW WHAT WE'RE UP FOR...OR WHAT WE'VE BEEN THROUGH.
HEH... REMIND YOU OF ANYBODY?
NO.
REALLY? SIXTEEN-YEAR-OLD KID, CAN'T TAKE NO FOR AN ANSWER?
GO DIE...
WE WON'T KILL ANYONE. THERE'S BEEN TOO MUCH DEATH LATELY.
BUT WE WANT TO HELP... WE KNOW WHO HYDRA IS.
MORE IMPORTANTLY, WE KNOW WHAT THEY DO.
LISTEN TO 'EM...THEY'RE GOOD. AND WITH THEM PITCHIN' IN, YOU CAN STILL MAKE YOUR APPOINTMENT.
DAMN IT...

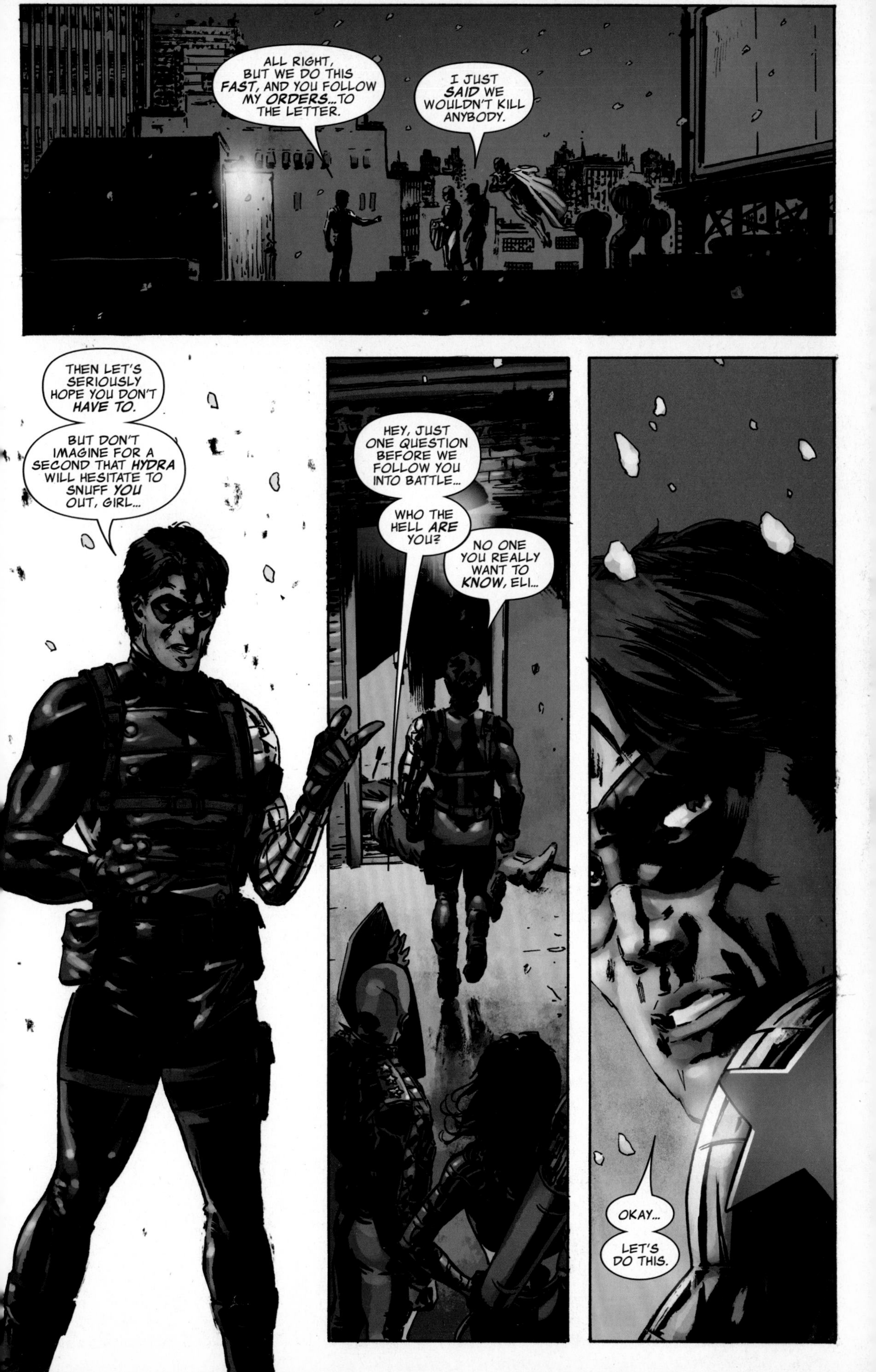
ALL RIGHT, BUT WE DO THIS FAST, AND YOU FOLLOW MY ORDERS...TO THE LETTER.
I JUST SAID WE WOULDN'T KILL ANYBODY.
THEN LET'S SERIOUSLY HOPE YOU DON'T HAVE TO.
BUT DON'T IMAGINE FOR A SECOND THAT HYDRA WILL HESITATE TO SNUFF YOU OUT, GIRL...
HEY, JUST ONE QUESTION BEFORE WE FOLLOW YOU INTO BATTLE...
WHO THE HELL ARE YOU?
NO ONE YOU REALLY WANT TO KNOW, ELI...
OKAY...
LET'S DO THIS.

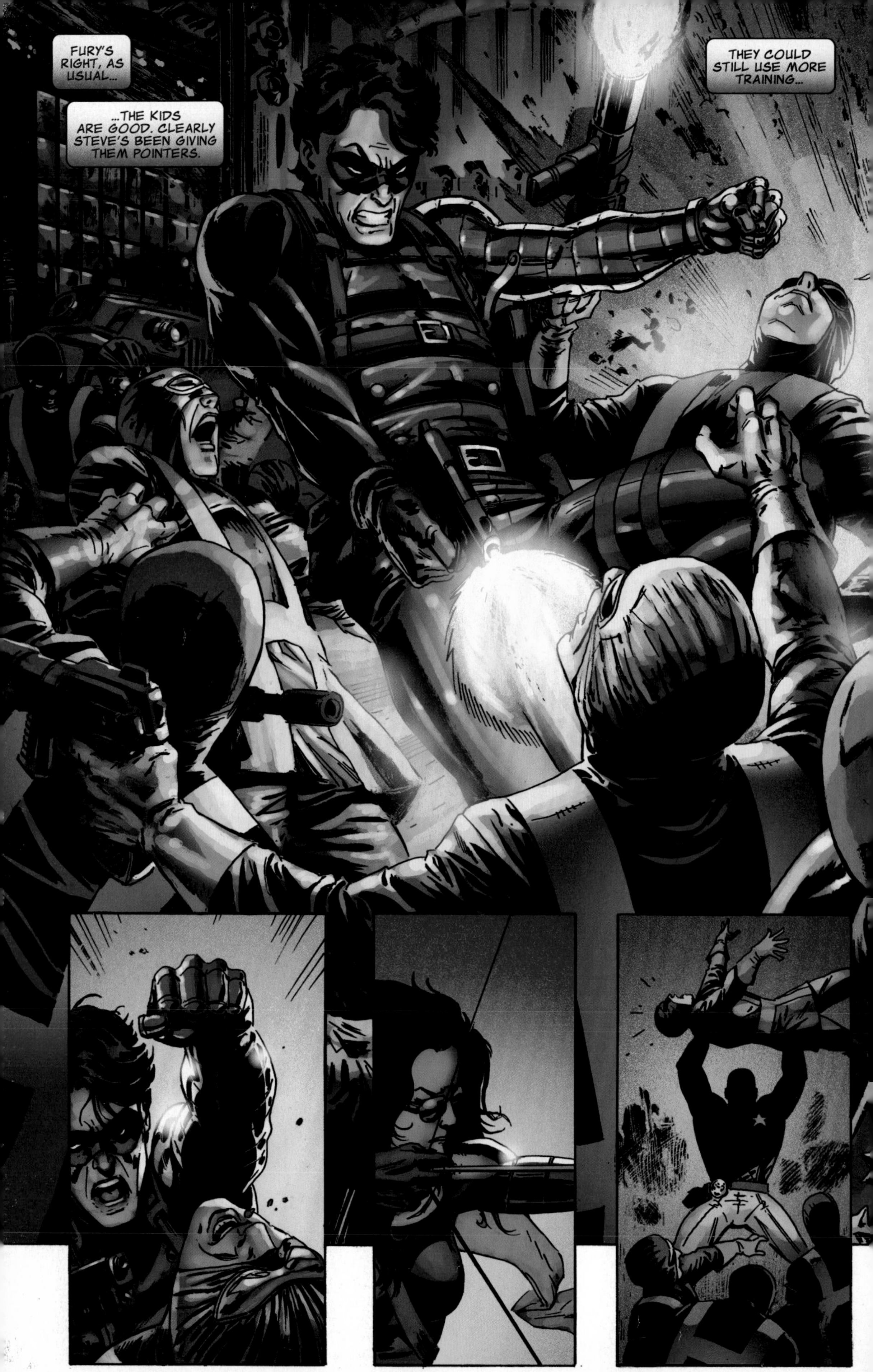
FURY'S RIGHT, AS USUAL...
...THE KIDS ARE GOOD. CLEARLY STEVE'S BEEN GIVING THEM POINTERS.
THEY COULD STILL USE MORE TRAINING...

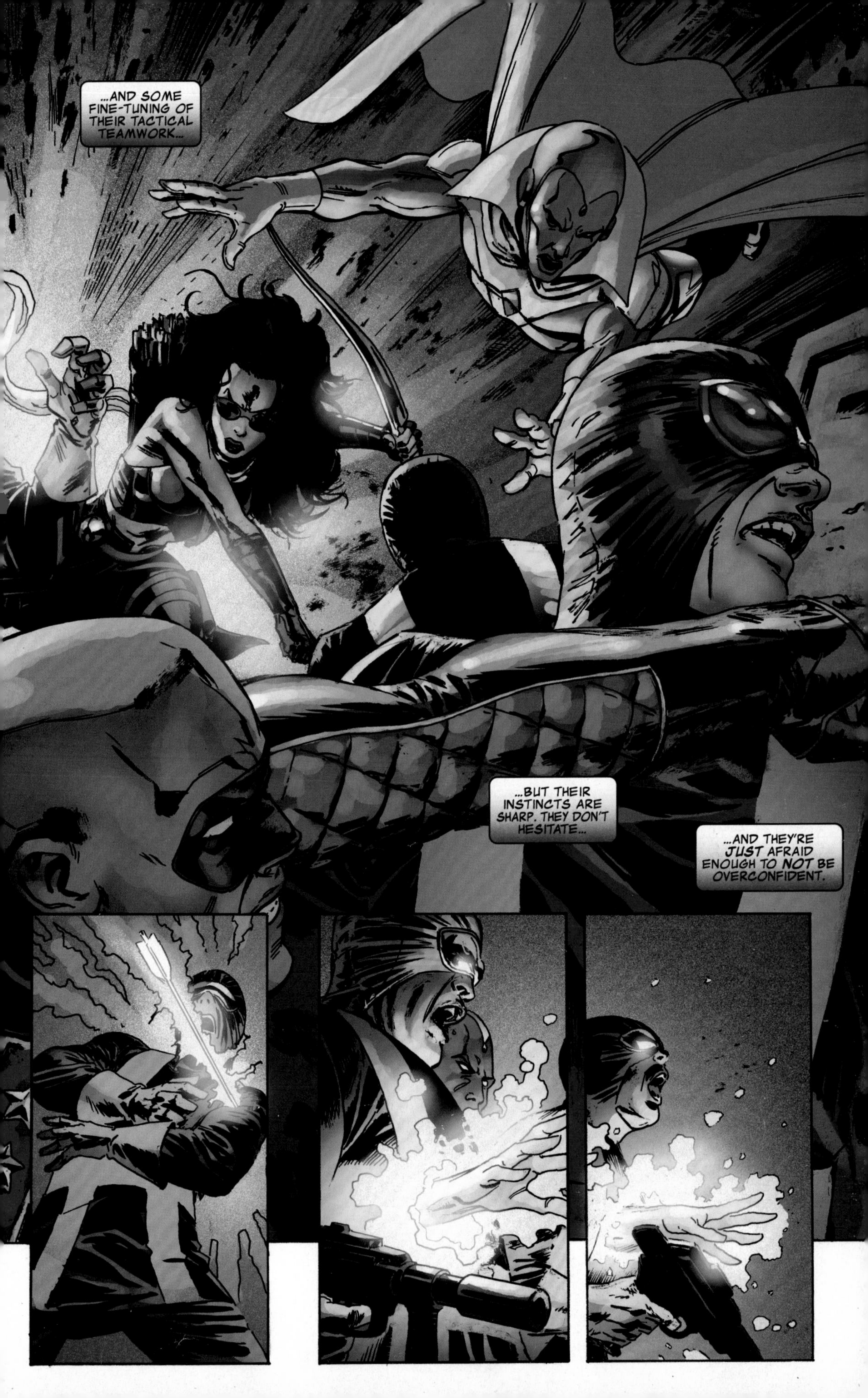
...AND SOME FINE-TUNING OF THEIR TACTICAL TEAMWORK...
...BUT THEIR INSTINCTS ARE SHARP. THEY DON'T HESITATE...
...AND THEY'RE JUST AFRAID ENOUGH TO NOT BE OVERCONFIDENT.

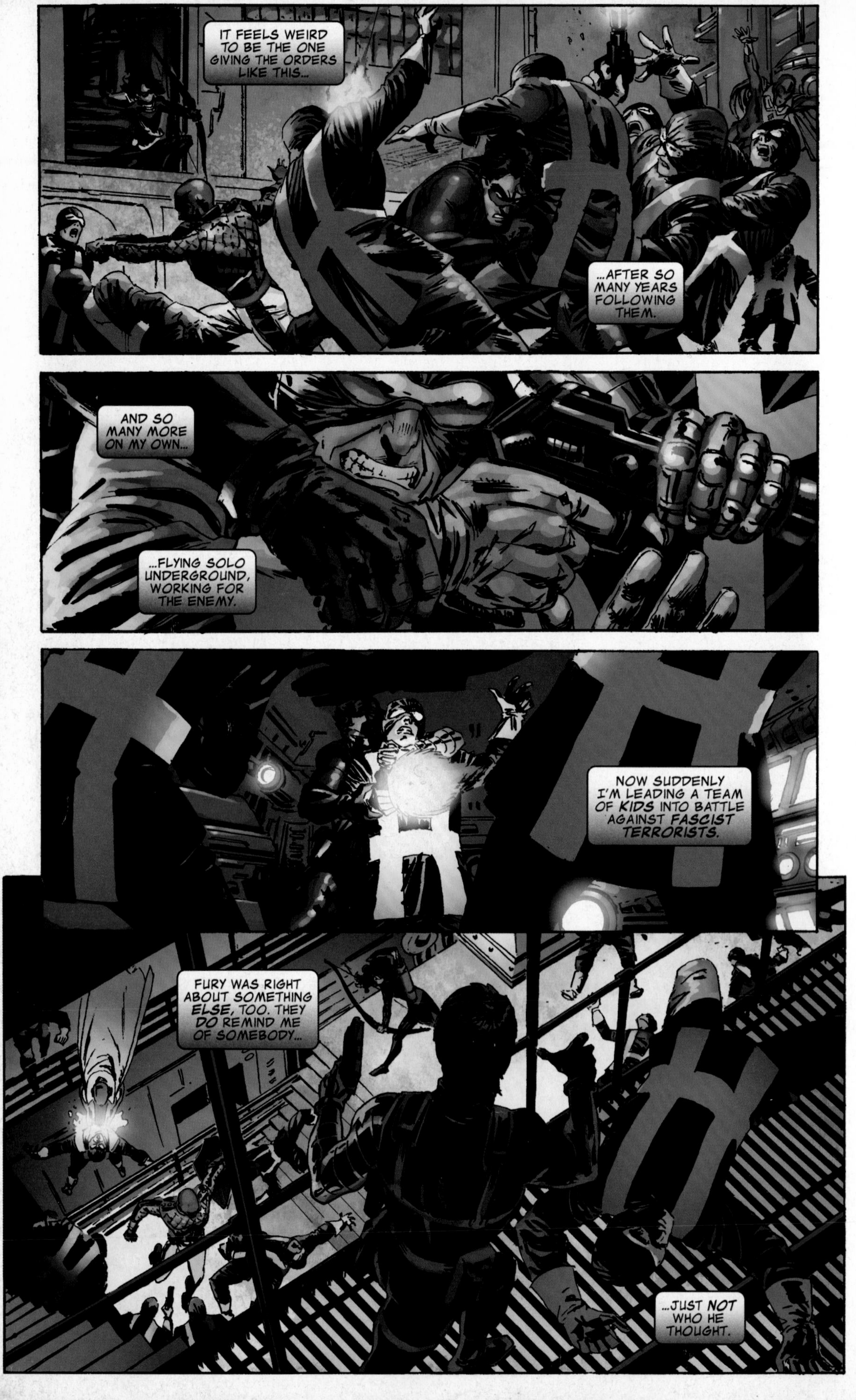
IT FEELS WEIRD TO BE THE ONE GIVING THE ORDERS LIKE THIS...
...AFTER SO MANY YEARS FOLLOWING THEM.
AND SO MANY MORE ON MY OWN...
...FLYING SOLO UNDERGROUND, WORKING FOR THE ENEMY.
NOW SUDDENLY I'M LEADING A TEAM OF KIDS INTO BATTLE AGAINST FASCIST TERRORISTS.
FURY WAS RIGHT ABOUT SOMETHING ELSE, TOO. THEY DO REMIND ME OF SOMEBODY...
...JUST NOT WHO HE THOUGHT.

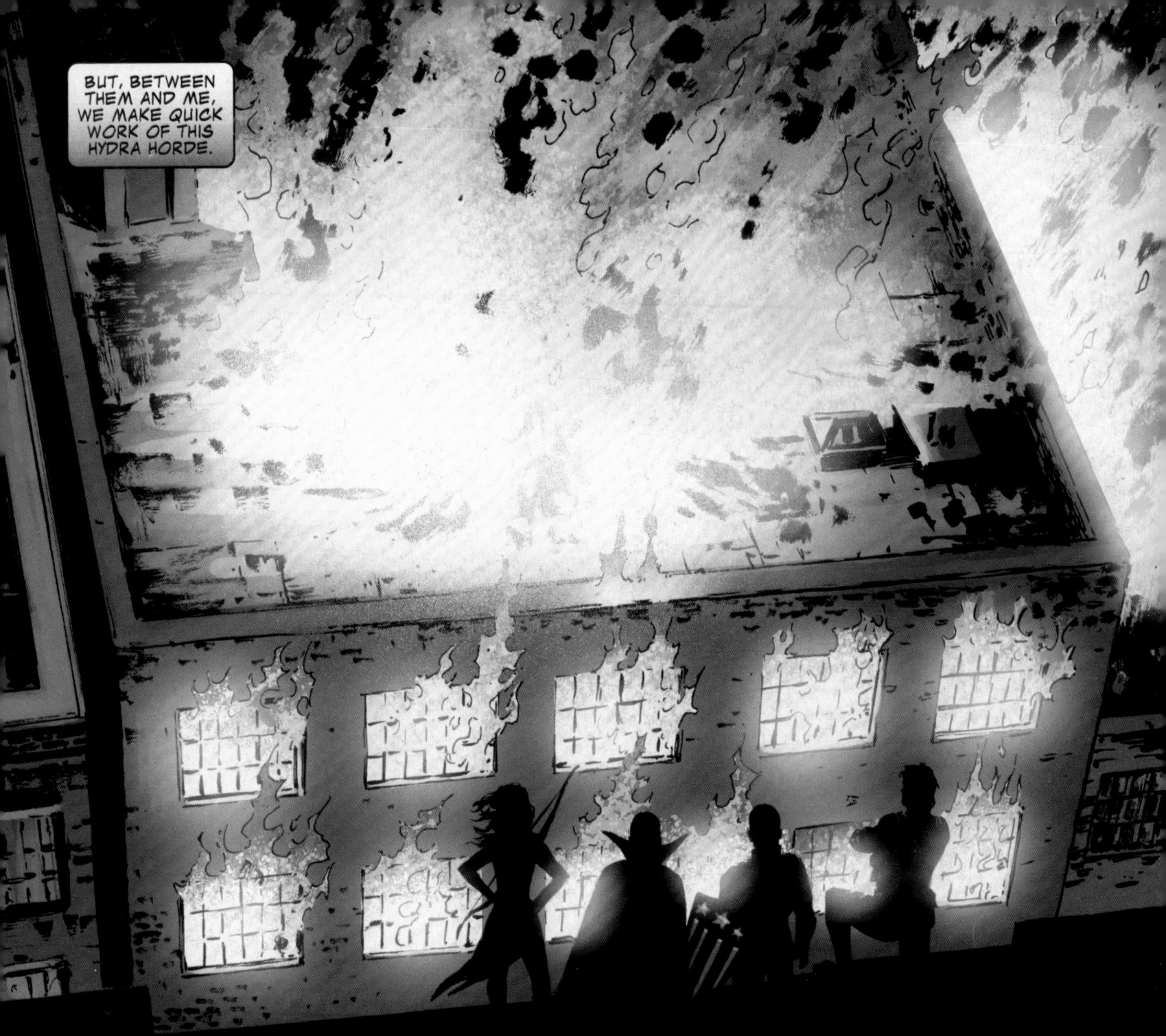
BUT, BETWEEN THEM AND ME, WE MAKE QUICK WORK OF THIS HYDRA HORDE.

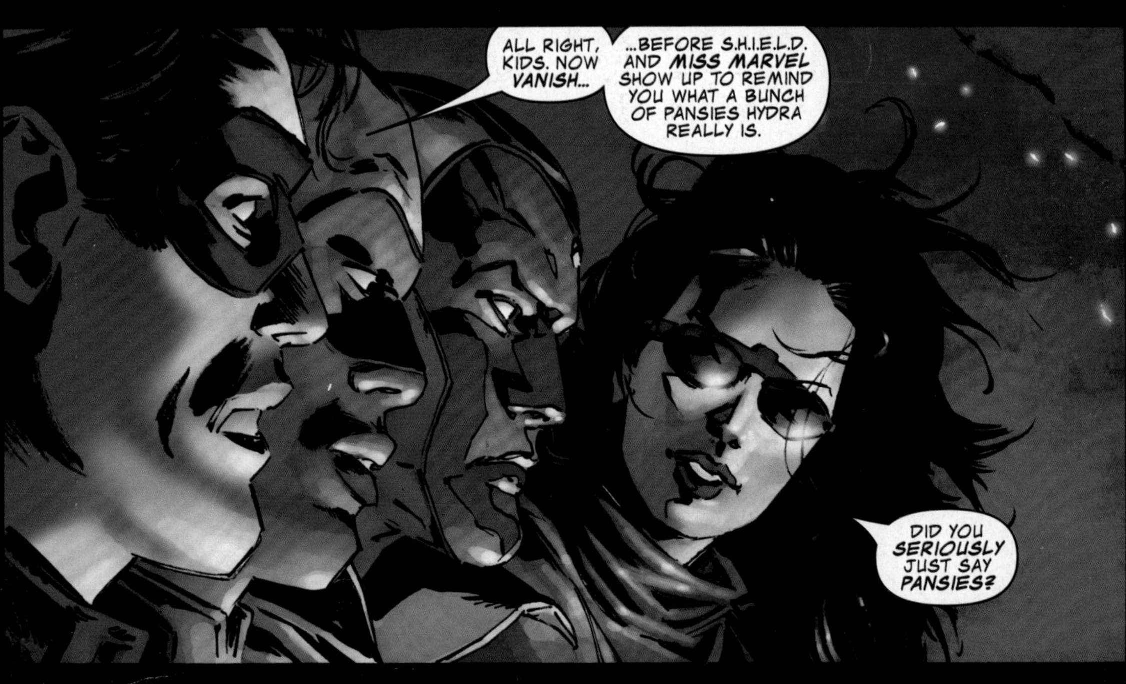
ALL RIGHT, KIDS. NOW VANISH...
...BEFORE S.H.I.E.L.D. AND MISS MARVEL SHOW UP TO REMIND YOU WHAT A BUNCH OF PANSIES HYDRA REALLY IS.
DID YOU SERIOUSLY JUST SAY PANSIES?

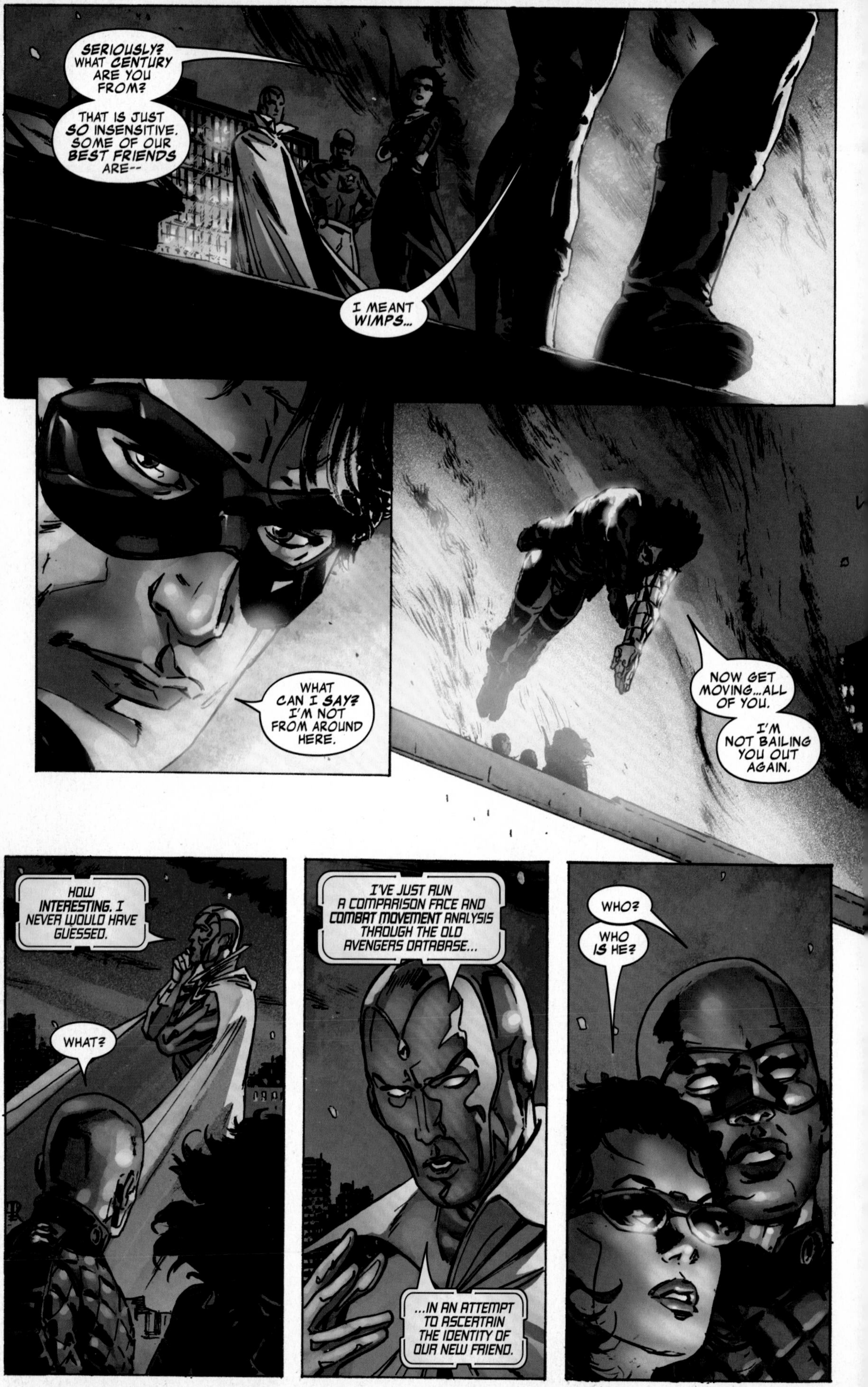
SERIOUSLY? WHAT CENTURY ARE YOU FROM?
THAT IS JUST SO INSENSITIVE. SOME OF OUR BEST FRIENDS ARE--
I MEANT WIMPS...
WHAT CAN I SAY? I'M NOT FROM AROUND HERE.
NOW GET MOVING...ALL OF YOU.
I'M NOT BAILING YOU OUT AGAIN.
HOW INTERESTING. I NEVER WOULD HAVE GUESSED.
WHAT?
I'VE JUST RUN A COMPARISON FACE AND COMBAT MOVEMENT ANALYSIS THROUGH THE OLD AVENGERS DATABASE...
...IN AN ATTEMPT TO ASCERTAIN THE IDENTITY OF OUR NEW FRIEND.
WHO?
WHO IS HE?

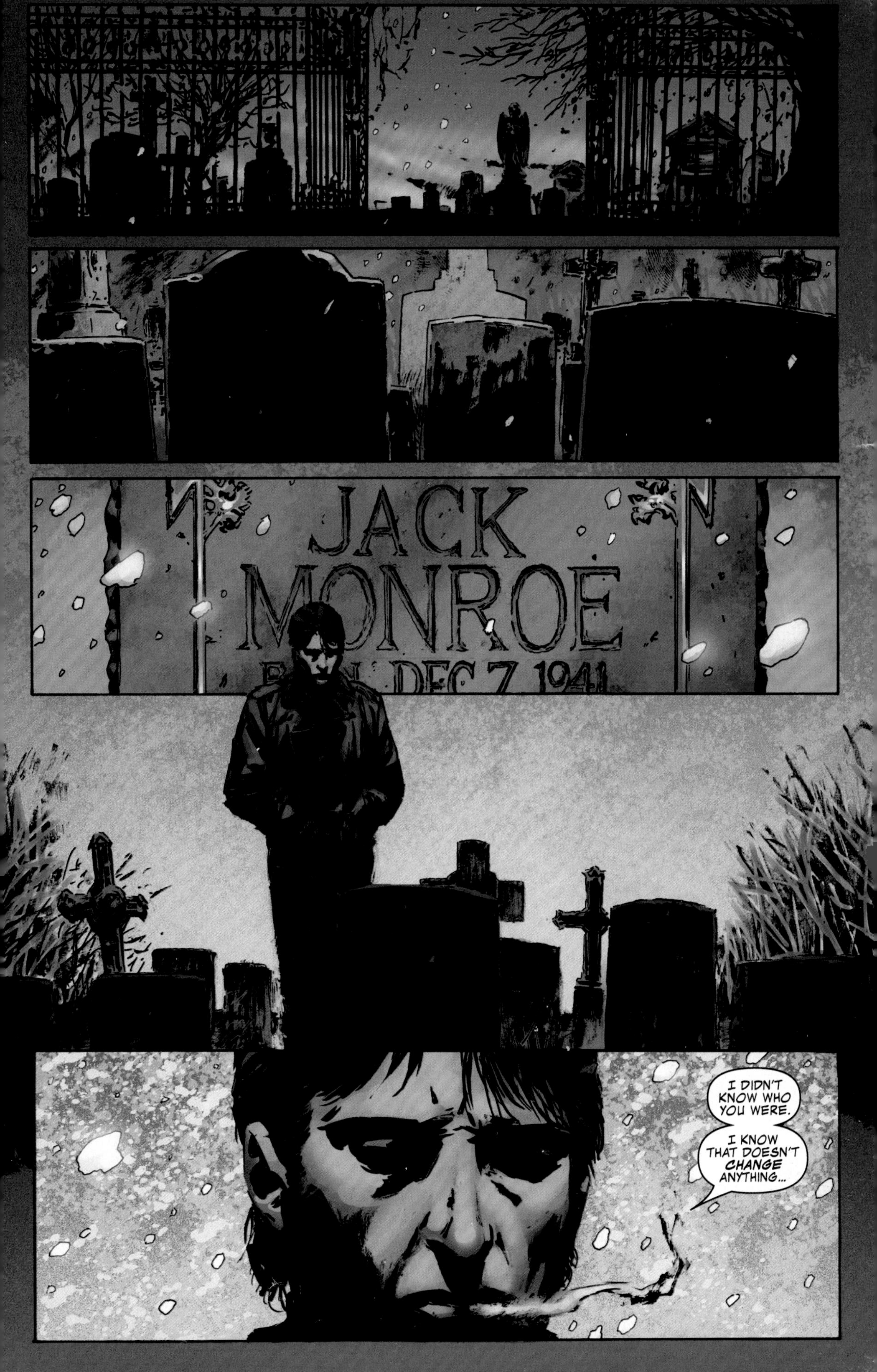
JACK
MONROE
DEC 7 1941
I DIDN'T KNOW WHO YOU WERE.
I KNOW THAT DOESN'T CHANGE ANYTHING...

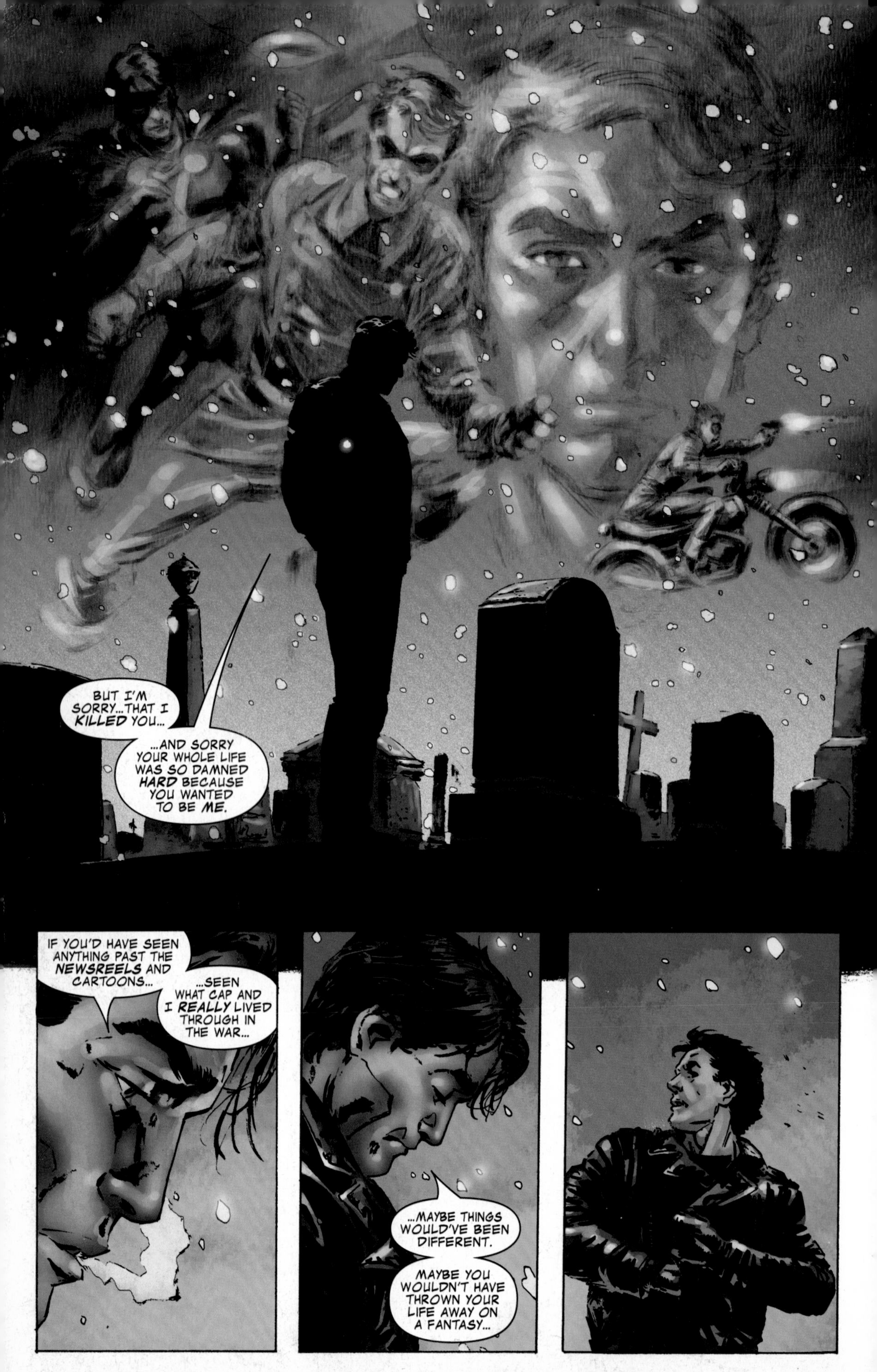
BUT I'M SORRY...THAT I KILLED YOU...
...AND SORRY YOUR WHOLE LIFE WAS SO DAMNED HARD BECAUSE YOU WANTED TO BE ME.
IF YOU'D HAVE SEEN ANYTHING PAST THE NEWSREELS AND CARTOONS...
...SEEN WHAT CAP AND I REALLY LIVED THROUGH IN THE WAR...
...MAYBE THINGS WOULD'VE BEEN DIFFERENT.
MAYBE YOU WOULDN'T HAVE THROWN YOUR LIFE AWAY ON A FANTASY...

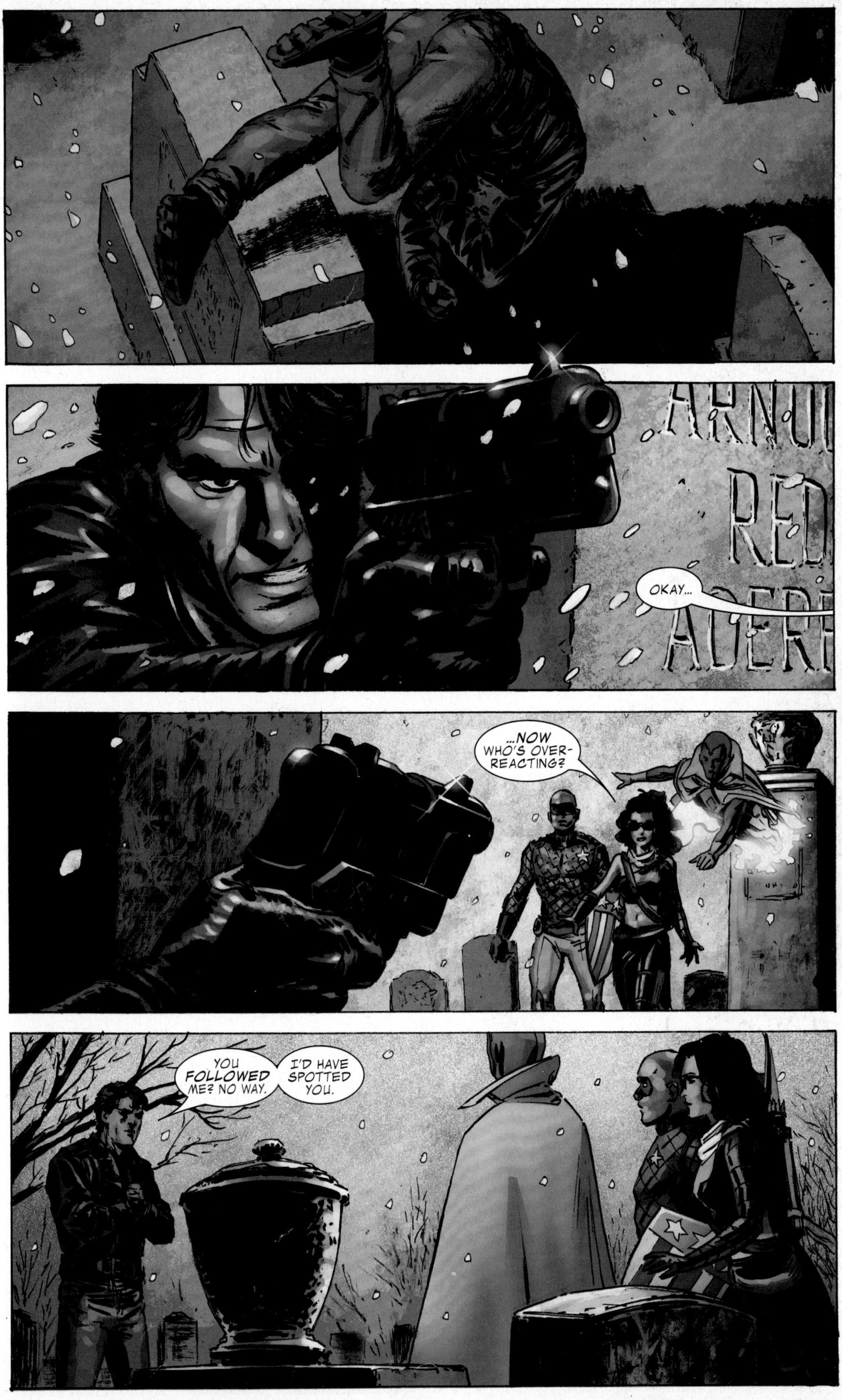
OKAY...
...NOW WHO'S OVER-REACTING?
YOU FOLLOWED ME? NO WAY.
I'D HAVE SPOTTED YOU.

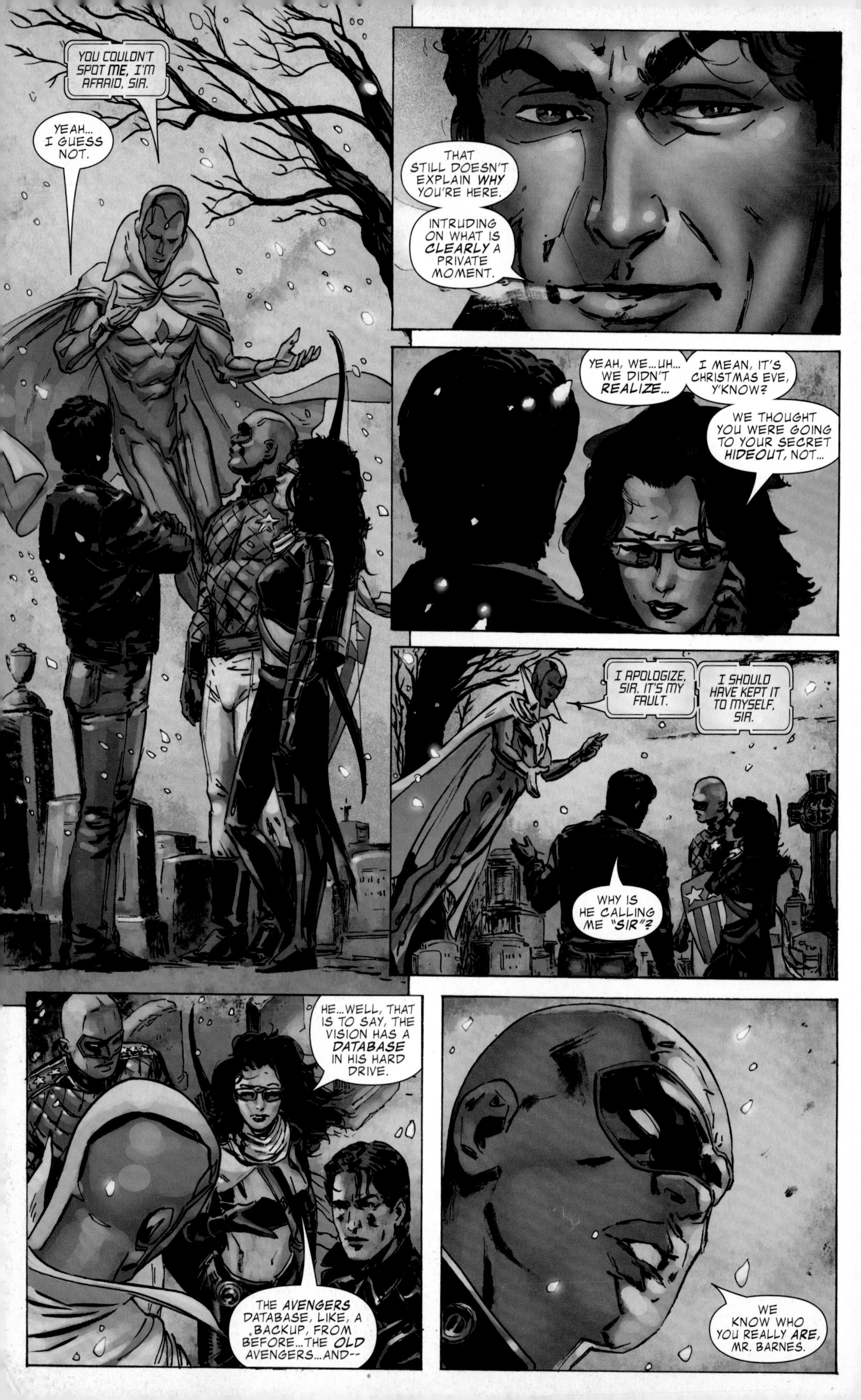
YOU COULDN'T SPOT ME, I'M AFRAID, SIR.
YEAH... I GUESS NOT.
THAT STILL DOESN'T EXPLAIN WHY YOU'RE HERE.
INTRUDING ON WHAT IS CLEARLY A PRIVATE MOMENT.
YEAH, WE...UH... WE DIDN'T REALIZE...
I MEAN, IT'S CHRISTMAS EVE, Y'KNOW?
WE THOUGHT YOU WERE GOING TO YOUR SECRET HIDEOUT, NOT...
I APOLOGIZE, SIR. IT'S MY FAULT.
I SHOULD HAVE KEPT IT TO MYSELF, SIR.
WHY IS HE CALLING ME "SIR"?
HE...WELL, THAT IS TO SAY, THE VISION HAS A DATABASE IN HIS HARD DRIVE.
THE AVENGERS DATABASE, LIKE, A BACKUP, FROM BEFORE...THE OLD AVENGERS...AND--
WE KNOW WHO YOU REALLY ARE, MR. BARNES.

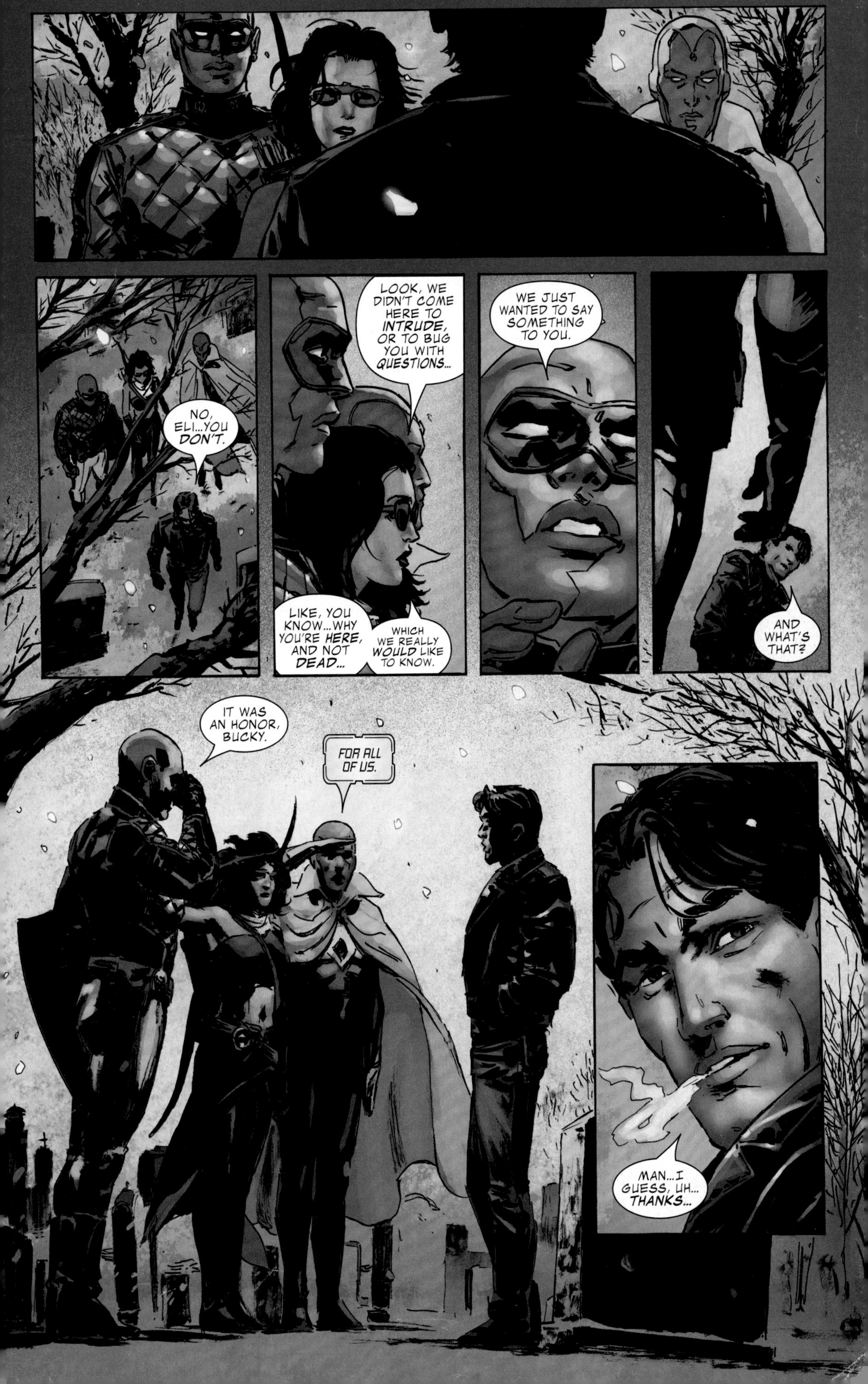
NO, ELI...YOU DON'T.
LOOK, WE DIDN'T COME HERE TO INTRUDE, OR TO BUG YOU WITH QUESTIONS...
LIKE, YOU KNOW...WHY YOU'RE HERE, AND NOT DEAD...
WHICH WE REALLY WOULD LIKE TO KNOW.
WE JUST WANTED TO SAY SOMETHING TO YOU.
AND WHAT'S THAT?
IT WAS AN HONOR, BUCKY.
FOR ALL OF US.
MAN...I GUESS, UH... THANKS...

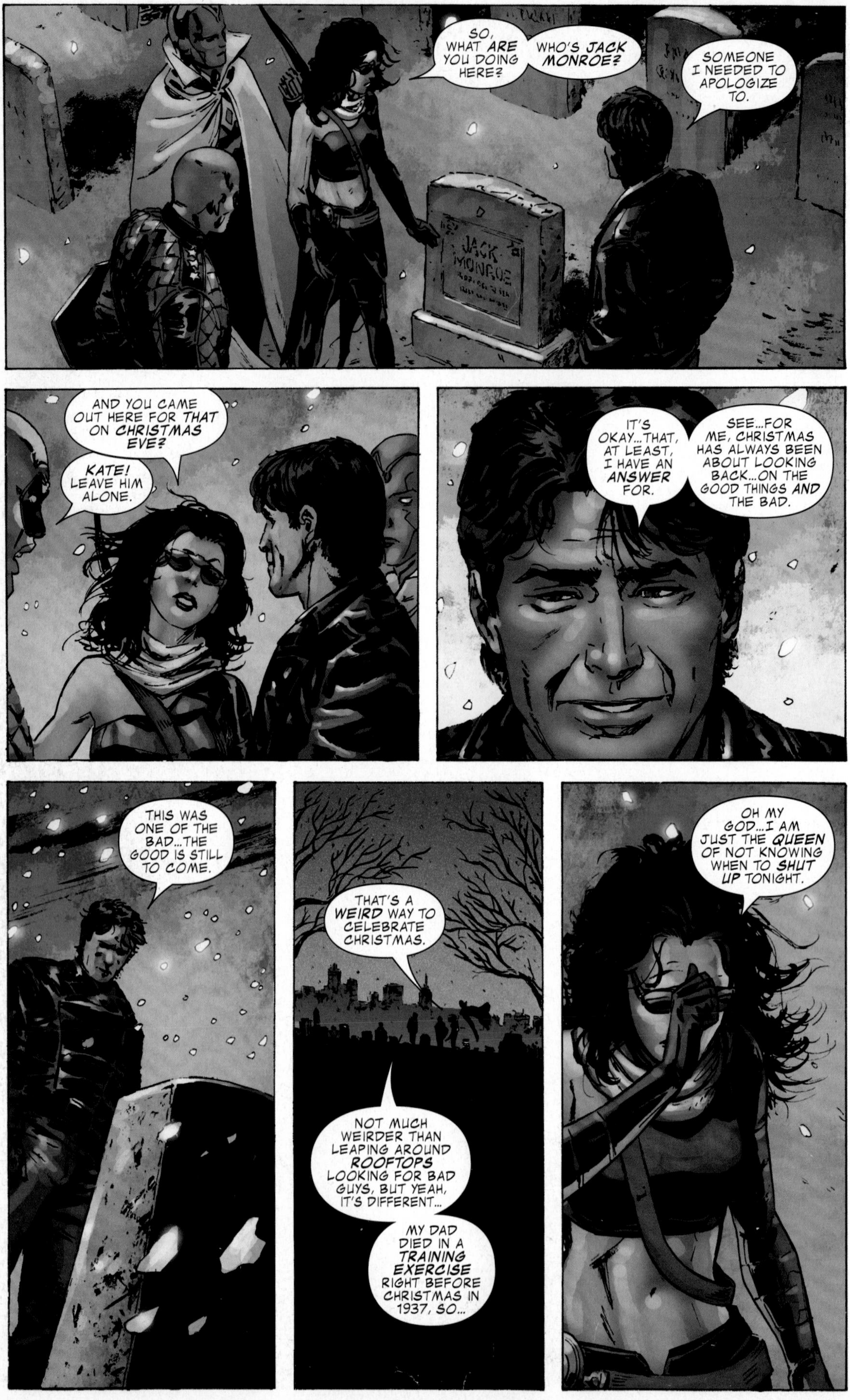
SO, WHAT ARE YOU DOING HERE?
WHO'S JACK MONROE?
SOMEONE I NEEDED TO APOLOGIZE TO.
JACK MONROE
AND YOU CAME OUT HERE FOR THAT ON CHRISTMAS EVE?
KATE! LEAVE HIM ALONE.
IT'S OKAY...THAT, AT LEAST, I HAVE AN ANSWER FOR.
SEE...FOR ME, CHRISTMAS HAS ALWAYS BEEN ABOUT LOOKING BACK...ON THE GOOD THINGS AND THE BAD.
THIS WAS ONE OF THE BAD...THE GOOD IS STILL TO COME.
THAT'S A WEIRD WAY TO CELEBRATE CHRISTMAS.
NOT MUCH WEIRDER THAN LEAPING AROUND ROOFTOPS LOOKING FOR BAD GUYS, BUT YEAH, IT'S DIFFERENT...
MY DAD DIED IN A TRAINING EXERCISE RIGHT BEFORE CHRISTMAS IN 1937, SO...
OH MY GOD...I AM JUST THE QUEEN OF NOT KNOWING WHEN TO SHUT UP TONIGHT.

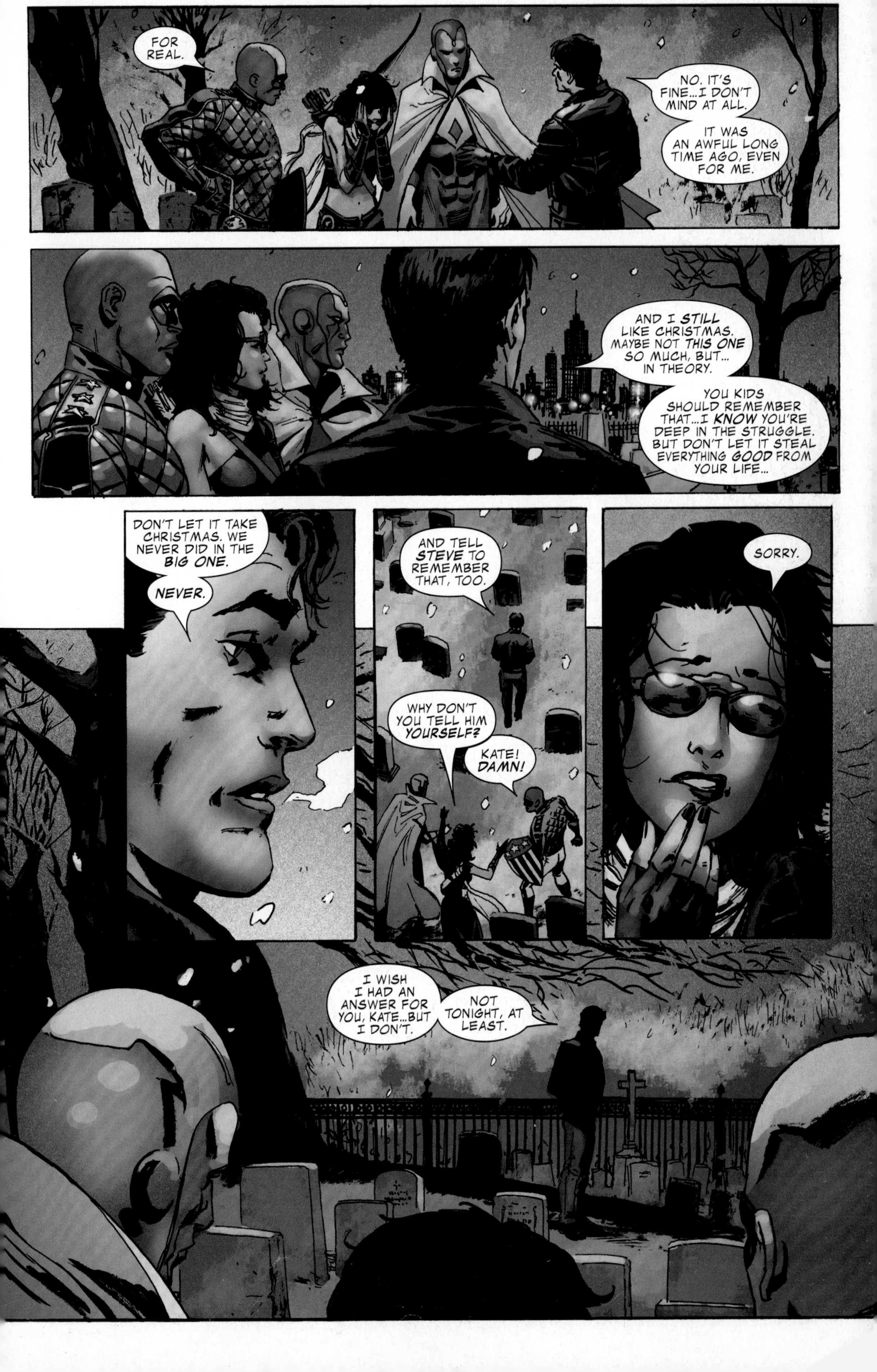
FOR REAL.
NO. IT'S FINE...I DON'T MIND AT ALL.
IT WAS AN AWFUL LONG TIME AGO, EVEN FOR ME.
AND I STILL LIKE CHRISTMAS. MAYBE NOT THIS ONE SO MUCH, BUT... IN THEORY.
YOU KIDS SHOULD REMEMBER THAT...I KNOW YOU'RE DEEP IN THE STRUGGLE. BUT DON'T LET IT STEAL EVERYTHING GOOD FROM YOUR LIFE...
DON'T LET IT TAKE CHRISTMAS. WE NEVER DID IN THE BIG ONE.
NEVER.
AND TELL STEVE TO REMEMBER THAT, TOO.
WHY DON'T YOU TELL HIM YOURSELF?
KATE! DAMN!
SORRY.
I WISH I HAD AN ANSWER FOR YOU, KATE...BUT I DON'T.
NOT TONIGHT, AT LEAST.

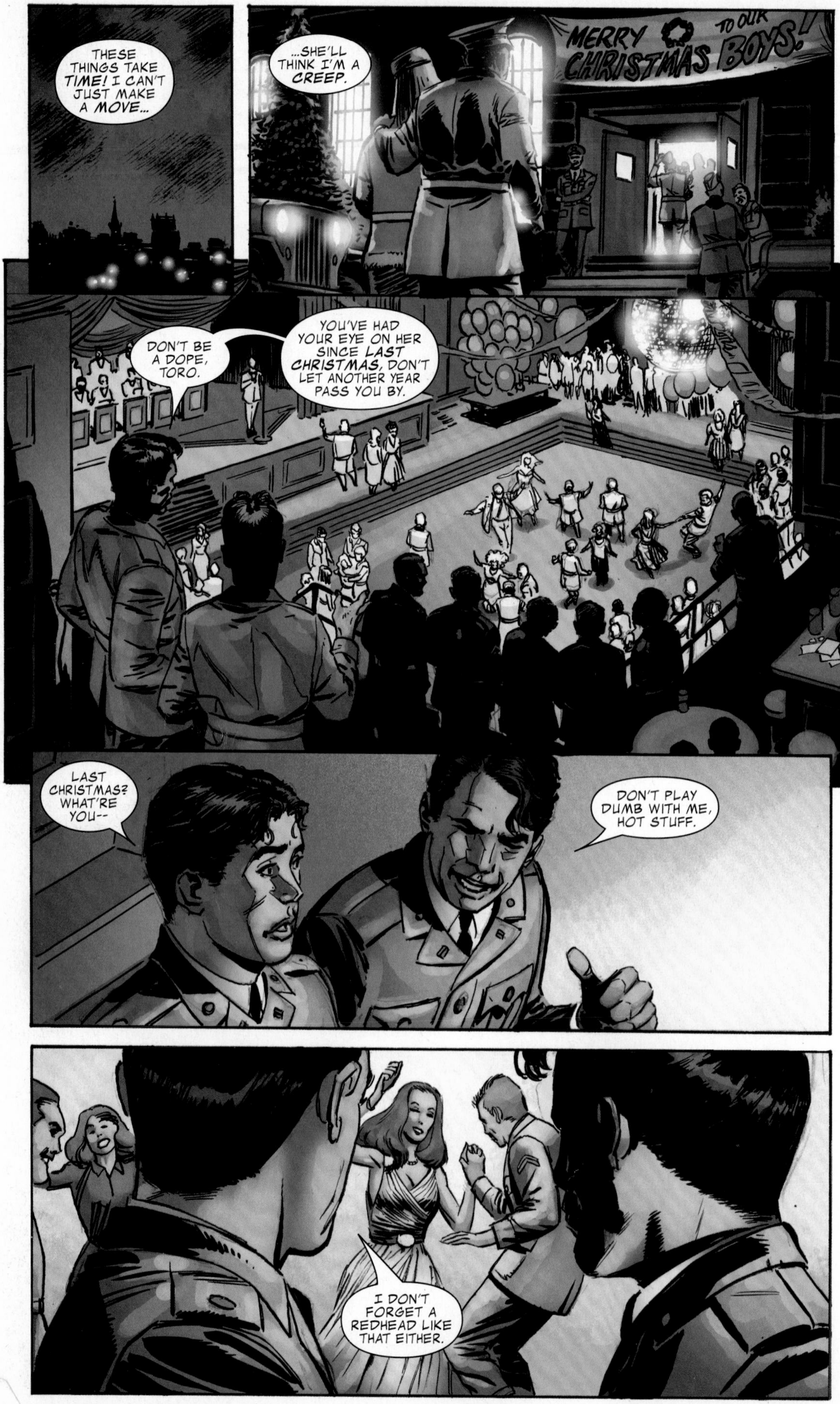
THESE THINGS TAKE TIME! I CAN'T JUST MAKE A MOVE...
...SHE'LL THINK I'M A CREEP.
MERRY CHRISTMAS TO OUR BOYS!
DON'T BE A DOPE, TORO.
YOU'VE HAD YOUR EYE ON HER SINCE LAST CHRISTMAS, DON'T LET ANOTHER YEAR PASS YOU BY.
LAST CHRISTMAS? WHAT'RE YOU--
DON'T PLAY DUMB WITH ME, HOT STUFF.
I DON'T FORGET A REDHEAD LIKE THAT EITHER.

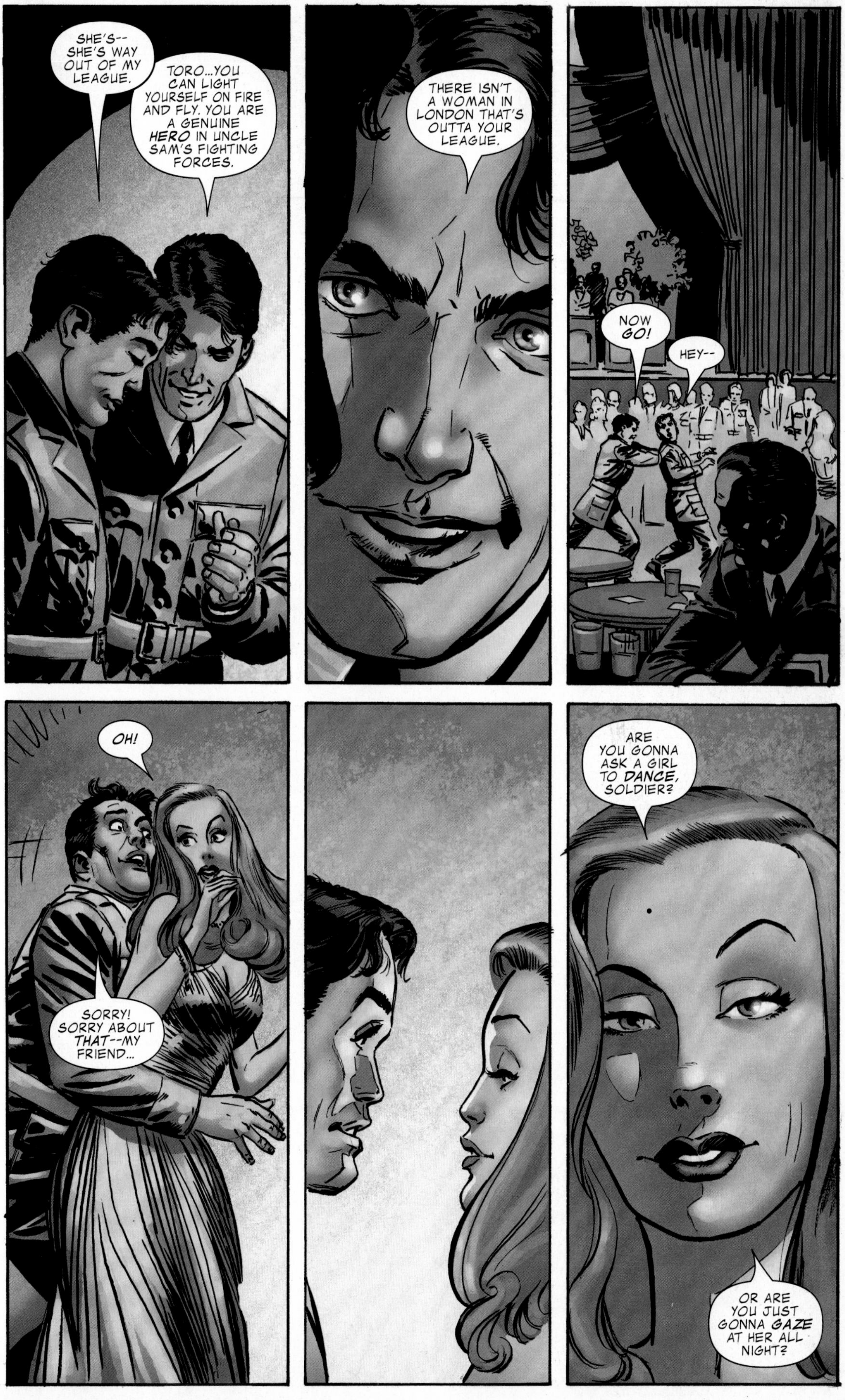
SHE'S-- SHE'S WAY OUT OF MY LEAGUE.
TORO...YOU CAN LIGHT YOURSELF ON FIRE AND FLY. YOU ARE A GENUINE HERO IN UNCLE SAM'S FIGHTING FORCES.
THERE ISN'T A WOMAN IN LONDON THAT'S OUTTA YOUR LEAGUE.
NOW GO!
HEY--
OH!
SORRY! SORRY ABOUT THAT--MY FRIEND...
ARE YOU GONNA ASK A GIRL TO DANCE, SOLDIER?
OR ARE YOU JUST GONNA GAZE AT HER ALL NIGHT?

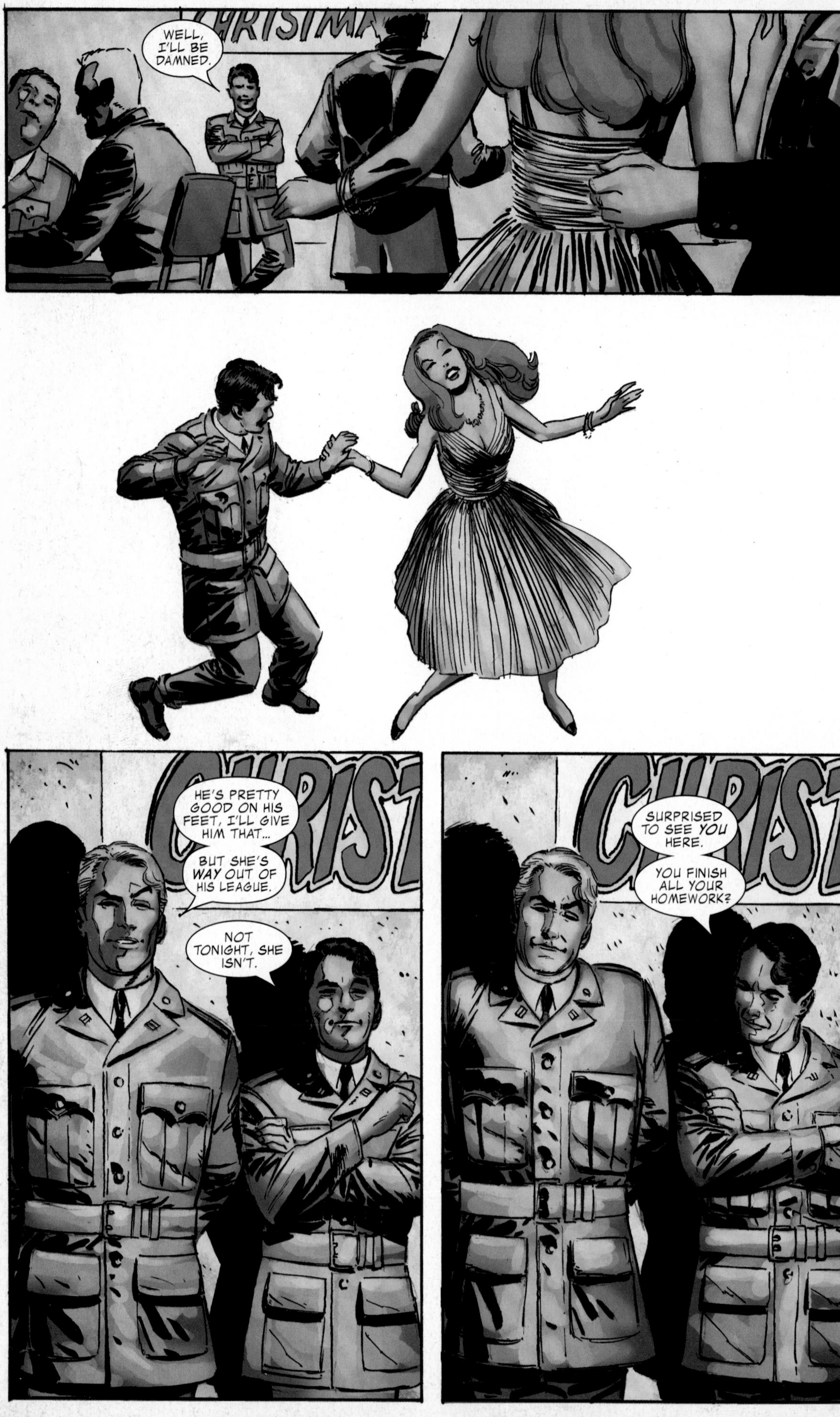
WELL, I'LL BE DAMNED.
HE'S PRETTY GOOD ON HIS FEET, I'LL GIVE HIM THAT...
BUT SHE'S *WAY* OUT OF HIS LEAGUE.
NOT TONIGHT, SHE ISN'T.
SURPRISED TO SEE *YOU* HERE.
YOU FINISH ALL YOUR HOMEWORK?

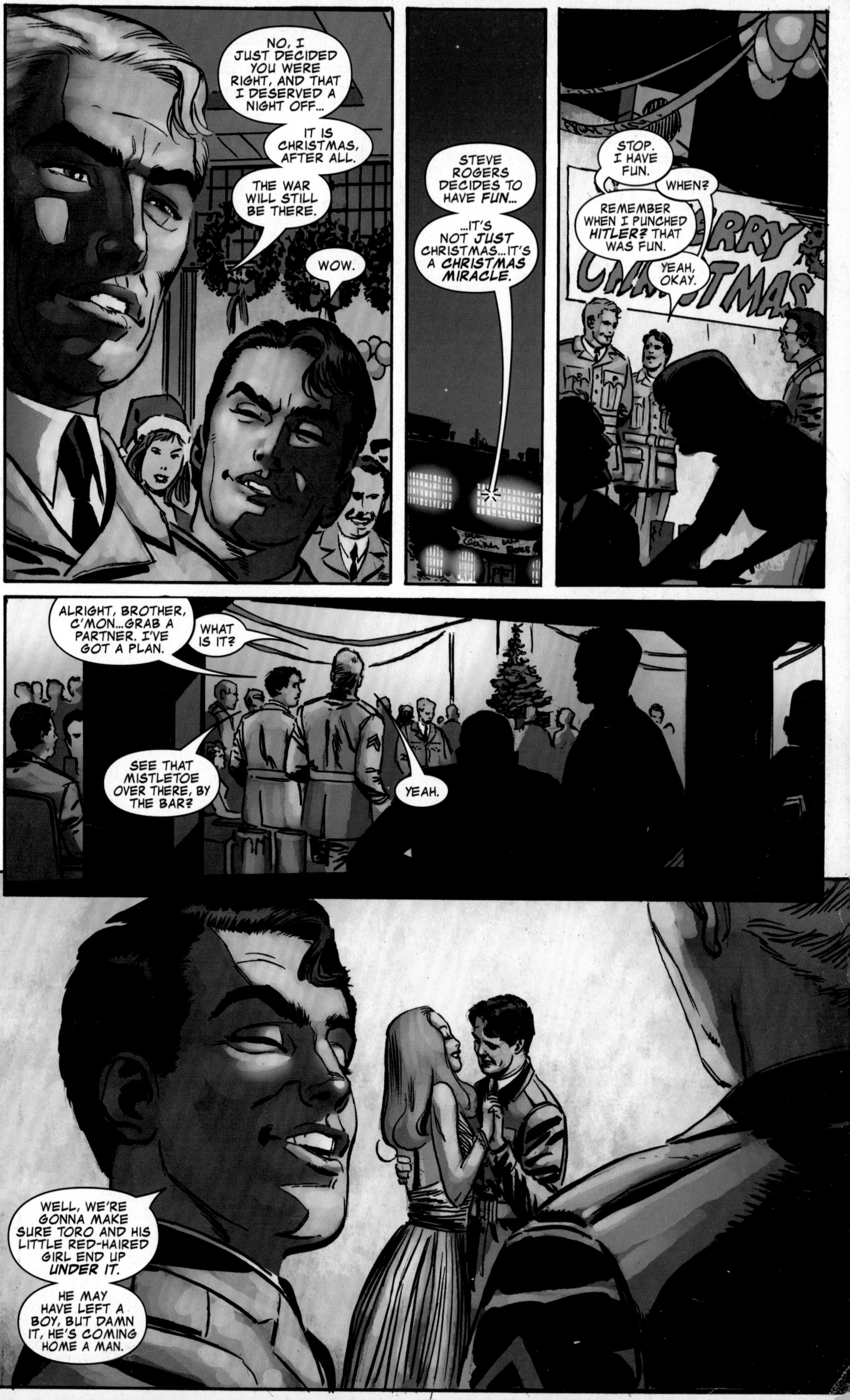
NO, I JUST DECIDED YOU WERE RIGHT, AND THAT I DESERVED A NIGHT OFF...
IT IS CHRISTMAS, AFTER ALL.
THE WAR WILL STILL BE THERE.
WOW.
STEVE ROGERS DECIDES TO HAVE FUN...
...IT'S NOT JUST CHRISTMAS...IT'S A CHRISTMAS MIRACLE.
STOP. I HAVE FUN.
WHEN?
REMEMBER WHEN I PUNCHED HITLER? THAT WAS FUN.
YEAH, OKAY.
ALRIGHT, BROTHER, C'MON...GRAB A PARTNER. I'VE GOT A PLAN.
WHAT IS IT?
SEE THAT MISTLETOE OVER THERE, BY THE BAR?
YEAH.
WELL, WE'RE GONNA MAKE SURE TORO AND HIS LITTLE RED-HAIRED GIRL END UP UNDER IT.
HE MAY HAVE LEFT A BOY, BUT DAMN IT, HE'S COMING HOME A MAN.

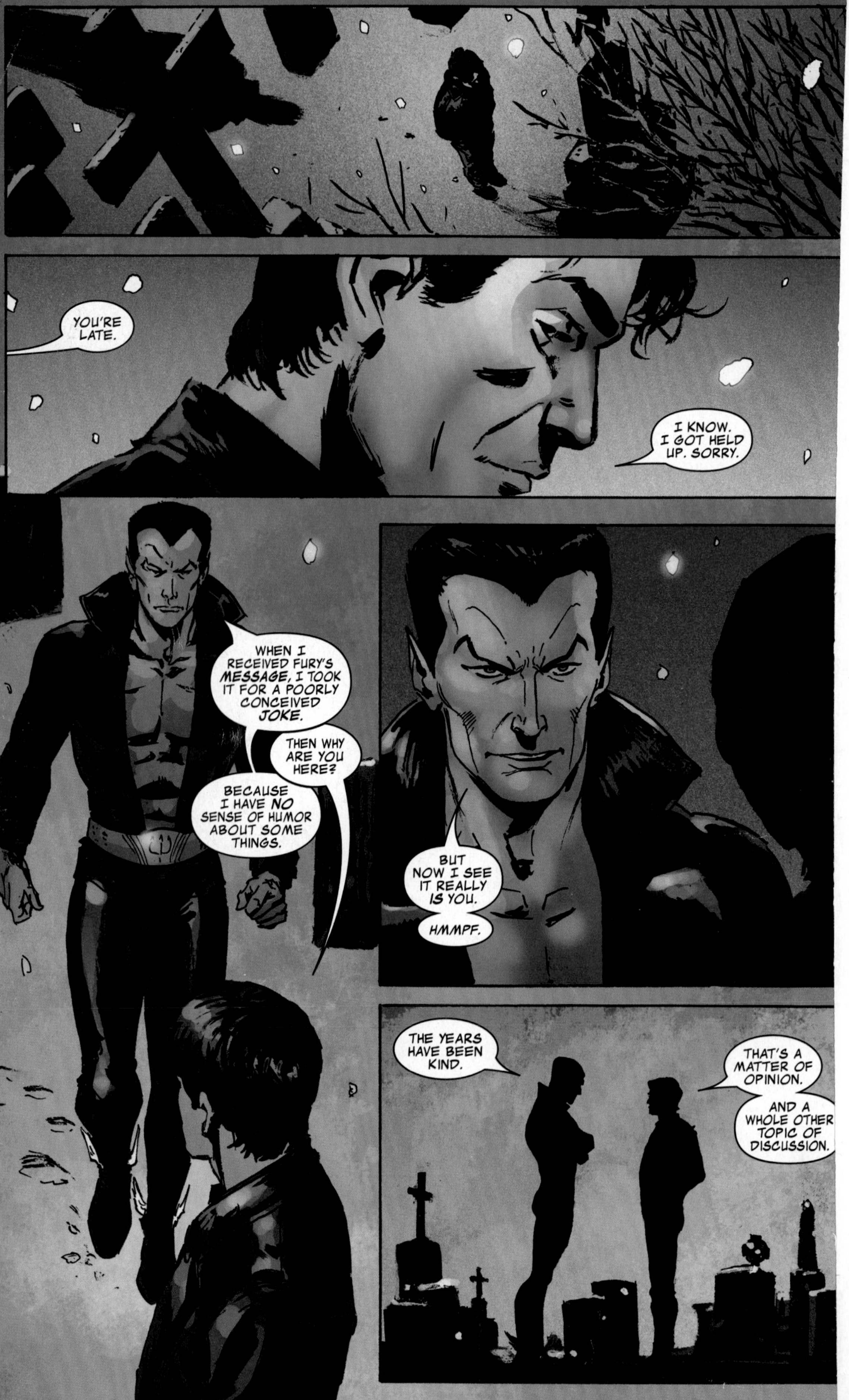
YOU'RE LATE.
I KNOW. I GOT HELD UP. SORRY.
WHEN I RECEIVED FURY'S MESSAGE, I TOOK IT FOR A POORLY CONCEIVED JOKE.
THEN WHY ARE YOU HERE?
BECAUSE I HAVE NO SENSE OF HUMOR ABOUT SOME THINGS.
BUT NOW I SEE IT REALLY IS YOU.
HMMPF.
THE YEARS HAVE BEEN KIND.
THAT'S A MATTER OF OPINION.
AND A WHOLE OTHER TOPIC OF DISCUSSION.

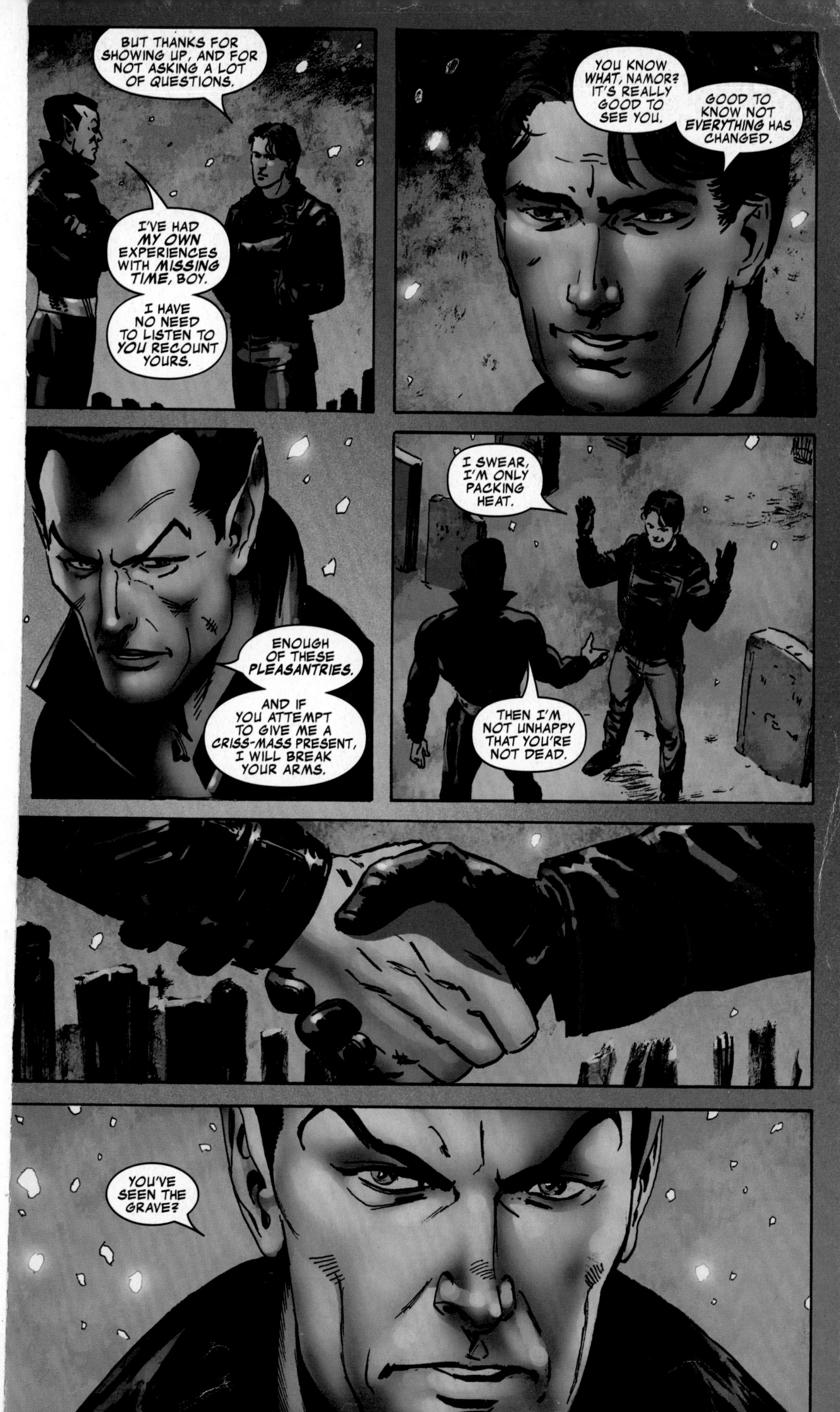

BUT THANKS FOR SHOWING UP, AND FOR NOT ASKING A LOT OF QUESTIONS.
I'VE HAD MY OWN EXPERIENCES WITH MISSING TIME, BOY.
I HAVE NO NEED TO LISTEN TO YOU RECOUNT YOURS.
YOU KNOW WHAT, NAMOR? IT'S REALLY GOOD TO SEE YOU.
GOOD TO KNOW NOT EVERYTHING HAS CHANGED.
ENOUGH OF THESE PLEASANTRIES.
AND IF YOU ATTEMPT TO GIVE ME A CRISS-MASS PRESENT, I WILL BREAK YOUR ARMS.
I SWEAR, I'M ONLY PACKING HEAT.
THEN I'M NOT UNHAPPY THAT YOU'RE NOT DEAD.
YOU'VE SEEN THE GRAVE?

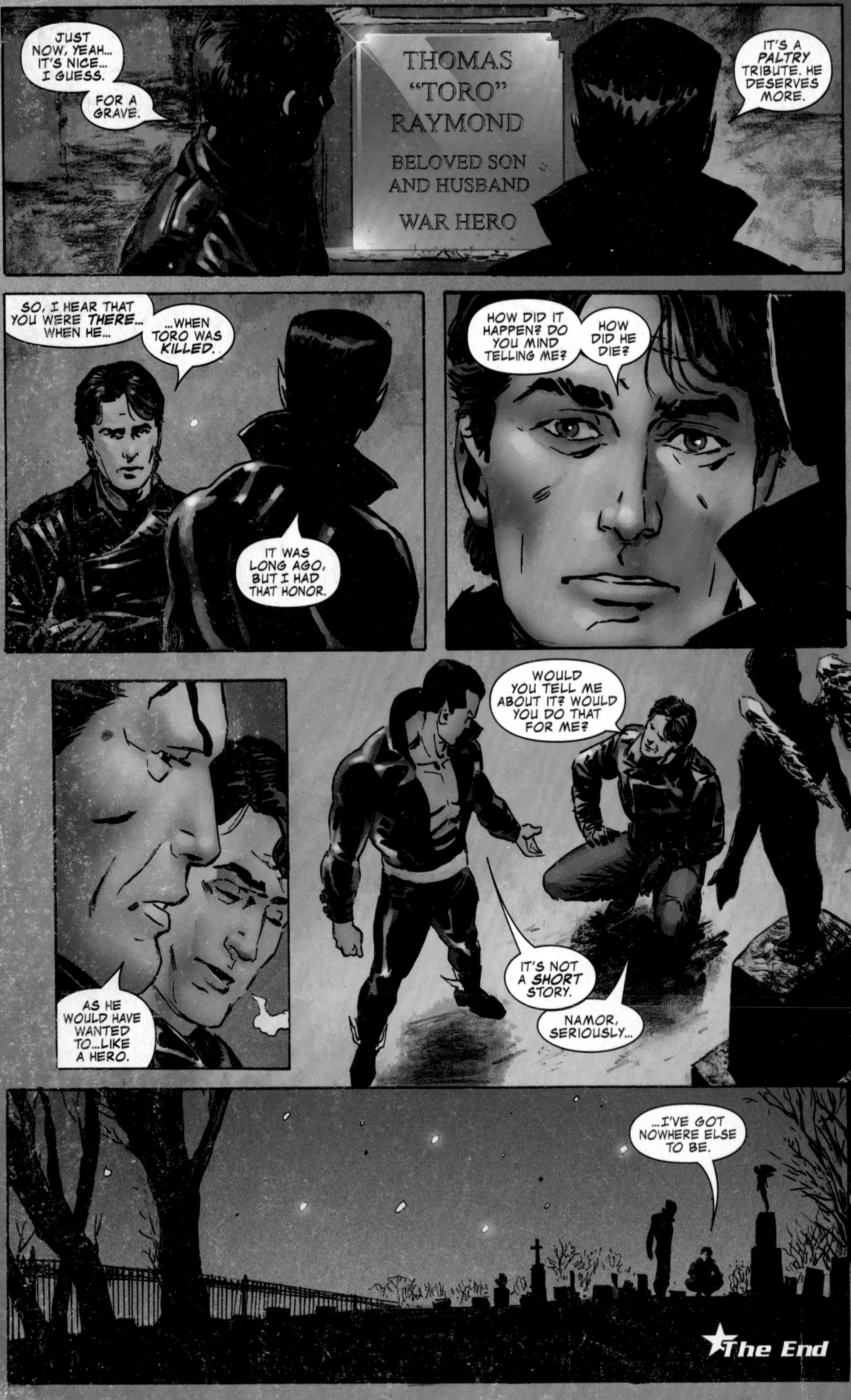
JUST NOW, YEAH... IT'S NICE... I GUESS.
FOR A GRAVE.
THOMAS "TORO" RAYMOND
BELOVED SON AND HUSBAND
WAR HERO
IT'S A PALTRY TRIBUTE. HE DESERVES MORE.
SO, I HEAR THAT YOU WERE THERE... WHEN HE...
...WHEN TORO WAS KILLED.
IT WAS LONG AGO, BUT I HAD THAT HONOR.
HOW DID IT HAPPEN? DO YOU MIND TELLING ME?
HOW DID HE DIE?
AS HE WOULD HAVE WANTED TO...LIKE A HERO.
WOULD YOU TELL ME ABOUT IT? WOULD YOU DO THAT FOR ME?
IT'S NOT A SHORT STORY.
NAMOR, SERIOUSLY...
...I'VE GOT NOWHERE ELSE TO BE.
The End